Ethnic Minorities, Electronic Media and the Public Sphere

A Comparative Approach

About Euricom

The European Institute for Communication and Culture (Euricom) is a non-profit organization devoted to research and publication in the general areas of mass communication, media studies, and cultural studies. In keeping with its unique position bridging the two parts of the formerly divided Europe, Euricom is concerned with the relationship of the mass media and democracy. For more than a decade Euricom has organized annual scholarly colloquia dedicated to this theme. Contributions to the colloquia have been published in theme issues of the journal *Javnost-The Public* and in scholarly monographs.

Euricom publishes the quarterly interdisciplinary journal *Javnost-The Public*. Based in the social Sciences, *Javnost-The Public* addresses problems of the public sphere on an international level and stimulates development of theory and research in the field. For further information on Euricom and *Javnost-The Public*, see: http://www.euricom.si/.

About *Euricom Monographs*

Euricom Monographs is an initiative of Euricom and considers book-length manuscripts on aspects of democratic theory grounded in empirical investigations of recent communicative innovations. Although the primary objective of *Euricom Monographs* is to contribute to intellectual understanding of transformations in the democratic process, some titles are oriented towards improving political practice, policy and action. Topics of interest to *Euricom Monographs* include:
- Internet-based discussions and political discourse
- Politics and political action online
- Tele-democracy initiatives and e-voting
- Implications of the digital divide for public discourse
- Online media as arenas for public information and debate
- Community networks and community development.

Forthcoming titles in the series Euricom Monographs include:

Challenges of E-democracy: New Forms of Communication, Political Engagement and Public Sphere
    Tanja Oblak, University of Ljubljana

For further details, see:
http://oase.uci.kun.nl/~jankow/Euricom_Monographs/index.htm. Queries about Euricom Monographs may be addressed to: Nicholas W. Jankowski, editor Euricom Monographs, Department of Communication, Raboud University Nijmegen, P.O. Box 9104, 6500 HE Nijmegen, The Netherlands. Email: N.Jankowski@maw.ru..nl.

Ethnic Minorities, Electronic Media and the Public Sphere

A Comparative Approach

Donald R. Browne
University of Minnesota

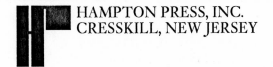
HAMPTON PRESS, INC.
CRESSKILL, NEW JERSEY

Printed in the United States of America

Library of Congress Cataloging-in-Publication Data

Browne, Donald R.
    Ethnic minorities, electronic media, and the public sphere : a comparative approach / Donald R. Browne
        p. cm. -- (Euricom monographs)
    Includes bibliographic references and index.
    ISBN 1-57273-604-6 (cl) -- ISBN 1-57273-605-4 (pb)
    1. Digital media--Social aspects. 2. Ethnic mass media. 3. Minorities--Services for. 4. Minorities--Effect of technological innovations on. 5. Social participation. I. Title. II. Series.

HM851.B77 2005
302.23'089--dc22

                                                           2004060941

Hampton Press, Inc.
23 Broadway
Cresskill, NJ 07626

Contents

Preface

It has been a labor of love to compile this volume, chiefly because I am more convinced than ever that the self-expression of ethnic minorities through the electronic media is a vitally important part of our increasingly migratory world. Although it is evident that much more can and should be done to bring ethnic minority voices and images into the public sphere, the past 20 years have seen considerable activity along those lines where the electronic media are concerned. Furthermore, that activity has taken many different forms and has led to both problems and successes, so that there is much to be learned from its many manifestations.

This is not my book so much as it is my attempt to convey the rich variety of the ethnic minority media experiences themselves, as I learned of them from the accounts furnished by their practitioners and by those few individuals who had studied those experiences. In conducting my research, I became aware again and again that most of the individuals engaged in ethnic minority electronic media operations knew little about what their counterparts in other parts of the world had done or were doing. I see that as the major reason for their willingness to share information with me: They were confident that I would pull their singular experiences together in a more or less orderly fashion and produce a collective account of what was occurring, why, and what they could learn from each other. I can only hope that their faith has been rewarded.

I cannot begin to register the hundreds of names of individuals who have contributed to this study, although many of those names appear in the bibliography. But I do wish to convey my particular thanks to those who were especially helpful in one respect or another: Mike Cormack, Myria Georgiu, Hans Heintze, Bruce Jenkins, Lyn Jones, Martin Kilgus, Ed Klute, Carmino Leicester, Adrian Loew, Catherine MacNeil, David Mathlany, Michael Meadows, Helen Molmar, Paul Pearman, Clemencia Rodriguez, Javed Sattar, Vijay Sharma, Roger Silverstone, Mike Thompson, Friedrich Voss, and Gualtiero Zambonini.

My thanks also go to Nicholas Jankowski, the editor of the Hampton Press EURICOM series, for his encouragement of my study and his careful shepherding of its component parts in their various manifestations; and to Leen d'Haenens, who read the draft of the study and provided me with helpful guidance and many useful suggestions. Thanks also to my departmental colleagues for their many insightful comments on my presentations of various aspects of this subject over the years, and to the Department of Communication Studies, the Office of International Programs, and the Graduate School at the University of Minnesota for their financial support of my research. I attach the usual proviso: no other party is responsible for whatever errors the text may contain. They are my responsibility.

—Donald R. Browne

Laying the Groundwork

Immigration has a long and often legendary history.[1] If humans originated in Africa, large numbers of them sooner or later fanned out to populate the world. The sacred texts of Islam, Judaism, and Christianity are replete with stories of individuals, families, and tribes seeking or forced into residence elsewhere. Indigenous tribes in Africa, the Americas, Australia, and Asia often moved in search of better hunting or growing conditions, or were displaced by other tribes and by nonindigenous peoples coveting their lands. Where nonindigenous incursions took place, the end result often was that the original inhabitants of the land became just one more of its ethnic minorities. The institution of the slave trade meant that millions of individuals, most of them African, were forcibly removed from their homelands to become ethnic minorities in the Americas, Europe, and North Africa.

The Industrial Revolution saw the migration of many rural families to the towns and cities where factories were established, with roads and railways facilitating the population shift. But it also saw the industries reaching out beyond national borders to recruit workers from other countries. By the beginning of the 20th century, large ships and extensive railway networks made it easier than ever for those recruits and others to move great distances at relatively low cost. Regional and global wars were a further inducement for many to seek their fortunes elsewhere. And finally, increasingly rapid and inexpensive means of communication (mail service, and later, the telephone) between those who had emigrated and those they left behind served as impetus for still more movement. "Old" émigré groups were joined by new groups, and the two often competed for employment.

1

Until well into the 20th century, the term *ethnic minority* was not in general use. The industrialized nations either had no ethnic minorities (at least that they were ready to acknowledge as such) or pursued a policy of assimilation, whereby *all* minorities, ethnic or not, would be absorbed into the mainstream. They were expected (and sometimes required) to learn and accept the mainstream language(s) and culture(s), and were discouraged from using or celebrating their own. Those certainly were not propitious conditions for the development of ethnic minority media services, and did not encourage mainstream media to pay much attention to ethnic minorities, either. The result was that ethnic minorities were invisible to the mainstream population, even as their numbers were growing.

World War II had a profound effect on the growth of ethnic minority populations throughout the industrialized world. Germany and France, decimated by the war, found that they needed to import manual labor to rebuild their industries; part of that workforce came from southern Europe, but part came from Turkey and North Africa, introducing sizable numbers of ethnic minorities to nations that had had little experience with them. The military forces of the Allied nations often featured units made up of ethnic minorities, for example, Maori in New Zealand and African Americans in the United States, which provided minorities with some experience in leadership positions, but also a larger claim to recognition for their contributions in the war. The colonial empires of France, Great Britain, Spain, Portugal, The Netherlands, and Belgium began to dissolve shortly after the war. That led to the birth of dozens of newly independent nations, but also to the migration of many individuals and groups from Africa, South and Southeast Asia, the Caribbean, and wherever else the empires had reached. With few exceptions, those migrations were to the colonial homelands themselves, meaning that Great Britain's Caribbean and South Asian populations burgeoned, as did North African populations in France, Indonesians and Surinamese in The Netherlands, and so on.

Many of those postwar population shifts led to civil strife and to movements for civil rights for various ethnic minority groups. That in turn helped to spur reexamination of longstanding assimilationist policies and to encourage the development of ethnic pride, with "Black is Beautiful" and other slogans proclaiming the right of ethnic minorities to be treated as equals in political, social, and cultural arenas as well as in the courts. It is at this time, as is seen in later in this chapter, that ethnic minority media really begin to gain a foothold in the industrialized nations.

By the end of the 20th century, large aircraft were making it easier and often cheaper than ever for individuals and families to seek what they hoped would be better lives in distant lands. Many came from nations with what some of their citizens regarded as harsh regimes: Cambodia, Afghanistan, Ethiopia, Iran, and Nicaragua. Civil wars in some Central American nations and rural poverty in many of them resulted in an influx of refugees where the United States was concerned, and the Hispanic[2] population of the United States soon began to challenge African Americans as "largest U.S. ethnic minority group." The smuggling of would-be émigrés from those and other lands, usually under horrendous physical conditions, had grown to the point where each year thousands and possibly tens of thousands of people around the world were relying on it to get them to countries where they might stand a better chance of improving their lot.

Over the past few decades, certain channels of communication have served to make the new homelands somewhat more congenial for newly arrived as well as long-resident émigrés and indigenous minorities. The electronic media—cassettes, radio, television, and internet—have followed (and sometimes supplanted) the print media in serving the needs of at least some ethnic minority populations, with one major difference; the electronic media (with the exception of the internet)[3] rely chiefly on aural and visual material rather than on printed symbols. Therefore, emigrés who are not literate in the language(s) of their new homelands or even those of their old ones can reap some benefit from listening to the radio and to audiocassettes, as well as watching TV and videocassettes.

Most electronic media services that are available to ethnic minority groups, recently arrived and long-resident alike, provide material intended primarily for the mainstream, and usually majority, population. The emphasis is on mainstream culture, and depictions of ethnic minority cultures are rare; when such depictions occur, they often distort those cultures, whether through concentration on stereotypical images (usually negative) or through exhibition of exemplary émigrés whose depictions are "proof" that other émigrés can do just as well, if only they make the effort. But more and more industrialized nations are experiencing the growth of ethnic minority electronic media services that provide the opportunity for those minorities to speak and act on their own behalves. Why and how those services were established, how they are structured, what they provide, and how they contribute to participation in society is the subject of this book.

WHAT IS IMPORTANT ABOUT ETHNIC MEDIA

By now, most ethnic groups have had at least the opportunity for direct access to electronic media in ways that have allowed them to present themselves in their own terms. However, their self-presentations remain minuscule in comparison with the electronic media output of majority culture. Furthermore, their electronic media outlets for the most part are underpowered and underfinanced. Many audience members living in rural areas and in smaller cities never have heard or seen self-presentations by ethnic minorities. Even in larger cities, where such self-presentations are more apt to occur, audiences are likely to be small, if only because the few ethnic minority services available there are less apt to be noticed among the plethora of choices. Furthermore, few ethnic services have the sort of financial support that would enable them to attract the attention of viewers and listeners with promotional advertising. Why, then, do they merit our attention?

First of all, ethnic minority populations are growing throughout the industrialized world. European nations, and particularly the Member States of the European Union (EU), find themselves receiving ever-increasing numbers of North African Arabs, South Asians, Kurds, Somalis, Afghanis, and others, especially those coming from regions experiencing internal conflict. Nations such as France, Germany, and The Netherlands now find ethnic minorities comprising as much as 10% of their population. All EU members expect increases in ethnic minority populations in the years ahead, even as some of them enact legislation designed to slow down the pace of those increases. To put it succinctly, ethnic and linguistic minorities increasingly will be a part of *all* our futures.[4]

Second, ethnic minorities can enrich the life of any member of the ethnic majority, or mainstream, who will take the time to learn just what is different, as well as similar, about their lives. That enrichment may take several forms: appreciation of a wider range of artistic expression; appreciation of a greater variety of religious beliefs; appreciation of social structures that may emphasize differing values and relationships; and finally, appreciation of difference itself, along with increased tolerance (and hopefully acceptance) of difference. In short, ethnic minorities promote the growth of richer and more civil societies.

NATURE OF THE STUDY

My examination of ethnic minority media is guided by five questions:

1. How do the electronic media serve as part of the public sphere where ethnic minority participation is concerned?
2.. What sorts of policies have governments developed to assist or discourage ethnic minority participation in the public sphere, and how have those policies shaped the nature of ethnic minority participation?
3. How do ethnic minority media services interact with their communities?
4. What types of program-making activity have characterized ethnic minority electronic media services, and how do those programs affect participation? What sorts of audiences are they intended to reach?
5. How "public" is ethnic minority media participation in the public sphere? Who participates in it, who does not, and why or why not?

One of my aims in searching for answers to those questions is to discern more clearly the sorts of effects that the structural elements of *policy* and *institutional form* have on participation, program type, and content. The answers should help ethnic minority groups to identify the sorts of media policies (including those yet to be formulated or enacted) and institutional forms that are likely to be most helpful in meeting the goals they set for themselves as they prepare to participate in the public sphere, or as they consider altering their present practices. Because I present numerous specific examples of practices in many different nations, I also hope that it will be easier for anyone with an interest in establishing or assisting an ethnic minority electronic media service to respond to those who say "It can't be done" with "Yes it can. It already *has*."

My *modus operandi* in searching for those answers is a combination of three sources of material: examination of documentary evidence, including such audience research as exists regarding ethnic minority and mainstream use of ethnic minority media; on-site observation; and personal interviews with those who are involved with ethnic minority media as participants, as regulators, as observers, and as beneficiaries. Mine is not a study of the depiction of minorities by the mainstream media. There is a great deal of excellent literature on that aspect of ethnic minorities and the media.[5] Instead, I have concentrated my attention on the actual practices of ethnic minority electronic media services, and have taken the approach of articulating the structural elements that influence the creation and practices of those services. My analysis is comparative, and contrasts the experiences of such services in more than two dozen nations around the world. This has been an ongoing research project since 1987, and has its roots in some of my earlier research on local broadcasting in Europe (Browne, 1984, 1988, 1991) and on indigenous peoples (Browne, 1996). It has taken me to more than 20 nations[6] and to well over 100 ethnic minority electronic media services (including support structures such as advisory or financial bodies) and regulatory agencies. The services themselves have ranged in size and scope from local ethnic groups with as little as thirty minutes of broadcast time per week to national services with radio programs in 68 different languages (Australia's Special Broadcasting Service [SBS]).

SCHOLARLY TRADITIONS

Aside from the large body of work on ethnic minority depiction through mainstream media, there are two traditions where the scholarly literature on ethnic minorities and the electronic media are concerned: the study of *minority languages* and how they operate through and are affected by those media; and the study of specific *ethnic minority experiences* in seeking to portray themselves through those media. Although neither body of literature[7] is large, both have grown quite rapidly since the late1980s.

Works representative (to varying degrees) of the first tradition include Cisler (1998); Davies (1994); Glaisne (1982); Gorter (1989); Lemke (1995); Maybury-Lewis (1998); Moseley, Ostler, and Ouzzate (2001); and many of the articles appearing in the Mercator Media Forum's volumes. They tend to emphasize the acts of individuals and groups seeking to maintain the relative purity of ethnic languages, given the overwhelming presence of mainstream language media; to revive dying languages; and to broaden those languages so that they remain relevant in contemporary society.

Works representative (again, to varying degrees—some are more heavily centered on ethnic minority experiences than are others) of the second tradition include Alia (1999); Barlow (1999); Bosch (2003); Browne (1996); Carmen Marquez (1993); Cottle (1995); Davies (1994); Davies (1998); Davila (2001); Dowmunt (1993); Fairchild (2001); Fero (1990); Girard (1992, 2003); Gumicio-Dagron (2001); HAM (2001); Heatta (1984); Hein (1988); Horn (1999); Husband (1994); Ismond (1994); Karim (2003); Keith (1995); King and Wood (2001); Lemke (1995); Madden (1989); Meadows (1992); Michaels (1986); Molnar (1993); Molnar and Meadows (2001); Naficy (1993); Noriega (2000); Riggins (1992); Rios and Mohamed (2003); Rivas-Rodriguez (2003); Rodriguez (1998); Rodriguez (2001); Stocker (1984); Ter Wal (2002); UNESCO (1986), and Vargas (1995). They often include brief histories of the attempts of ethnic minority groups to establish their own media services, and usually provide case study-like examples of what the services disseminate to their communities. Many of them deal with single nations or population groups.[8]

The present work draws on both of those traditions, although more heavily on the second than on the first if only because it offers a greater array of documented experiences, and thus a richer basis for comparison. However, very few of the authors whose work I have noted above and in the bibliography have much to say about policymaking, about the role of audience research, or about the nature of the societal structures within which the ethnic minority media services operate, which is one reason why I have emphasized those aspects of the subject in my treatment. Nor do many of those authors present much by way of comparison of experiences and approaches.

WHAT IS AN ETHNIC MINORITY?

What do we mean by the term *ethnic minority*? Although there are many dictionary definitions, there is nothing that approaches universal agreement concerning the correctness or acceptability of any of them. My working definition of the term *ethnic minority* includes anyone who identifies him or herself as part of a group that maintains a distinction in language and/or culture between itself and the majority (mainstream)[9] population. That definition does not include distinctions in gender, sexual orientation, or religion, although there are many examples of activity by women, gays and lesbians, and individuals and groups connected with religious organizations in my study. And finally, although I do include "foreign origin" as part of my definition, I understand that to mean not only first-generation émigrés, but also the children, grandchildren, and others of those émigrés who have grown up in the "new" (to the first generation) homeland. I also include indigenous groups. I have devoted a book (Browne, 1996) to their experiences with electronic media, and do not cover them in similar detail here, but many of their media experiences are germane to my present consideration.

Part of the problem in creating any definition here lies in the term *minority* and the level of aggregation it entails. At the most general level—human beings—there are no minorities. At every other level, anyone can be a minority. For example, if you are White (Caucasian), live in the United States and mark that box on the U.S. Census Form, you will be counted as a member of the majority (nonminority, if you prefer) for now. If projections of U.S. population growth are accurate (and they often are criticized for various inaccuracies), you will not be in the majority after anywhere from 2030 to 2050, although you still will be a member of the plurality. If you identify yourself as a speaker of one of the Bantu languages and live in the Republic of South Africa, you are part of the majority now, and almost certainly will be for the foreseeable future. Still, very few South Africans identify themselves in that way, but rather as Zulu, Xhosa, N'debele, or other tribes or groups, in which case *all* of you are minorities in the larger society. But the concept of *minority* is not just numbers; it also is about who holds *power.*

The term *ethnic* is just as slippery. In part, this is because our ethnicities generally are blends of more or less (increasingly less) "pure" ethnic strains. Although ethnicity can be measured to some extent, self-identification and peer identification are very powerful influences here. If we accept that each of us is a mixture of strains, we may perceive ourselves and others may perceive us as looking, acting, feeling, thinking like one strain in one set of circumstances and like another strain in another set of circumstances.[10] Our self-perceptions and the perceptions of others may or may not agree. Although that also can hold for perceptions of minority status, the scope of perceptions is much wider for ethnicity, and far more subjective.

In certain cases, we may have to meet someone else's standards in order to lay valid claim to a specific ethnicity, as many Native Americans must do in order to qualify for membership in a particular tribe, or even band within a tribe. We may "feel" (or claim that we feel) Anishinabe (Ojibway), or Lac Court Oreille Band of the Ojibway, but that claim alone would not lead to our admission. *That* usually requires documented ancestry, which may or may not be readily available, especially if the tribe or band relies heavily on oral tradition in such matters. Or it may be the display of a specific skill: For some Basques, the ability to speak Basque with reasonable fluency is sufficient indication of someone's "Basqueness."

In my presentation, I refer to the experiences of three sometimes overlapping groups of minorities: indigenous, linguistic, and ethnic. Indigenous groups appear to have little problem with their identification as ethnic minorities so long as it is clear that their indigenous status is recognized: They were the chief residents of the land before more recent arrivals came to or created the present nation, and as such feel that they have a particularly valid claim on its resources and services. Linguistic groups may or may not think of themselves as ethnic minorities,[11] but they certainly are aware of their minority status where recognition of the social validity of their languages is concerned: its usage in schools, government, the courts, the media, and others. As for the term *ethnic* I already have indicated that it is not easy to define. However, it does seem to me to be an appropriate umbrella term for all three groups where their media experiences are concerned, since all three were (and in many cases still are) largely ignored or misrepresented by the mainstream media, and usually have had to struggle to acquire the means to speak in their own right.

CIVIL SOCIETY AND PUBLIC SPHERE

My admittedly broad-brush consideration of a highly complex issue is intended chiefly to serve as an introduction to another issue: Why should we even attempt to think in terms of ethnic minorities? Perhaps the term itself may be invalid if there is so much disagreement about what it means or includes, or if, as some claim, there is no way to use either half of the term without insulting at least some of those to whom it might apply. My answer is that we need not use it in some circumstances, and should not do so in others, but that it *is* important to employ it when we consider why and how the electronic media may, can, and already do play important roles in the establishment and maintenance of a truly *civil* society: one where people with differing backgrounds and priorities can communicate on roughly equal terms with one another, can celebrate their similarities as they come to better understand their differences, and can discover ways to work together to improve the quality of life for all.

There is another issue to be dealt with before we consider the civil society and the public sphere, and the place of the ethnic minority media within them. At one time, we could assume that society would be understood as part of what made up the *nation-state*.[12] More recently, the concept of the nation-state has been challenged as possibly outmoded. Ironically, the electronic media themselves often are cited as one of the elements informing that challenge, with the communication satellite and the internet allegedly helping to break the hegemony of the nation-state by opening the world to the free flow of information and entertainment and to the possibility of creating electronic communities of interest wherever there are computers and modems.

However, neither medium has *carte blanche* to go wherever it wishes, or to proceed without obstruction once its products (e.g., the U.S. TV series *Baywatch*, various Usenet groups discussing such topics as swimming suit fashions, Islam and women, political correctness, and others) enter national media delivery systems around the world. Economic, technological, cultural, and political barriers exist in every nation-state. Some of those barriers would exist without it—poverty and intolerance are not limited by national boundaries—but the nation-state is likely to remain influential in its role as gatekeeper for some time to come. Thus, I assume the continuing relevance of the nation-state for my consideration of civil society and the public sphere.

The civil society is a crucial element in understanding German philosopher Jürgen Habermas' concept of the public sphere. The first cannot exist without the second, and the second depends on the first for its own continuation. That is why I have employed Habermas' concept in my consideration of the roles that have been/could be played within the public sphere by the electronic media. Those media would appear to be well-suited to support the ongoing dialogue among the diverse and sometimes conflicting forces in society that Habermas regards as the *raison d'etre* for the public sphere. Most electronic media are in part or wholly oral, they are increasingly economical to operate, and large numbers of people own the equipment needed to receive them. However, his voluminous writings make little specific reference to the electronic media, and such references as there are do not indicate just how they might be used to that end. Therefore, my work is an extrapolation on Habermas' concept, and I suspect that I may be taking the concept in directions that he would not have imagined, and might find curious or irrelevant.

I provide here a brief summary of those aspects of Habermas' concept that I find especially relevant to my consideration of the ways in which ethnic minorities use the electronic media. I follow that summary with a set of *structural factors* that appear to affect the nature of electronic media participation by ethnic minorities in the public sphere. I concentrate on those factors because I regard them as having particularly important effects on the existence and ultimate uses made by ethnic minorities of the various electronic media outlets. Furthermore, a structural analysis is well-suited to a comparative study of media practices: It foregrounds the frameworks that support the manner in which the media are used in similar and dissimilar ways within different nations. I then offer some theoretical considerations, and close the chapter with a brief history of the overall development of ethnic minority electronic media.

HABERMAS AND THE PUBLIC SPHERE

When German philosopher Jürgen Habermas introduced his concept of the public sphere in the late 1950s,[13] his homeland was a very different place. It had made a remarkable recovery from World War II—so remarkable, in fact, that most Germans no longer were willing to take menial or dangerous jobs such as garbage collecting, toilet cleaning, or even (*mirabile dictu* in the land of Mercedes-Benz) automobile assembly. Thus, "foreigners" from Yugoslavia, Spain, Italy, Morocco and other southerly locales were beginning to appear on the streets of the larger German cities. They were relatively few in number; in any case they were *gastarbeiter* ("guest workers") and therefore temporary residents. Still, they were widely regarded by the mainstream population as "different": Darker-skinned, -haired and -eyed, sometimes oddly dressed, loud of speech and flamboyant of gesture. They cooked and worshiped in strange ways. Few of them

spoke German. But they were *invited* guests, and a few of the State (*Land*) radio
stations then comprising the West German public radio service ARD—a public
service monopoly radio service at the time—began in the early 1960s (Voss,
2001) some of them with informational programs in their own languages, usually
for 15 minutes or less per language per day.

There is no indication in Habermas' early writings that his public sphere
might have room for those new guests. To him, it was at that time a realm in
which political discussion and debate could/should take place among the citizenry, meaning the mainstream population. The passage of time and the massive
changes within Germany itself—nearly 10% of its population now is foreign-
born—have led him to speak increasingly of a public sphere in which economic
issues are nearly as prominent as political issues, and in which ethnic minorities
do have a place (see the appendix). How much of a place is uncertain. For example, in a 1995 seminar session at Stanford University, Habermas appeared to indicate that he regarded citizenship as a requirement for participation in the
sphere,[14] and a fair number of ethnic minorities have faced barriers to acquiring
citizenship in their "new homelands," including Germany.

Habermas' writings about the public sphere never have been very specific
concerning ways in which participation within it might be facilitated through the
media. He makes numerous historical references to the mass media as relevant
agents, but can be quite disdainful when speaking of electronic mass media ("The
world fashioned by mass media is a public sphere in appearance only"
[Habermas, 1989: 171]). He pays far more attention to face-to-face spoken communication as the customary and preferred vehicle for dialogue among individuals and within/between groups.[15] He also appears to regard the public sphere as
functioning primarily at the national level, at least in terms of the sorts of topics
and concerns that might be discussed or debated within its confines.

Habermas might be challenged by Hartley and McKee's (2000: 210) depiction
of the public sphere: "(T)he public sphere is entirely encompassed, like a Russian
doll, by the mediasphere, which in turn is encompassed by the semiosphere."
They go on to state that

> The mediasphere is not set in opposition to the public sphere. . . . Instead
> the mediasphere is conceptualized as the very medium that *connects* the
> world of political and public dialogue with the larger universe of culture.
> It is the inter-penetration of politics, media and "semiosis" that renders so
> much of what passes for politics as *narrative*, turns "rational" sciences like
> government into *drama, story, image, symbol*, and others. At the same time, it
> shows how those same apparently immaterial objects have very real
> political impact.

I find their approach very congenial, as is evident in Chapter 5.

Whether Habermas would accept my present use of his concept of the public sphere as a place where ethnic minorities and the mainstream culture might acknowledge, understand, and value their similarities and differences, I do not know. Certainly, he has stimulated me to think about the ways in which such a sphere might be created. Nor do I know whether he would accept the concept of alternative (mini-) spheres.[16] I have drawn on the work of Dahlgren and of Curran,[17] as well as Fraser (who uses the term *subaltern counterpublic* when describing the media activities of the women's movement),[18] in broadening my interpretation of Habermas to include such spheres, as well as a wider range of electronic media formats than Habermas acknowledges. Dahlgren's (1995) division of the public sphere into *political* and *cultural* spheres also has been useful in my study. Downing and Husband's (2002: 11) assertion of a "Right to be Understood" within the mediated public sphere, where they warn against the privileging of unidirectional "communication," has led me to feature a wider variety of ethnic media approaches to dialogue than I might otherwise have done. Anderson's (1991) concept of the *imagined community* and Appadurai's (1996) treatment of the development and maintenance of community among diaspora groups have aided my understanding of why many ethnic minority groups, and émigré/diaspora groups in particular, may use the electronic media as they do in maintaining links with their old/ancestral homeland cultures, thus creating mini-spheres.

In my application of Habermas' concept of the public sphere to the realities faced by ethnic minorities working through the electronic media, I have separated *policy* and *institutional form* so as to make their component parts clearer. They are of course intertwined, but not always in ways that one might have predicted, or even that the policymakers may have intended or that the institutions themselves may have anticipated. My definition of policy admittedly is quite liberal, including as it does not only presidential decrees, major court decisions and laws passed by legislative bodies, but also the actions of government- or license fee-supported broadcasters, as well as commercial operations, in developing specific program services for ethnic minorities, codes of practice treating their on-air depiction, and others I have defined *practices* as including both *structural* and *programming* components.

I begin with the identification of where, how and in what forms certain nations already have begun to do so, whether intentionally or not. That in turn has led me to develop a schema which provides a more precise indication of the component parts of an electronic public sphere.

A STRUCTURAL SCHEMA

What follows is an outline of the structural elements that are examined in detail in Chapters 2 through 6. My intent in setting it forth here is to provide readers with a comprehensive indication of what I mean by *structural elements*, and why I regard those elements as central to understanding ethnic minority electronic media activity in a broader societal context.

Types of Outlets

Although most studies of electronic media concentrate on governmentally licensed media, few raise questions concerning the sorts of problems that ethnic minorities may face when applying for electronic media licenses. The presence of *un*licensed electronic media services that might foster ethnic minority activity attracts even less attention. The issue of accessibility to services for ethnic minority users rarely receives attention aside from allegations of "red-lining"[19] by cable companies.

- *Licensed outlets.* Terrestrial radio? Terrestrial TV? Cable Radio? Cable TV? Satellites?
- *Unlicensed outlets.* Internet? Audio- and videocassette?
* *Accessibility.* For ethnic minority audiences? For "majority" audiences?

Levels of Service (Geography)

When we consider level of media service, we generally think in terms of national or local, but there are others. Furthermore, the level of a service will make it more appropriate for some kinds of material and less so for others.

- International?
- Regional (supranational)?
- National?
- State/province?
- Local?
- Neighborhood?

Policy

There are several types of policies: those generated by governments, by media services themselves, by advertisers. Some policies encourage, whereas others discourage. They may or may not take into account the presence, absence or nature of portrayal of ethnic minorities.

- Are there state-licensed electronic media outlets specifically for minorities?
- Are there preference policies that assist minorities in acquiring or sharing licensed outlets?
- Are there laws/statutes mandating balanced portrayals, reasonable amounts of airtime, and others, for ethnic minorities? What recourse do minorities have if they feel that their rights have been violated?
- Do electronic media services and organizations (networks, individual stations, professional associations) have codes of practices that address issues of portrayal, amount of airtime, and other such issues?

Financing

Advertising in its various guises seems increasingly dominant as financial support for electronic media services in general, but not for those operated by ethnic minorities. Why that situation exists, what forms of support do predominate, and the advantages and disadvantages to each where minority services are concerned, all are vital to the growth and impact of ethnic minority electronic media.

- What forms (Annual government appropriation? Annual license fee? Advertising? Corporate/Individual donation? Media operation sale of services/merchandise/programs?
- How *stable* are those forms? How *adequate* are they for each minority operation's (self-) perceived needs?
- How do the various forms affect each operation's *programming* policies? (What sorts of influence might be expected in connection with each form?)

Operational Goals

Electronic media services differ in the extent to which they establish and revise their operational goals. Ethnic minority services often perceive themselves as facing a broad array of choices where goals are concerned, which makes it all the more important to articulate and prioritize them.

- What does each operation regard as its chief *raison(s) d'etre?* How do those top priorities affect minority participation in the public sphere?
- Are those priorities likely to be attractive to other minority groups? To the mainstream?"

- Which goals appear to predominate:
  - Maintaining links with the "ancestral homeland?"
  - Preserving, restoring or advancing the use of a minority language?
  - Providing and/or restoring a sense of pride in minority accomplishments (cultural, social, political, economic)?
  - Combating negative stereotypes, especially those provided by mainstream media?
  - Indicating how minorities and mainstream can/do work together?
  - Serving as source of information on employment, health care, education, financial aid, and others?
  - Illustrating that ethnic minorities are capable of operating media services?

Media Service-Minority Community Links

Perhaps because ethnic minority electronic media were comparatively recent arrivals on the media scene, they face high expectations where their communities are concerned. Satisfying those expectations will rely to some degree on how a media service keeps in touch with its community.

- Does the service have a community board? If so, how *representative* is it of the community? Is it strictly *advisory*, or does it have some real power?
- Does the "larger" minority community (beyond the board) *participate* in selecting goals and priorities? Working within the service itself? Does the service itself facilitate participation, or does most of the initiative to participate come from outside?
- Does the service conduct audience research? Does it share results with the larger community?

Primary Audiences

It is difficult to develop a meaningful program schedule if one lacks knowledge of which audience(s) one hopes to reach or might expect to reach, given the medium through which one operates and the level at which one operates. Furthermore, the pressures to favor some groups or individuals and to disfavor others can be especially strong where ethnic minority services are concerned.

- One's own minority group? Other minority groups? Mainstream? Children? Adolescents? Younger adults? Older adults? Women? Men? Rural? Urban?
- Who is favored (amounts of airtime, times of day, days of week, frequency of guest appearances)? Who is disfavored or excluded? Are newly significant minority groups (recently arrived groups such as Somalis in Minnesota, Kurds in Sweden) accommodated?
- Who initiates the contact—the media service or the group?

Programming

Ultimately, this is why any media service exists. Although the basic formats are common to electronic media services of all sorts, the opportunity exists for ethnic minorities to devise new uses for old formats so that they can reflect themselves more accurately and appropriately. For various reasons, that is not always easy to manage. Relevant categories are:

- *Information.* News, commentary, feature interviews, call-in shows; roundtable; talk shows; discussions; coverage of meetings; documentaries; advertising.
- *Education.* Teaching the language; teaching cultural and political history; teaching teachers how to teach minorities; linking with schools to provide production experience for students.
- *Entertainment.* Music (contemporary, "traditional," popular, classical, minority, "world," "mainstream;" local performers, national/international recording artists), dance, sports, comedies and dramas, game shows, "reality" programs.
- To what extent is programming *representational* ("displaying" others)? To what extent is it *participatory* (others speaking for themselves)?

THEORIES AND CONCEPTS

As was the case with society itself for much of the 20th century, ethnic minorities by and large were ignored when sociologists, psychologists, political scientists, and communication scholars considered the various elements that made societies what they were. Minorities were invisible, and perhaps unimportant, especially where the dominant societal paradigm was assimilationist. In such a climate, theorizing about their place within society would have been considered a waste of time, even if closer examination of their particular mores, customs, and others might hold a certain inherent fascination.

Where the field of communication is concerned, relevant theory begins to appear in the late 1950s, when intercultural communication gains prominence as a potentially important realm of scholarly investigation. Anthropologist Edward Hall's *The Silent Language* (Hall, 1959) sets forth the then-revolutionary (to U.S. residents, at least) concept that "other" people in other parts of the world have other ways of communicating than those with which most of "us" (again, U.S. residents) are familiar. Although Hall does not proclaim a theory, he certainly inspires others to think along theoretical lines. He tends to illustrate those "other" ways of communicating primarily through reference to the practices of cultures in other parts of the world (quite typical among anthropologists at the time), which may reduce their relevance to the situations of ethnic minorities living in a "majority" culture. Also, his approach would appear to be more directly applicable to studies of the *portrayal* of ethnic minorities through the electronic media, which makes it less valuable for my structurally based study.

The two sets of theories that have greater value for my study are those related to *hegemony* and to *dependency*, particularly as exercised through *cultural/media imperialism*. They originally were stimulated by Herbert Schiller's 1969 *Mass Media and American Empire* (Schiller, 1969), which drew on both theories. Schiller set in motion a serious, if not always academically rigorous, consideration of the possible effects on other cultures of U.S. television, and to a lesser extent, other U.S. mass media. The theories achieved greater prominence during the 1970s, as debates over the New World Information (and Communication) Order (NWICO), inspired to some degree by Schiller's work, got underway.[20] In the course of that consideration, there was frequent reference to the likelihood or unlikelihood that those other cultures, and particularly those in Third World ("developing") nations, would become dependent on U.S. culture as portrayed through U.S. media, and would consciously and/or unconsciously allow it to displace their own cultures. There also was some reference to the question of whether those in the United States who were responsible for exporting U.S. culture through U.S. television and other media, for example, TV network executives, were exercising a kind of cultural hegemony in a deliberate, calculated way, or whether it simply did not occur to them to consider the possible impact of their material on other cultures.

When I began to study the ways in which indigenous peoples used the electronic media, I was struck by the fact that many of their radio and TV broadcasts seemed to be a mixture of presentational styles. Although some of the broadcasts sounded much like what one would hear on mainstream stations, some of them decidedly did not. As I watched and listened to them over several years, and as I spoke with the indigenous announcers, reporters, disc jockeys, interviewers and others who produced and delivered the broadcasts, I learned that they themselves often were not conscious of the extent to which they did or did not sound like their mainstream counterparts. (I also encountered a very few who consciously modeled their delivery on a specific mainstream individual or on a composite of such individuals.) I noticed much the same thing about administrative practices around the stations themselves.

I already was familiar with theories of dependency and hegemony. Taking into account one aspect of the former (that those importing radio and TV programming from the United States or Europe often are not conscious of its effects on their beliefs and behaviors) and one aspect of the latter (that those who determine what should go into a production, how it should be presented, and what effects it might have, often are not even aware that they are making choices or that there will be any impact), I have come to believe that something similar occurs in the behaviors of ethnic minority media staff.[21] However, I also believe that the dependency exhibited here is not as pervasive as some media scholars, Schiller in particular, have contended.[22] I have listened to and watched many ethnic minority radio and TV productions and have visited many ethnic stations and media centers, as well as ethnic minority-operated Web sites, in coming to that conclusion. Although I cannot totally reject or accept the theories of dependency and hegemony, I do see them as applicable in some circumstances. I also believe that they apply to ethnic minorities as well as indigenous peoples.[23]

I have not discovered any theories relating to institutional structures and their effects on programmatic outcomes that strike me as relevant for my study, but I have been aided by a perspective on *regulatory* structure as set forth by Krasnow, Longley, and Terry (1982). That perspective takes into account the influences of six agents—the Federal Communications Commission (FCC), the broadcast industry, citizen groups, the legislative branch, the courts and the executive branch—in determining regulatory policy. Their multidimensional approach has served as a model for my own structural schema. I also have found a similar, although less thoroughly articulated perspective offered by Hirsch (Hirsch, Miller, & Kline, 1977: 13-42) to be of assistance in assessing the nature and importance of organizational structure, particularly in terms of his consideration of interorganizational relationships. Finally, Giddens' (1984) concept of institutional *structure* as both a limiting and an enabling factor where a society's use of the media is concerned has influenced my utilization of a structural framework in the present study.

A BRIEF HISTORY

Although it has become fashionable in some circles to minimize the importance of history when considering a highly contemporary phenomenon such as ethnic minority media activity, I feel that it is essential for us to do so for four reasons. First, it serves to place on stage the essential characters—who is involved, in what forms, for what reasons—at the beginning of my structural analysis, so that we have a general idea of how they interact, but also of what set them in motion in the first place. Second, it should remind us that things have not happened by chance, and that very often they have happened because of events and actions that have taken place in the context of the larger society. Third, it should help to answer the question of why it took so long for such an activity to develop. And fourth, it can highlight ways in which changing societal climates have affected and may still affect the development of ethnic minority media.

Beginnings

There was a minority presence of sorts in the electronic media from early on, at least in a few nations. In the United States of the 1920s, local radio stations in the larger cities where émigrés (largely from Europe) were most numerous often broadcast a weekly "German (Polish, Swedish, and others) Hour." It usually featured music from the ancestral homeland, perhaps a live performance by a local German/Polish/Swedish choir/band/soloist, a community calendar, all of it held together by a German/Polish/Swedish and others speaking host (and occasionally, hostess). Stations were anxious to fill out their program schedules, and German-American, Swedish-American and other émigré societies might pay for the airtime.

Other minority groups—long-resident ones, certainly—fared less well. Opportunities for airtime were rare, and usually were limited to occasional appearances by African-American musicians or Native American storytellers. There is no record of an ethnic minority-operated radio station during the decade, although an association of African-American businessmen, the Harlem Broadcasting Corporation, operated radio recording studios, purchased a block of air time on New York City station WRNY for programs showcasing African-American talent (Barlow, 1999: 24), and attempted in 1929 to purchase an existing station in New York City, but without success. The 1930s were much the same, although by late in the decade a few stations in major northern cities (e.g., New York City, Chicago) had begun to provide more substantial blocks of airtime for African-American listeners, since they had become sufficiently numerous to constitute a promising commercial target. Programs usually featured recordings of what was called "race" music by record companies such as RCAVictor.

Other nations offer even fewer examples of minority broadcasting during the 1920s and 1930s, but generally speaking they are along much the same lines: Bits and pieces of "minority culture."[24] Nations continued to follow assimilationist policies, and minorities, ethnic or otherwise, could expect little more than occasional appearances as cultural exotica on the airwaves. This was the case for all types of radio services, whether national or local and whether supported by advertising revenue, annual license fees, or government appropriations. The BBC began broadcasts in Welsh and in Scots Gaelic in 1923, but they were sporadic, although Welsh fared considerably better over time than did Scots Gaelic.[25] The Norwegian public service broadcaster, NRK, started occasional broadcasts in Sami ("Lapp") in 1934, but did not make them part of the regular schedule until 1946.

World War II

By the early 1940s, the presence of African Americans and Native Americans in the U.S. military, along with the migration of substantial numbers of the former to northern U.S. industrial centers (Cleveland, Detroit) led to the establishment of further African-American-oriented (but still White-owned and operated) radio stations. The radio networks began to broadcast individual programs and short series about ethnic minority contributions to the war effort (Savage, 1999). In a few other nations, the war also led to some ethnic minority broadcast "firsts," such as the creation in 1942 by the New Zealand Broadcasting Service of a 5-minute weekly news program in Maori (Lemke, 1995). But most of the industrialized nations had minuscule ethnic minority communities, and the war did nothing to alter their "media invisibility."

Some of the wartime broadcasts involving ethnic minorities ceased at war's end, although others continued: The Maori radio newscasts ran until 1972. Also, the occasional one-time radio programs or short series continued to appear now and again during the immediate postwar years.[26] Television, which had been viewed by relatively few individuals before or after World War II, began to develop into a truly mass media in some industrialized nations by the early 1950s. It followed the pattern set by radio, in that it was owned, operated by and programmed for the white majority, and the few shows that featured ethnic performers and lifestyles confined portrayals to servants, entertainers or comic figures (Barlow, 1999; MacDonald, 1979). *The Amos n' Andy Show,* carried over from radio by CBS Television, was heavy with "Negro dialect" and negative stereotyping, but did manage on occasion to include some positive images of family coherence. Also, it was acted by African Americans, whereas BBC-TV's *Black and White Minstrel Show* (on air from 1958 to 1978) featured Whites made up as Blacks and performing song and dance routines that came straight out of the old minstrel show tradition, where stupidity and gullibility frequently took center stage (Andrews & Juilliard, 1986; Ely, 1991).

The Postwar Period and Ethnic Minority Ownership

The immediate postwar years also saw the beginning of something that, in its modest way, was revolutionary: An ethnic minority owned and operated electronic media service. Frequency-modulated (FM or UHF) radio broadcasting had barely appeared before World War II, and was slow to resume its progress after the war. Where the United States was concerned, few potential owners cared to take the risks associated with the new medium, since few people owned FM receivers. That made it relatively simple for anyone willing to take those risks to acquire an FM broadcast license. However, the first station to attempt an all-ethnic minority-format (music) was an AM station purchased by a Hispanic American businessman in San Antonio, Texas, in 1946 (Meyer, 2001). WDIA in Memphis,

Tennessee (U.S.) came soon after, and also was on AM; it moved (gradually) to a music format in 1948-49.[27] It was White-owned and managed, although management did depend heavily on African-American disc jockey (DJ) Nat D. Williams to develop the format and to recruit African-American DJs, but did not increase his pay or provide him with an administrative title (Barlow, 1999: 111-115).

WDIA was an important precedent for the development of ethnic minority-owned- and operated broadcasting in the United States, simply because it showed that an "all ethnic" format could be successful: It had risen from no. 6 to no. 1 among Memphis radio stations by fall 1949. In 1949, another AM station, WERD (Atlanta, Georgia), was purchased by an African American, J.B. Blayton, and managed by his son, who also hired an African-American program director (Barlow, 1999: 124). WERD was another powerful example for African-American investors, and during the 1950s, numerous African-American-owned and operated stations came on air, and by the 1960s there were a few Hispanic-American-owned and operated radio[28] and television stations, as well. (The first African-American-owned and operated TV station appeared in 1971.)

Still, U.S. ethnic-owned and operated stations remained relatively few in number, for three main reasons. First, few banks or other potential sources of financial support were willing to risk loans to would-be ethnic minority broadcasters; they were an unknown quantity and so were the services that they intended to provide. Second, specific ethnic minority groups (African American, Hispanic-American, and others) were not all that sizable in most U.S. cities, and size of audience did matter to potential investors. And third, the commercial model remained dominant, so that it was difficult to sell investors on a venture that did not have the presumably essential characteristics of experienced administrators and reasonably large and affluent audiences that would attract advertisers. Because very few surveys (and none by "reputable" organizations) revealed anything about the size and/or purchasing habits of ethnic minorities, it was difficult to produce solid evidence that would give investors the requisite confidence to back such stations.

The European Public Service Tradition

In most other nations, the possibility of obtaining a license to broadcast was not simply difficult; it was impossible. With one exception, European nations operated broadcast services as public service broadcasting (PSB) monopolies, and there were no licenses to be had. That exception—Great Britain's BBC—had a PSB monopoly until 1954, when Parliament passed legislation authorizing the creation of a commercially supported television service. The BBC derived its income from annual license fees paid by households owning radio and TV sets, while the Independent Television companies (14 in all, and free from commercial competition) derived theirs from advertising. Commercially financed radio would not come along until 1973; it, too, was a monopoly.

Great Britain had experienced considerable growth in its ethnic minority population following World War II. However, the BBC did little to serve the more recently arrived ethnic minority audiences (those other than the Welsh, Scots, and Northern Irish living within their respective regions) until the late 1960s, when BBC local radio got underway. Because many of the new local stations were located in or near major urban areas where South Asians, Caribbean Islanders, and other "nonindigenous" ethnic minorities were most numerous, some of them began to provide airtime for programs highlighting the various ethnic cultures, largely through their popular music. There also were programs that served as sources of assistance and advice for members of those ethnic communities. When local commercial radio stations came on air, some of them followed the BBC's lead. In neither case was service to ethnic communities mandatory, and few stations offered more than 1 or 2 hours per week for such programs, which usually were scheduled during the less popular hours and days. Also, although ethnic minorities were involved in producing the programs, they were subject to BBC and Independent Local Radio (ILR) control in terms of program content.[29]

Operating out of a similar public service tradition, where the PSB was supported largely through annual license fees paid by each household owning a set, New Zealand took a quite radical approach to the question of who was to be served by the public broadcaster. Several decades of pressure from Maori, who claimed that they, too, paid license fees, but received very little programming featuring their culture or in their language, brought change: Parliament passed a law (the Broadcasting Act of 1989) under which a newly created agency, the Broadcasting Commission, would disburse some of the license fee money for the specific purpose of "promoting Maori language and culture" [through broadcasting]. The financial support that this provided—several million U.S. dollars a year—permitted the development of a number of Maori tribal radio stations (Government of New Zealand, 1989: 2).

Most of the other European public service broadcast monopolies were slower than the BBC had been to serve not just the national audience but also the country's regions. They remained national, with little or no regional service and no local services until the 1970s. Commercial services, national and local, were not introduced until the 1980s or even 1990s, and few of them afforded opportunities for minority broadcasters. But another form of broadcasting already had begun to emerge by the 1940s, and it provided airtime for ethnic minority groups large and small, not to mention many non-ethnic minority groups. In an often used phrase, it became a "voice for the voiceless."

Community Radio and Ethnic Minority Involvement

Community radio (and later, television) could have existed much earlier than it did in most nations, if only. . . . The *ifs* ranged from abandoning the monopoly approach and the assimilationist philosophy to licensing low power services to developing low-cost production and transmission equipment. In fact, the U.S. FCC began to license low power (10 watt) radio stations in 1948, and a few venturesome individuals tried their hands at something that had the potential to be a truly alternative radio service. One such station, KPFA-FM Pacifica Radio in San Francisco, California, came on air in 1949 and soon began to broadcast programs in which Communists, "beat" poets (e.g., Allan Ginsberg,) and ethnic minorities (including the more radical Black Panthers) spoke, some of them for the first time over radio.[30]

The development of community radio in the United States and Canada[31] was glacially slow until the 1960s. But that decade, rich with civil rights demonstrations and anti-Vietnam War protests, became the catalyst for the greatest period of growth in ethnic minority electronic media activity that North America has experienced. Although community radio itself was a major incubator, there were other dimensions to it, and one was particularly noteworthy: citizen involvement in station license renewals. It began with the filing of complaints, most of them from African Americans, about the ethnically biased broadcasts of two Jackson, Mississippi, television stations. The FCC placed both stations on 1-year license renewals, and warned each to improve its record of hiring and of reporting about African Americans (who constituted more than half of the population in the stations' coverage area). When the year was up, one of the stations could show enough improvement in both respects to receive a full-term license renewal. The other, WLBT-TV, showed very little improvement, but after lengthy discussion by the FCC, it too received a full-term renewal. The original complainants, assisted by the United Church of Christ, took the case to the U.S. Circuit Court of Appeals—twice. Ultimately, the court ruled in 1969 that the FCC's licensing process was deeply flawed, in that it appeared to deny citizens any meaningful role in determining whether a station licensed to serve them was actually doing so. The result of that ruling was that citizens gained the explicit right under the law to have their complaints considered as a material part of the FCC's renewal of a station's license.[32]

It took a few years for the ruling to have real impact, but by the mid-1970s the license renewals of several hundred stations had been challenged, with ethnic minority groups prominent among the challengers. Only a handful of those challenges resulted in FCC action against the stations, because the stations themselves usually managed to reach agreements with the challengers that would answer the latter's concerns. Often that meant increased coverage of ethnic minority community and individual activities, which often involved members of those communities as direct participants in the production of appropriate programming. Sometimes it meant the establishment of training programs for ethnic minority individuals who wished to seek employment in meaningful positions, for example, announcing, reporting, studio operations, sales, and occasionally management.[33]

Community radio was helped by start-up, training and other U.S. Government grants, but also by the rapidly decreasing cost of studio equipment and the general spirit of citizen activism that pervaded the 1970s. Although there was no requirement that a community station commit airtime to broadcasts by and/or for ethnic minorities, most of the stations did and still do provide some airtime for the purpose; a few, for example, KMOJ-FM in Minneapolis, Minnesota, and WPFW-FM (a Pacifica Radio operation) in Washington, DC are wholly African American. Because community radio stations have had to operate on a non commercial basis, they often have subsisted on donated (used) equipment and have relied heavily on unpaid volunteers for everything but management and engineering (themselves low-wage positions at those stations). Still, most of the stations have remained on air, and have served as training grounds for many individuals, ethnic minority and otherwise, who have distinguished themselves in the field of broadcasting.

Community broadcasting in other parts of the world blossomed during roughly the same period, and for some of the same reasons: anti-Vietnam War protests, civil rights activism, and demands for "voices of our own." The Canadian and Australian experiences form the closest parallels with the U.S. experience. That is not surprising, since those two nations have featured strong commercial broadcasting sectors for many decades, and the community broadcasting sector of each has an element of anti-commercialism. Furthermore, civil rights demonstrations and anti-Vietnam War protests were prominent in both countries. Neither nation's broadcast regulators went as far as did the U.S. FCC in developing preference policies for ethnic minority license-seekers, but they did create what was in effect a special category of license available only to community broadcasters, some of whom were ethnic minorities.

Each nation provided funding earmarked for specific ethnic minority services, namely those provided by and for Native Americans and Inuit in Canada[34] and by and for Aboriginal Australians. In addition, Australia created a special licensing category for radio stations that were dedicated *solely* to ethnic minority broadcasting. In the late 1970s, the Australian government also authorized the development of a temporary national radio broadcasting service exclusively for ethnic minority groups—this in order to reach as many group members as possible, and in their own languages, with information about a new government health program. It turned out to be useful in still other ways, the ethnic minority groups themselves fought for its survival, and it became a permanent organization: the SBS. SBS is one of very few national broadcast services for ethnic minorities, and far and away the largest.[35]

Preference Policies in the United States

The FCC took a highly significant step in the early 1970s where ethnic minority media access was concerned: It began to develop a set of preference policies for its licensing process (see Chapter 3). Taken *in toto*, those policies made it more likely that ethnic minorities would receive broadcast licenses. Dozens of stations, most of them radio, owned and operated by African Americans, Hispanic-Americans, Native Americans, Inuit, and others, came on air during the 1970s and on into the 1980s. There also were various forms of financial assistance offered by U.S. government agencies: The Corporation for Public Broadcasting offered a Minority Station Improvement Project Grant, and the National Telecommunications and Information Administration provided funding through a Minority Station Start-Up program. Interestingly, stations receiving their licenses through preference policies were not *required* to serve ethnic minority audiences, although all of them did.

Europe in the 1970s and 1980s

European nations took somewhat different approaches.[36] Although it could be argued that the protests, demonstrations, and "power to the people" movements had some influence on government policy in the United States, Australia, and Canada, it is more difficult to sustain that argument in the case of Europe. Sweden and Norway, for example, had featured public service broadcasting monopolies since the 1930s. When the two nations decided to open up their systems in the late 1970s, it was pressure from non-Lutheran religious organizations that played the most important role in winning parliamentary approval for the creation of a state-supported set of low-power transmitters that would serve as access radio channels (Tomlinson, 1994). Both the parliaments and those religious bodies were quite surprised to discover that ethnic minorities in the larger cities and in some university towns soon were among the heaviest users of the new *närradio* ("nearby-radio") services.

Where Great Britain was concerned, the 1970s saw a number of extra-legal challenges to the system. Nonindigenous minorities were among the challengers, but they had to do so largely by operating *unlicensed* radio services as "land-based pirates," which meant that they were frequent targets of the authorities.[37] Finally, in the 1990s, interested parties were permitted to apply for limited power radio licenses, and Caribbean, South Asian and other ethnic stations, as well as many others, took to the airwaves legally.

Some of the West German public radio stations had provided broadcasts in the languages (Italian, Serbian, Croatian, Spanish) of Germany's so-called "guest workers" by the early 1960s, but usually for 15 or fewer minutes per day, and not necessarily on all days (Voss, 2001). The Second German Television service (Zweites Deutsches Fernsehen) began to offer a weekly television magazine program, *Nachbarn* ("Neighbors") in the mid-1960s, in the same languages. Unlicensed radio services began to appear in the 1970s, most of them short-lived (Radio Dreyeckland was an exception, and remains on air) and few of them offering airtime for ethnic minority groups. The growth of cable television in the

1980s (see later) stimulated the development of cable access radio and TV in the northern *Länder* (states), and many ethnic minority groups took advantage of that opportunity. The southern *Länder* followed a different path: They began to license independent, noncommercial radio stations as *Freies Radios* ("Free Radio") starting in the late 1980s. Those stations in the larger cities, for example, Munich and Stuttgart, often have made blocks of airtime available to ethnic minorities.

France liberalized the licensing of radio (and soon, television) largely because the opposition Socialist Party had promised to end the public service broadcasting monopoly if it won the 1981 national election, which it did. Initially, the Socialist-led government attempted to restrict the licensing of new radio stations to noncommercial license-seekers, which included a good many ethnic minorities, but that restriction was lifted within 2 years, and commercial licensees soon became predominant (Browne, 1999: 98-101, 129-131). Even so, various ethnic minority groups managed to obtain a foothold, and some of the stations operated by North African Arabs living in France developed into a modest national network, Radio Beur, based in Paris.

Italy, which also had a public service monopoly system, found itself in the position of having to license "pirate" radio stations (most of them operated by labor unions and student groups) in the late 1970s simply because the existing broadcast law did not provide the government with a sound basis for forbidding their existence. Relatively few of them served ethnic minorities, although Milan's Radio Popolare did and still does. Under Generalissimo Franco Spain maintained a public service broadcast monopoly and forbade most forms of self-expression on the part of the country's regions (Basque, Catalan, Galician, and others). After he died in 1975, national elections were held and the Socialist Party came to power. One of its early acts was to provide the regions with more autonomy, which included having their own broadcast facilities in their own languages. Losing no time, Catalonia and the Basque region were on air by 1977, first with radio, but soon after with television (Howkins, 1983; de Moragas Spa & Corominas, 1992; Rodriguez, 2001).

The Netherlands, which had seen considerable growth in its ethnic minority population starting in the 1960s, began to provide very limited amounts of airtime for ethnic minority languages (e.g., Moluccan) in 1966, through its public radio service (NOS). The public television service (also NOS) began in 1976 to carry even more limited amounts of ethnic minority material. The government also permitted some experiments with local and regional cable TV during the 1970s, but there was little ethnic minority involvement in them. However, the pressure for local radio and TV services mounted in the early 1980s, and in 1983 an Amsterdam cable TV channel began to carry a service specifically for ethnic minorities: *Migranttelevisie* ("Migrant TV"). It featured a mix of programs, some imported from ethnic minority homelands but others produced by ethnic minorities living in the city.[38] In 1985, the city government and other organizations helped to establish a cable radio and TV access service: SALTO (Stichting Amsterdamse Lokale Televisie/Radio Omroep) that was open to any and all interested parties, ethnic minorities included.[39] During the same period, local and regional radio spread to other parts of the country; most of the new services were transmitted through cable, and often featured programs made by ethnic minority groups (Browne, 1999; Gooskens, 1992).

The Soviet Union, as well as the People's Republic of China (PRC), supported ethnic minority broadcasting within their republics or regions and in their particular ethnic languages: Ukrainian, Armenian, Dai, Uighur, and many others.[40] But the broadcast time devoted to those languages was far outstripped by broadcasts in Russian and in Mandarin, and a speaker of Georgian or of Amoy who happened to live anywhere else in the nation generally would search the airwaves in vain for any trace of her or his language.[41] In other words, for the most part these were ethnic majority languages within the areas where they were broadcast, but unavailable elsewhere. The USSR and the PRC appeared to have three policy objectives here: to reach illiterate people; to "keep the locals happy," and to reinforce the notion that both countries featured "unity with diversity."

The same current of activism on behalf of social change helped motivate members of religious groups, particularly Roman Catholic priests in Latin America, to use radio to assist and even empower many of the indigenous groups in Mexico, Central America, and South America. Such a movement had begun on a small scale in 1947, when Father Salcedo established a tiny community radio station in Sutatenza, Colombia, although its primary goal was to ensure that the local population did not fall prey to Communist propaganda. "Liberation theology" and other teachings by individuals such as Paolo Freire inspired numerous priests to follow Salcedo's example and create local radio services for Mayan, Incan, Aztec, and other indigenous populations, usually with broadcasts in their own languages and often with "the locals" themselves as program producers.[42]

External Broadcasting and Ethnic Minorities

The use of external radio services to reach ethnic minorities in other countries with broadcasts in their own languages became quite widespread starting in the 1950s, in part because some of the communist nations began to support independence movements in Africa and Asia at that time. A few of the former colonies and protectorates—India, Pakistan, Indonesia, Egypt—had achieved independence by the early 1950s. However, most had not, and in many of them the European colonial powers either had not introduced radio broadcasting in the indigenous languages or provided little airtime for them. In essence, the indigenous peoples were treated as ethnic minorities. Radio Moscow and Radio Peking (later, Beijing) provided broadcast services in various African and Asian languages (among them minority languages such as Bambara and Zulu), and often employed political exiles fluent in those languages and living in Moscow or Peking to produce some of the programs carried by those services. Radio Cairo followed a similar path when Egypt under President Nasser began to identify itself as an African nation in the mid-1950s; political exiles formed the core of Shona, Ndebele, Fulani, Zulu, and other minority language services to Africa, where the usual message was encouragement of liberation from British, French, or other European rulers (Browne, 1982).[43]

The Union of South Africa was reacting to external broadcasts (but probably not those of Radio Cairo) when it created an unusual radio service for Black South Africans in 1964.[44] Radio Bantu featured programs in seven different Bantu languages—Zulu, Xhosa, and others—as well as English and Afrikaans. Unlike the Soviet and Chinese services, there was some likelihood that listeners could receive broadcasts in their particular languages in areas other than the tribal regions and so-called Black homelands;[45] it also could be heard in some of the Black townships housing the miners, garbage collectors, and others filling various undesirable or dangerous jobs in the cities. The service was available on FM only, which was a deliberate move to discourage the target audience from listening to short- or medium-wave broadcasts from surrounding nations—thus, external broadcasts. Most of those nations at that time had Black governments sympathetic to the overthrow of the Union's White government and its policy of *apartheid* (separation of the races). Tanzania, Southern Rhodesia (now Zimbabwe), and other neighboring States already had begun to broadcast to South Africa, and were voicing their support for South African Blacks. They also made their radio studios and transmitters available to individuals and groups belonging to or allied with the outlawed (in the Union) African National Congress, which developed (1967) an anti-*apartheid* radio service that it labeled Radio Freedom. The service broadcast in the same languages as did Radio Bantu, but could not be picked up by FM receivers, so its staff also distributed audiocassette recordings of some of its material in order to reach FM-only households, as well as to circumvent the Union's jamming of its broadcasts from nearby countries (Phelan, 1987; Tomaselli et al., 1985).

It was not all that unusual for newly independent Black African nations to provide external services in the languages of neighboring countries, many of them colonies but some of them independent. The Republic of Guinea, which became independent of French rule in 1958, soon initiated broadcast services through Radio Guinea for Equatorial Guinea (a Spanish colony) as well as for Sierra Leone and The Gambia (British colonies), but also to Senegal following its independence from France in 1960 (Browne, 1963: 113-122). Political exiles again provided the necessary command of indigenous languages, with differing messages for the present colonies ("Get rid of your colonial rulers") and for the former colony ("Get rid of your present rulers, who serve only as the stooges of France").

There is little evidence to indicate that the various external services directed to indigenous minorities had much success in fomenting rebellion. They often did serve to encourage the development or enlargement of indigenous language services within the target areas, and a few of them—Radio Freedom, for example—helped to sustain the hope of indigenous government over a prolonged period of time. The effectiveness of such external services often has been compromised by poor reception quality in target areas, limited amounts of airtime in each indigenous language, and, for the more ideological services (communist, Christian), messages couched in highly doctrinaire language that either is unclear or uninteresting to the intended audience. However, if the external service happens to be the only one providing a specific language, it may improve its chances of attracting listeners.

Ethnic Minorities and Cable, Satellites, Cassettes and the Internet

With a few exceptions, chiefly African and Hispanic-American, television services owned and operated by ethnic minorities did not appear until the 1990s (Frachon & Vargaftig, 1995; Moragas Spa & Garitaonandia, 1995; Rodriguez, 2001).[46] The medium simply was too expensive. Minorities usually had to content themselves with *access cable* services.[47] Perhaps the earliest of these was in 1965, when two cable companies were licensed by the New York borough of Manhattan to supply cable television service to the north and south halves of the island. One condition of the licenses, set by local government, was that the companies provide channels through which the citizenry could express itself. The companies also were to provide training and equipment for the purpose, at low cost or even free of charge. Many individuals and groups, ethnic minorities among them, soon took advantage of the opportunity. The FCC's Cable Television Report and Order of 1972 (36 FCC 2d 143) made it a requirement that cable systems serving cities with 3,500 or more subscribers provide similar access services.[48]

Cable television was slower to spread in other nations, although it did so very quickly in Canada, where 75% of all households had subscribed by 1980 (Murphy, 1983: 51). Many nations did not require that cable companies provide access channels or training programs, but cable operators often discovered that doing so helped to increase the cable subscriber base.

A number of German cities have impressive access channel operations (*Offener Kanale*) for both cable radio and TV, financed in part through a modest surcharge on the monthly cable bill, and they are heavily used by ethnic minorities living in the larger cities, Hamburg and Berlin in particular. The Netherlands, too, have seen heavy ethnic minority participation in cable access programming, as noted earlier.

Still, there are many nations with very low cable subscriber rates. Italy, for example, has a rate of less than 10% as of 2003. As a result, cable access has remained largely undeveloped there, and opportunities for ethnic minority participation in that form are rare. Spain, Portugal, Greece, and the Balkan States are in much the same situation, as are Australia and New Zealand. Japan had a cable subscriber rate of more than 50% as of 2002, but just slightly over half of the subscribers can receive anything more than terrestrial stations. In any case, there are few cable access services, and even fewer possibilities for ethnic minority electronic media participation in that highly homogeneous nation.[49]

Cable radio is widely available as part of most cable TV systems, but does not usually attract anything like the number of TV subscribers, so audiences for it tend to be very small and to include relatively low percentages of ethnic minority subscribers, probably because of the monthly subscriber fees. (In general, one cannot receive cable radio without subscribing to cable TV.) No nation requires that access cable radio or TV time or production assistance be provided specifically to ethnic minorities.

Satellite television is beginning to reach sizable numbers of subscribers in a few nations—the United States, Germany, Great Britain, Japan—but most satellite services do not relay locally originated programming, so there is no opportunity for cable access channels to find an additional outlet through satellites. However, satellites *have* been keys to success for the few nationally distributed ethnic minority services that have come into existence or have expanded their scope during the past decade or so. The Aboriginal Australian, Maori, Canadian and Alaskan Inuit, Native American (U.S.), South Asian (U.K.), African-American and Hispanic-American services such as American Indian Radio on Satellite (AIROS), BBC Asian Service (U.K., radio), the Aboriginal Peoples' Television Network, or APTN, in Canada, BRACS (Broadcasting for Remote Aboriginal Communities Scheme—Australia), Black Entertainment Television (BET), Univision (Hispanic-American) and others owe their existence, at least as national services, to the availability of reasonably priced satellite channels.

However, most listeners or viewers receive the services through cable, although some services—AIROS, for example—serve primarily as relays to feed individual terrestrial radio stations.[50] The annual cost of leasing a satellite channel is high enough that only operations with sizable target audiences (thus, good commercial potential) or financial support from the government, sponsors, or their parent corporations such as the BBC in the case of the BBC Asian Network can afford them, which often tends to exclude the smaller ethnic groups.

Audio- and *videocassettes* also have played important roles as instruments of ethnic minority self-expression. They saw some use along those lines during the 1970s, but the rapidly declining cost of equipment (including cassettes and their duplication) in the 1980s and 1990s saw numerous manifestations of one-time and serial employment of cassettes for subjects as diverse as parental and spousal abuse, language instruction and substandard working conditions. Often, the tapes are meant for home use, although some of them have been broadcast, as well. They are particularly useful in situations where there have been no readily available domestic broadcast outlets, as well as those where the government has discouraged or even forbidden ethnic self-expression.[51]

Many of the cassette-based projects have been supported by religious and nongovernmental organizations (NGOs). The main reason seems to be that such organizations often are interested in fostering a spirit of self-reliance among people who have been ignored, neglected, disadvantaged or otherwise mistreated by the majority culture. Taping a presentation that displays how the mistreated feel about their situations and what they attempt to do to improve matters is regarded as an empowering act in itself, and sharing the presentation with others is a way to remove the feeling of isolation common among the mistreated.

The *internet* has seen an expansion of activity on the part of ethnic minorities over the past decade, as more minority users have come online. Some of that activity has been through radio over the World Wide Web (Webcasting), but much more of it has been through the establishment of Web sites containing everything from ethnic language lessons to exhibits of ethnic minority video art, as well as online newspapers for specific groups, for example, a southern California Latino "Webspaper" (Rivas-Rodriguez, 2003). Web radio is comparatively expensive, but the other Web sites are quite low in cost, especially if they are relatively simple in design (and not counting time spent in updating or otherwise modifying them). Most governments in industrially developed nations do not license internet activity, so the Web sites also allow for a fairly free range of expression, depending on who is in charge of them.

Ethnic minority access to the necessary computer equipment and hookup varies a great deal, but there are indications of increasing, and in some cases rapidly increasing, ethnic minority access in the United States—certainly on the part of Asian-Americans, but also to a lesser degree by African and Hispanic-Americans.[52] Ethnic minority associations and activity centers in other nations increasingly are installing computers and connecting to the internet so that their members and other users can go online.[53] Some media services in Third World nations also are beginning to use the internet, especially in educational activities and as a means of data collection and distribution to individual users, but also to still other media services.[54]

The Lessons of History

Now that most of the characters are on stage, so to speak, we see that they exhibit considerable variety. Also, increasing numbers of channels are available to carry the ethnic minority messages, there is a greater variety in those messages, and there is relatively broad freedom to speak about what one wishes and as one wishes, although that freedom can vary from country to country and can be affected by specific events, for example, 9-11 and the war on terrorism.

Perhaps the first thing that history shows us concerning ethnic minority electronic media services is that broad circumstances and significant events have played the largest roles in the development of those media. The chief circumstance appears to be the sheer growth in numbers of any given ethnic minority group. Wars and economic hardship have played major roles in leading people to migrate, and various media of communication—transportation, mail services, radio, the internet—have made it easier for them to consider such a course of action and to then realize it. The principal significant event (really a series of events) clearly is civil rights movements in various industrialized societies around the world. The U.S. Civil Rights Movement led the way, and the coverage of that movement by both U.S. and foreign media certainly helped to ensure that it came to the attention of ethnic minorities and those who supported their struggle for equal rights elsewhere. However, that coverage also fell on fertile soil, and most civil rights movements in other nations found their own ways to carry on the struggle. Opposition to the war in Vietnam added fuel to the fire, so to speak, in that it meant one more major element in the call for "power to the people."

Civil rights movements and opposition to the war had one other important effect: They underlined the power of the media (the electronic media in particular) to influence public opinion, while at the same time underscoring the need to find ways of presenting alternative viewpoints through those media. Some learned to manipulate the mainstream media services; others developed their own media outlets. The growth during the 1970s and early 1980s of community radio, of "pirate" radio, of access channels on cable radio and TV, all were fueled by the desire for alternative (and often self-) expression, and ethnic minority groups usually were prominent among those leading the charge. It helped greatly that the FM (UHF) band was just beginning to open up in Europe and Australia/New Zealand at the time, because the common argument of the PSBs—there is not enough spectrum space to accommodate new (especially 'alternative') services—no longer was sustainable.[55]

The ethnic groups soon discovered that maintaining alternative media services was much harder than creating them, but the effort persisted: Most of the ethnic minority electronic media services established during that period remain active today, even if staff turnover generally has been high, financial support a persistent worry, and goals often a subject of (sometimes bitter) dispute. Government regulatory policies and financial support sometimes have been helpful and even crucial, but they have not been all that common, generous or consistent, as we shall see when we consider policy in Chapter 3.

By the end of the 1990s, very few industrialized nations were without some form of electronic media service for and by ethnic minorities. Even Ireland, which had very few ethnic minorities until the 1990s, had developed a service by the year 2000, first for Albanians only, but later for several other groups, as well. Known as "One World Radio," it quickly expanded into a several hour per day, seven day per week service. However, its parent corporation, the Irish PSB Raidio Telefis Eirann (RTE), experienced budgetary problems with Ireland's economic slump in 2002, and cut the service back to 1 day a week, for a few hours only (RTE, 2001).[56]

The goals of the various ethnic minority services have shifted over time, to varying degrees. Telling one's own story and celebrating one's own culture in one's own way have remained at the top of the list of priorities. How best to present those things and for whom have proven more likely to be contested terrain; we shall consider that issue in Chapter 4. What those media messages signify in terms of their contribution to the societal dialogue envisaged by Jürgen Habermas in his concept of the public sphere is taken up in subsequent chapters.

NOTES

1. There are thousands of books about immigration, most of them devoted to the experiences of specific ethnic groups leaving or coming to specific nations or regions at specific moments in time. A useful summation of such experiences can be found in Eltis (2002), Adler and Gielen (2003), Benmayor and Skotnes (1994).

2. There are many different groups that might come under the broad term *Hispanic*, for example *Chicano, Latino,* and *Tejano.* Furthermore, female members of those groups may choose to label their identities as *Chicana, Latina,* and *Tejana.* I have chosen to utilize the collective term *Hispanic* chiefly in the interests of space, aside from a few instances in which I cite an example that involves a more specific designation of identity by a group.

3. With Web-streamed radio stations increasingly available through the World Wide Web (WWW), even the internet can play a role in the lives of illiterate émigrés. However, the costs of a computer, modem, and monthly connection charges are likely to restrict its utility where low-income households are concerned.

4. A brief "note" in *The New York Times,* October 10, 2003: A17, indicated that the principal language of close to 20% of all U.S. households in 2002 was something other than English, compared with a 1992 figure of 14%.

5. There are many useful accounts, most with bibliographies, regarding the depiction of minorities through the mainstream electronic media, including those contained in the following more recent books: Berry and Manning-Miller (1996); Bogle (2001); Boyer and Lochard (1998); Cottle (1995; (2000); Coupe and Jakubowicz (1993); Cumberbatch and Woods (1994); Daniels and Gerson (1989); Dates and Barlow (1990); Dines and Humez (1995); Ely (1991); Fero (1990); Frachon and Vargaftig (1995); Givanni (1995); Gray (1995); Hall (1997); Hamamoto (1994); Hartley and McKee (2000); Jakubowicz (1994); Jhally (1996); Jhally and Lewis (1992); Kamalipour and Carili (1998); Lee and Wong (2003); Malik (2001); Means Coleman (1998); Navarrete and Kamasaki (1994); Noriega (2000); Rodriguez (1998); Ross (1996, 2001); Savage (1999); Spoonley and Hirsh (1990); Torres (1998, 2003); Tuning into Diversity (2002); U.S. Commission (1977, 1979); Wilson, Gutierrez, and Chao (2003). Most of those accounts are based on some form of content analysis, although Boyer and Lochard (1998) take a more philosophical approach to the depiction of North African and Black populations by French television. Yet another body of literature on that same subject is ethnic minority reactions to their depiction, particularly through mainstream television but in some instances through ethnic minority media. Those studies, generally based to varying degrees on survey research, include Ang et al. (2002); Anwar (1978); Anwar and Shang (1982); Bostock (1993); Cunningham and Sinclair (2000); De Sipio (2003); Entman and Rojecki (2000); Gillespie (1995); Karam and Zuckernick (1992); Kolar-Panov (1997); Lind (2003); Mullan (1996); Nihohiho and Young (1983); Ogan (2001); Ruohuoma (1995); Soruco (1996); Sreberny and Ross (1995); Sreberny (1999); Wober and Fazel (1984).

6. In Europe: The United Kingdom (England, Wales, Scotland, Cornwall); Ireland; France; The Netherlands; West, East and united Germany; Poland; Slovenia; Switzerland; Italy; Spain; Denmark; Finland; Norway; Sweden; and Austria. In North America: The United States and Canada (Quebec and Ontario). In Africa: The Republic of South Africa. In Asia and the South Pacific: Japan, Australia (all seven states and the Capital Territory), and New Zealand.

7   The works to which I refer here are books or larger reports. There are many articles in academic journals, and I cite a number of them throughout this book.

8   Also, several of the more general studies of community/local/regional media,
including Beaud (1980); Jankowski, Prehn, and Stappers (1992); Jankowski (2002);
Lewis (1977, 1993); Lewis and Booth (1989); Milam (1974); Moragas Spa et al.
(1995, 1999); Mowlana and Frondorf (1992); and Walker (2001) provide considerable information relevant to the study of ethnic minority media activity.

9.   I use the term *mainstream,* throughout the book to designate the majority culture,
without any qualitative implication that it is correct, superior, or anything other
than most prevalent.

10.   Husband (1994: 10) offers a wise cautionary note when he states that "The media-
related behavior of members of an ethnic minority community cannot be
'explained' by their ethnicity. They are not merely ethnic, nor is their ethnicity a
permanent element of their consciousness. In certain situations they may be acutely
aware of their ethnic identity, while in others it may be irrelevant to their thoughts
and actions."

11..   A Scots Gaelic-speaking colleague who studies the use of that language in the
media has told me that he doubts that most Scots Gaelic speakers would think of
themselves as ethnic minorities, given the many peoples that have come to
Scotland in peace or in war (Cormack, personal communication, April 2003).

12.   Schlesinger (1991) provides a thorough consideration of the mass media and the
nation-state.

13.   Habermas (1989). This is a translation of Habermas' 1962 book *Strukturwandel der
Oeffentlichkeit: Untersuchungen zu einer Kategorie der buergerlichen Gesellschaft* (Neuweid:
H. Luchterhand). Hans Kleinstüeber offers an interesting examination of the ways
in which Habermas' concept was perceived by German academics when it first
appeared in the 1962 book (as part of a long-running discussion of *Offentlichkeit* as a
literary and aesthetic phenomenon), and the ways in which it was perceived by
European scholars (with emphasis on the spatial aspect implied by "public sphere")
(Kleinstüeber, 2001).

14.   However, it is possible that he was mistranslated, or, if he spoke in English, that he
expressed himself inaccurately Habermas (1995). The passage in question
(Habermas, 1995: 853) reads "Once they become citizens themselves, they in turn
get a voice in public debates, which may then shift the established interpretation of
the constitutional principles."

15.   My departmental colleague Professor Ron Greene regards Habermas as strongly
favoring person-to-person interaction, which could help to explain why Habermas
has so little to say about the electronic media (although the internet certainly serves
as a suitable vehicle for much person-to-person interaction). Stevenson (2002: 47-74),
also notes this, and specifically criticizes Habermas for his failure to acknowledge the
existence and relevance of micromedia for the public sphere. See also Peters (1993).

16.   Keane (1996: 169) refers to micropublic spheres ("dozens, hundreds or thousands of
disputants interacting at the subnational level"), mesopublic spheres ("millions . . .
interacting at the sub-national level"), and macropublic spheres ("hundreds of millions and even billions . . . enmeshed in disputes at the supranational and global levels of powers"). I find his triad interesting, but do have some reservations about the
extent of the "interaction," and "enmeshing" that takes place through the electronic
media, and express them in Chapter 6.

17. Dahlgren (1991) and Curran (1991). Few books address in detail the subject of the ways in which ethnic minority populations use the electronic media, and mainstream media in particular, in their daily lives. Gillespie (1995) presents Punjabi experiences in London; Cunningham and Sinclair (2000) deal with Chinese, Vietnamese, Thai and Fijian-Indian experiences with Australian media and VCRs as well as satellite-delivered material from the ancestral homelands (with SBS as the only Australian ethnic minority-centered service that is covered in any detail, and then only for the Chinese and Vietnamese). Ogan (2001) discusses Turkish viewing experiences in Amsterdam; Sreberny and Ross (1995) cover ethnic minority viewing in the United Kingdom; and Hargreaves and Mahjoub (1997) does likewise, chiefly for North African Arabs in France. Several of the contributions in Karim (2003) also center on studies of actual viewing habits, for example, Aksoy and Robins on Turkish-speaking viewers in London. Several of Ross' (2001) contributors also deal with ethnic minority viewing. However, radio listening receives very little attention from any of those authors.

18. Fraser (1992). Fraser includes "peoples of color" in her list of subaltern counterpublics; she also makes the astute observation (1992: 120) that "In stratified societies, unequally empowered social groups tend to develop unequally valued cultural styles. The result is the development of powerful informal pressures that marginalize the contributions of members of subordinated groups both in everyday contexts and in official public spheres."

19. The practice of avoiding areas of a city where minority populations predominate; the usual grounds for the practice are that minorities "really aren't interested in having cable," or that they do not pay their monthly service bills promptly or at all. The practice is illegal in the United States, but still occurs.

20. The report of the McBride Commission (McBride, 1980) made recommendations on a "New World Information and Communication Order." See also Nordenstreng and Schiller (1993); and McPhail (1987) for observations on NWICO.

21. Cruise O'Brien (1976) and Golding (1991) offer studies of such behaviors for Algeria and Senegal and for Nigeria. Those studies, all conducted in the 1970s, indicate some quite evident "modeling" (on "Western" practices). They also note attempts to break away from Western "models." I have not seen any more recent studies along those lines.

22. Hartley and McKee (2000: 4) criticize what they label the concept of the "victimized other, vulnerable to the influence of powerful agencies and incapable of self-determination or self-representation," and state that their book stems from a "longstanding discomfort with models of social and textual power that can be observed in media studies."

23. McPhail (2001) discusses several theories that draw upon the concepts of dependency and hegemony. Downing (2001: 12-22) covers theories associated with power, hegemony and resistance; as does Rodriguez (2001: 11-17).

24. Lemke (1995) covers the Maori experience in New Zealand during this period.

25. Davies (1994) has a very detailed account of the first several decades of BBC Welsh radio; McDowell (1992) provides similar information on BBC Scots Gaelic broadcasts; Withers (1984: 249) notes that a BBC Gaelic Department was created in 1935, and produced 35 minutes *per week* in the language.

26. That sort of activity was not confined to the national networks: For example, in 1948 WCCO-AM in Minneapolis, Minnesota produced and broadcast a radio play with racial prejudice as its central theme. The play was recreated and broadcast over Minnesota Public Radio on February 13, 2001.

27. Cantor (1992: 56) notes that WDIA continued to broadcast 5-minute newscasts once the station had gone "all Black," largely for White listeners at first, but "later" with stories about the Memphis African-American experience. Barlow (1999: 121) mentions a 15-minute weekly roundtable forum, "Brown America Speaks," on WDIA, apparently begun in the early 1950s.

28. There were numerous instances of Hispanic-American time-leasing ("brokerage") arrangements during the 1950s, helped by the fact that the radio industry was losing ground to television. In the process of "re-inventing" themselves, many radio stations encountered economic difficulties, and some were quite willing to lease airtime to "outsiders," including ethnic minorities (Rodriguez, 1999: 26-45; 2001: 129-147).

29. Lewis and Booth (1989) provide a summary of the development of local radio in the United Kingdom during the 1970s and 1980s.

30. See Land (1999), Lasar (1999), and McKinney (1966) for the early history of Pacifica. See Milam (1974) for reflections (highly personal and colorful) on the early years of community radio in the United States. Walker (2001) provides a more extensive account of U.S. community radio, with several brief sections on Pacifica. See Lewis and Booth (1989), Beaud (1980), Berrigan (1977), and Lewis (1993) for general histories of community radio.

31. Fairchild (2001) provides some background detail on the development of community radio in Canada, as does Thomas (1992).

32. The WLBT-TV case is complex, and there still is disagreement over why it came out as it did. See Classen (1996).

33. In 1964, the U.S. commercial TV networks and the National Urban League developed a Broadcast Skills Bank for similar training (aside from management), but it could accommodate no more than a few dozen individuals at a given facility each year, and for the first few years of its existence, trainees had to come to New York City for the training sessions.

34. Canada's Northern Native Broadcast Access Program (NNBAP) was particularly generous by the standards of the times: From 1983 through 1987 it provided approximately CAN$40 million for the support of Inuit broadcast activity (Stiles, 1985: 24-25). It furnished another CAN$140 million between 1988 and 2003; annual funding levels began to drop in 1989, and have been level (c. CAN$8 million p.a.) over the period 1997-2003. Still, it continues to serve as a major source of financial support for Canadian Aboriginal and Inuit electronic media services. The Northern Development Program (NDP) helps to offset the costs of leasing, operating and maintaining the satellite distribution system that interlinks the services. Over the period 1989-2003, it furnished c. CAN$ 35.5 million, with annual support level at CAN$2.1 million over the period 1998-2003 (Whiteduck & Consilium, 2003).

35. Davies (1998) provides a detailed analysis of SBS. See Chapter 3 for a case study on the origins of SBS.

36. There are several accounts of European experiences with community radio: Berrigan (1977), Beaud (1980), Husband (1994), Jankowski, Prehn, and Stappers (1992), Lewis (1993), Lewis and Booth (1989).

37. Hind and Moss (1985) note several ethnic minority-operated pirate services, such as the Dread Broadcasting Corporation (Jamaican). Worpole, in a 1992 study quoted in Morley (2000: 163), mentions Liverpool's (pirate) Radio Toxteth as young Blacks' "most important form of public space and time."

38. Personal interviews with Gerard Reteig and Richard Troelstra, Migranttelevisie, Amsterdam, September 1995.

39. Personal visits to SALTO, September 1995 and April 2001.

40. There are no lengthy accounts of ethnic minority broadcast services in the USSR, although Mickiewicz (1988: 6-7) notes their existence. See also *Rising Voices* (1991: 203-215). For China, see UNESCO (1986: 88-91).

41. Krasny Most, a private commercial radio station founded in Moscow in 1998, broadcasts chiefly in Russian, but its target audience is Armenians, Georgians, Azeris, and other Russian speaker from some of the former Soviet Republics.

42. Gumicio-Dagron (2001) has several chapters on Radio Sutatenza and other Catholic church-supported local stations. See also Carmen Marquez (1993); Hein (1988); and Vargas (1995) for details on such services.

43. A useful general source on clandestine and other "unofficial" radio is Soley and Nichols (1987).

44. Tomaselli, Tomaselli, and Muller (1985: 39) note that the South African Broadcasting Corporation (SABC) provided a service in Zulu, Sotho, and Xhosa during World War II, delivered over telephone lines to "compounds, hostels and institutions" in all cities and major towns. It ceased operation in 1945, but SABC began a "Bantu program" in the 1950s, over medium wave and for "a couple of hours daily only." Eventually, it was discovered that some of the black announcers had been broadcasting "anti-Government propaganda," and the SABC tightened control over the service by installing white supervisors who could speak the various Bantu languages (Tomaselli et al., 1985: 94-95).

45. In fact, Wilkins and Strydom (1979: 1) indicate that the Broederband (a politically powerful Afrikaaner group of hard-core racial separatists) thought of Radio Bantu as a way of ensuring that Blacks would remain in their segregated "homelands." For more information on Radio Bantu, see Phelan (1987); and Tomaselli et al. (1985: 89-103).

46. A notable exception was the founding of KYUK-TV in Barrow, Alaska in 1976, to provide television service for the isolated and largely Inuit town on Alaska's North Slope. It carried limited amounts of locally produced programming.

47. Another outlet sometimes available to ethnic minorities in the United States is the provision of airtime on local public television stations, especially in those instances where a station has two TV channels at its disposal. The Minneapolis/St.Paul, Minnesota public TV stations, KTCA and KTCI, carry six ethnic minority-produced series, ranging from Hmong to Arab. The former is in Hmong, the latter largely in English (Tillotson, 2004).

48. Linder (1999: 7) states that two notable U.S. advocates of citizen involvement in broadcasting, George Stoney and Red Burns, aided FCC Commissioner Nicholas Johnson in creating the access requirements.

49. Broadcast activities of the more than 600,000 Koreans living in Japan are limited to blocks of airtime on local commercial radio stations in Tokyo, Osaka, and Fukuoka, and to "mini-FM" (very low power) radio stations in such cities (Sonnenberg, 1994). The Ainu, Japan's indigenous people, have small amounts of airtime on a

commercial radio station in Hokkaido, and also have a tape distribution service. Both outlets are used primarily to preserve the Ainu language (DeChicchis, 1992: 114-115; Kristof, 1996; Sterngold, 1992).

50. The AIROS-distributed daily discussion program "Native America Calling" also uses the satellite, along with the internet (www.nativeamericacalling.org) to allow listeners to join in on the discussions.

51. Dowmunt (1993), particularly Kuttab's (1993: 138-145) report on Palestinian use of videocassettes. Girard (1992), Riggins (1992), Thede and Ambrosi (1991), and White (2003) all have numerous examples of this activity.

52. Two reports offer interesting and somewhat different viewpoints on the issue of minority group usage of the internet in the United States: U.S. Department of Commerce (2002), Harris (2002). Although the former generally presents an optimistic view of increasing usage of the internet by ethnic minorities, the latter points out (2002: 6) that, according to data from 2001 presented in the former's study, African-American and Hispanic-American schoolchildren must rely much more heavily on using the internet within their schools, and that many of them lack internet access in their homes. Asian-American schoolchildren have even more home access to the internet than do their White counterparts.

53. Cisler (1998), Girard (2003), Gumicio-Dagron (2001), and *Hommes et Migrations* (2002) contain several articles and chapters on émigré experiences with the internet. Many of the "community media centers" that have developed over the past decade, although not exclusively for the use of ethnic minorities, have been helpful to them. In my visit to the La Plaza Community Media Center in Taos, New Mexico in August 2001, I saw video projects that had been guided by the center staff, a number of which featured the work of teenagers, some of them ethnic minorities. One of them, made by a Native American from the nearby Taos Pueblo, was a well-produced video portrait of the teen's grandfather in which the video-maker displayed his grandfather's "visual legacy" (what he regarded as important for his grandson to know).

54. Gumicio-Dagron (2001) reports on several such projects, perhaps most notably Pulsar (a regional service in Latin America; 2001: 241-246); and Kothmale Community Radio in Sri Lanka (2001: 127-132). See also Castells (2001).

55. The falling costs of transmitters and production equipment also made it much easier to develop the "alternative" services, radio in particular.

56. Theses observations are drawn from a descriptive brochure (RTE, 2001) and a personal interview with RTE Director General Bob Collins in Dublin, May 2002.

What *Are* the Ethnic Minority Electronic Media?

Audiences around the world are familiar with the variety of electronic media available nowadays, even if their own particular nations may lack one or more of the services. Certainly, the industrialized nations offer a wide range of choice, whereas much of the rest of the world is catching up where the newer media are concerned: China and India, with a total of more than 2 billion people, are sprouting cable and satellite services, with the internet not far behind. Subscriber rates for such services are low in many nations, including Italy, Greece, and Portugal, but they are growing, and so is public awareness of (and interest in) them.

That growth in interest is not limited to potential subscribers. Individuals and groups, including ethnic minorities, see those newer media as possible outlets for their self-expression, particularly because they seem almost limitless in terms of their ability to accommodate such users. They are not, of course: Limits of various sorts, cost of equipment and need for specialized skills among them, may discourage participation, and even the most sophisticated cable and satellite systems have channel space for hundreds rather than thousands of services. Still, there remain a few low-cost electronic media technologies, with radio, audio- and videocassettes and the internet leading the way.

The following is a brief consideration of each of the individual media, particularly in terms of a given medium's advantages and disadvantages where ethnic minority group usage is concerned.

THE ELECTRONIC MEDIA FAMILY

Radio (Terrestrial)

The oldest of the electronic media, aside from phonograph records, and the most heavily used by ethnic minorities. At its most basic level—control board, amplifier, turntable/cassette player/compact disc player, and microphone, plus a modest transmitter (say 50 watts)—the total package can cost as little as U.S. $1000. The studio can be an ordinary room fitted out with cardboard egg cartons fastened to the walls, and I have seen studios made from wooden shipping crates for automobiles[1] or located in house trailers (caravans).[2] The equipment can be very simple to operate, and is portable—a quality that was much appreciated by ethnic groups such as South Asians and Caribbeans living in the United Kingdom as they operated unlicensed ("pirate") radio services during the 1970s and 1980s. When law enforcement officials came to close down the service, its staff gathered up the equipment and left the premises. If they were caught and their equipment confiscated, it did not cost a fortune to replace it, and the services soon were back on the air.

Radio also has the advantage of near-universal reception: Nearly every household in industrially developed nations, and substantial numbers of households in other nations, own radio receivers, quite often more than one set per household. And if a given ethnic minority group features a strongly oral culture, radio is particularly appropriate for its delivery.

The chief disadvantage to radio is that, if its users intend to broadcast legally, there may be a shortage of available broadcast frequencies—a common problem where larger cities are concerned. The only alternatives aside from operating illegally are to lease a block of airtime on an existing station (if any is willing to do so) or to purchase an existing station, and many ethnic minority groups cannot begin to afford such costs. *Cable radio* may be another possibility, because there usually is channel space available; Germany began to develop quite extensive cable access radio services by the late 1980s. However, many households subscribing to cable television either do not bother to add cable radio or may not even know that they can do so. Also, audiences may pay less attention to radio than they do to television, often treating it as background ("musical wallpaper").

Low-power access radio stations have been around since the late 1970s in Sweden and Norway (*närradio*), New Zealand initiated them in the early 1990s,[3] and Great Britain began experiments with them in 2002; the 15 licensed services ran until December 31, 2003, with the likelihood that at least some of them will be relicensed by Ofcom—the new (as of December 29, 2003) regulatory agency for electronic media in the United Kingdom. Four of the 15 services are entirely ethnic minority operated: A South Asian station in Glasgow (Awaz FM), an Asian Women's/ Islamic station in Nottingham (Radio Faza), a Punjabi station in London (Desi Radio), and a Black station in Birmingham (New Style Radio).

Also, Sound Radio in East London and Bradford Community Broadcasting in Bradford both feature major commitments of airtime for ethnic minority groups.

Where ethnic minorities are concerned, access stations seem to offer a particularly viable alternative for the smaller, highly localized ethnic groups: They offer technical facilities and training to users at low or no cost; many of them allow users to come on air with one-time only programs or short series, rather than requiring long-term commitments; and users usually are encouraged to present their material in a natural way, rather than attempting to sound highly professional. The relatively small Spanish-speaking community in East London (U.K.) probably would not have had a radio service in its language if it had not been for the encouragement of Sound Radio, 1 of the 15 experimental access radio stations (Everitt, 2002: 93-94).[4]

Television (Terrestrial)

Although it is possible to assemble the components of a television studio at relatively low cost, television remains far more costly than radio, and considerably more complex to operate, as well. Inexpensive TV studios are a possibility, but not at the same level of economy as radio. Automobile crates and egg cartons do not begin to provide adequate studio conditions for television production. But television is a highly popular medium, commands the attention of most listeners far more completely than does radio, and offers a wider range of possibilities for different types of programs. Furthermore, it has far more prestige and higher believability scores (as indicated in audience surveys) than does radio. Ethnic minority groups cannot and do not ignore its usefulness where their goals are concerned, even if high costs often discourage them from doing very much.

Television set ownership is nearly as universal as radio in most of the industrialized nations, and growing but considerably less prevalent in other nations. Ethnic minorities in the former appear to place a high premium on owning television sets, and often subscribe to cable or satellite services, as well. They also display great interest in seeing people like themselves on TV, even if most of the programming available to them within the industrialized nations includes relatively few faces similar to their own. To the extent that ethnic minority groups can provide television services, there appears to be an audience eager to receive them, but cost and, in larger cities, channel availability, remain very large barriers. Lack of trained staff also can be a problem in some cases.

Cable Radio and TV

Channel availability is not as severe a problem on cable radio as it is on cable TV, and transmission costs for both media are lower on cable than they are for terrestrial services. That should make cable quite attractive to ethnic minority

program producers. Cable subscribership rates among ethnic minorities in industrialized nations generally are lower than they are for the mainstream majority,
but they are increasing, at least for cable TV: *Cable radio* is less popular, and aside
from *cable access radio*—quite heavily used by minority program producers—most
attempts to sustain ethnic minority cable radio stations have failed, often owing
to lack of audience.

There are *cable access TV* channels in many of the industrialized nations, and
ethnic minority producers are among the heaviest users of airtime. In part, that is
because many cable access TV (and radio) services make both production equipment and professional advice available to users at very low cost, or even free of
charge. The greatest drawback to attracting larger audiences to ethnic minority
cable TV programming, especially on the access channels, is letting audience
members know that such services exist. Cable TV in most industrialized nations
offers a minimum of 20 channels, and 50+ channel cable operations are increasingly common. It is easy for access channels to get lost in the myriad of choices,
especially because such channels rarely show up in printed program guides.
When they do, the listings usually are not very specific, because groups producing access programs cannot always be certain when their programs will be ready
for airing, or precisely what their contents will be. Production quality may be less
than stellar, which in turn may lead audience members to regard the programs as
amusing or bizarre rather than informative or interesting.

Access TV programs made by minorities also face the possibility of direct
competition on cable TV. Cable TV operations in many industrialized nations
have discovered that they can increase subscriber rates among ethnic minorities
by importing domestic television services from the ancestral homelands of many
of the larger ethnic groups, such as Turks in Germany and The Netherlands,
South Asians in the United Kingdom, and Hispanics in the United States. Such
services may satisfy the need of ethnic minority viewers to see people like themselves on TV, but it does nothing to speak to the reality of their lives in their new
homelands, nor can it help the mainstream audience to understand that reality.
However, it is well produced, it keeps alive a sense of contact with the ancestral
homeland, and it provides hours and hours of material, far exceeding the hour or
less per day (if that) provided by most ethnic minority producers working
through cable access or other outlets.

Satellite Radio and TV

With few exceptions, satellite subscriber rates are far lower than they are for
cable in industrialized nations. *Satellite radio* has gotten off to a slow start in
Europe and North America, and faces an uncertain future. *Satellite TV* seems to
be doing quite well, especially in Germany and, to a lesser extent, the United
States and United Kingdom. Still, most satellite services do not retransmit local
terrestrial TV stations, which cable TV routinely provides. This means that local

access TV services will not be available to audiences wishing to view them, depriving ethnic minority groups of what most of them would regard as their best opportunity to reach viewers. Some satellite services are beginning to retransmit the major local TV stations, but access TV services have lower priority.

A number of nations, Canada, Australia, and the United States chief among them, have seen the development of satellite services that assist in the distribution of programming to, but not necessarily by, indigenous groups: Native Americans and Inuit in Canada and the United States, Aboriginals in Australia. In each instance, the vast distances and small and scattered populations would have been almost impossible to serve through terrestrial broadcasting. The Canadian government began to use satellites for television program distribution to stations in Canada's far north in 1972, just a year after the U.S. National Aeronautics and Space Administration had begun to allow the use of its ATS-1 satellite for experiments in the transmission of various health care and educational services, including elementary school programs dealing with the traditions of Inuit and Native Americans. Australia's Broadcasting for Remote Aboriginal Communities Scheme (BRACS) came into service in the late 1980s, largely as a retransmission service for existing TV stations, including the Aboriginal TV station in Alice Springs, Imparja.[5]

Those services led to the development of more ambitious operations, and Canada's Inuit population now has its own satellite-delivered network, the Aboriginal Peoples Television Network (www.aptn.ca), which also is available through cable in Canada.[6] BRACS has faced problems in maintaining and updating equipment, as well as providing training, but it helps to support various activities of Aboriginal groups, particularly through radio information hubs coordinated by regional indigenous media centers.[7] It is likely to be some time before satellite radio and TV are of much value to most ethnic minority program producers, but satellite TV in many nations has followed cable TV's example, and provides retransmission of ancestral homeland TV stations, which again do not mirror the lives of the ethnic minorities now living in other lands.

Audio- and Videocassettes

The decreasing costs of *audio-* and *videocassettes*, coupled with the increasing availability of tape-duplication services, has meant that tape recorded material can achieve mass distribution without having to go through radio or television. The Iranian Revolution in 1979 was fueled in part by audiocassette recordings of the anti-Shah sermons preached by the exiled Muslim leader Ayatollah Khomeini from his headquarters in Paris. Many Iranians had access to portable cassette players, and the cassettes themselves could be smuggled into the country and distributed with relative ease (Mohammadi & Mohammadi, 1994: 119-121). Bush Radio, a Black township-oriented radio station in Cape Town, South Africa, began life as an anti-apartheid tape production and distribution service

(CASET) during the final years (early 1990s) of apartheid government rule. It was inexpensive, escaped detection by the authorities, and could be passed along from one user to another (Gorfinkel, 1992).

Videocassettes also have been used to counter the information monopolies held by autocratic governments in a number of nations. As one example, Black South Africans began in the mid-1980s to produce "video pamphlets" that would provide a Black perspective on the South African government's *apartheid* policies and the need for strikes and demonstrations to oppose those policies. Trade union, religious, civic, student, and other organizations showed and distributed the tapes (Currie & Markovitz, 1993: 94-96).

Cassette recordings can be passed around easily among interested viewers and listeners, and the compactness of audiocassettes in particular makes it simple to conceal them from the authorities. However, they are of limited utility in presenting highly topical material to a large audience unless the program producers are willing and able to invest in massive tape duplication so that all interested parties can have their own copies immediately. Even then, the sorts of distribution systems that exist would not be able to deliver the cassettes to everyone simultaneously. In those situations, cassettes are no substitute for radio or TV stations.

Finally, videocassettes often serve to furnish ethnic minorities lacking ready access to cable or satellite television with tapes of movies and other entertainment from the ancestral homelands, just as audiocassettes (and increasingly, CDs) provide traditional and contemporary popular music from the same sources. Anyone who has visited an Asian or African or Latin American grocery store in North America, Europe, Australia, or New Zealand will have seen racks of such tapes for sale or rental, and they remain popular with those wishing to retain links with the "old homeland." There also may be tapes of locally recorded ethnic groups available—usually of local rock, hiphop, or pop music—but they are far outnumbered by the imported material.

The Internet

The most recent of the electronic media, and the most open in terms of access to users of all sorts, the *internet* should be of considerable interest and value to ethnic minority groups, and for some, it is. Where computer ownership is widespread and where the costs of connecting to and spending time online are relatively low, many ethnic minority groups make ample use of the internet to communicate individually with each other. They also use the internet to present material highlighting the group's history, artistic endeavors, scientific accomplishments, teaching the group's language, encouraging demonstrations and letter-writing campaigns on issues important to the group, and so on. The internet appears to be particularly popular with various diaspora populations, thanks in part to its ability to link widely scattered groups simultaneously.[8]

Unfortunately for ethnic minority groups living in most of the European nations, online connections and time charges are far higher than they are in North America, and that alone has discouraged widespread use of the internet by ethnic minority groups in Europe, aside from the internet cafes and their numerous ethnic minority users. European libraries and, less often, religious institutions (mosques, synagogues, churches) are beginning to make internet facilities available to their users, but for the most part are behind their North American counterparts in that respect. Independent media centers also are gaining strength, particularly in North American but also in other parts of the world, and the internet is an important element in their use of a variety of media to highlight the problems and accomplishments of ethnic minority groups.[9] The Russian Penza Association has relied heavily on the internet in assisting refugees and migrants in such areas as Chechnya, Dagestan, Ingushetiya, and other strife-ridden regions of Russia to establishing citizenship, gaining migrant rights, and obtaining recognition of their social status (Sharipkov, 2002-2003).

Producing material for display on the internet can be done very economically at the level of e-mails and chat groups, but cost mounts if there is a perceived need for more elaborate links, visual displays, and so on. There also are the costs of purchasing and operating one's server, connecting with an internet service provider, and, if there is Web streaming of radio and television material for *Web radio* and *TV* services, equipment costs can run in the thousands of dollars for radio and tens of thousands for TV. Some ethnic minority groups would be willing to make the necessary investments, but not until the user rates among their target audiences (usually the members of their own groups, rather than the mainstream majority) improve.

Those ethnic minority internet services (aside from Web-streamed radio) that do exist tend to follow mainstream models, in that many of them have some sort of commercial dimension: subscription to access certain portions of the Web site; tie-ins with Web sites selling vacation packages, recorded music, and so on; "meeting" (dating) services operated by the group running the Web site; and advertising, with government departments as major advertisers in nations where there are meaningful equal opportunity laws. Often, there will be provision for a chat group, a forum, an events calendar, a job-finding service, all of them relevant to a particular ethnic minority group.

As one example, Black Britain (www.blackbritain.co.uk) carries channels of business reports, a dating service (OneLove), a user's forum, a job-finding service (JobsNow), ads (primarily from local, county and national governments, as well as job-training firms), news (plus a separate channel devoted to entertainment news), an events calendar, British civil service training programs, and BlackMarket, a free classified ad service (but each visual display costs 25 pounds, as it does for OneLove). The target audience is the roughly 550,000 African Caribbeans living in the United Kingdom, with 70% of the site users falling into the 18-35 age group.[10] The site owner (The Colourful Network, founded by Kofi Kusitor) also operates separate Web sites for Indian, Iranian, and Muslim users.

Web radio offers particular advantages for groups with limited financial resources, because it is far less expensive to develop and operate a Web radio service than it is to run a full-time terrestrial radio service. Furthermore, there are as yet no formal licensing requirements for Web stations in most industrialized nations, although some countries forbid any internet service from carrying material that glorifies war (Germany), distributes child pornography (most nations), or carries "hate" speech—especially as directed toward ethnic minorities (most European nations). However, there are costs connected with developing and operating Web radio, as already noted. Costs to listeners also are an issue, because computers must be linked by modem to the internet and must be equipped with a sound card in order to receive Webcasts. In addition, the high user time charges levied in many nations for the internet are particularly discouraging to continuous listening on the part of Web radio ethnic minority audiences.

Web TV is far more expensive than is Web radio, and far fewer computers are equipped to receive it. Image quality often is a problem, as well. Still, it is far less expensive to operate a Web TV station than it is a terrestrial TV station, and if Web TV ethnic minority users increase in number, it may be worth the investment to reach viewers through that medium. As with Web radio, most nations have no formal licensing requirements for Web TV stations, so groups that have not managed to obtain licenses for terrestrial TV stations will find space available to them on the Web. Very few ethnic groups have sought such space as yet.

Summarizing the Media Family

The levels and types of media activity available to ethnic minorities are numerous, but not equally accessible. Although cost appears to be the most important reason for ethnic minority producers to work through certain media, there are other factors to consider. There may be a relative scarcity of frequency spectrum space. Numbers of potential target group listeners or viewers for a given medium may be restricted because the cost of reception equipment or service fees may be high. There may be a greater or lesser degree of freedom to express one's viewpoints over various media, with the internet representing a relatively unrestricted medium and terrestrial broadcasting a relatively restricted medium in terms of what one can say. One medium may suit the expressive style or character of a group particularly well.

There is also the issue of coverage area. Do the producers wish to reach a neighborhood, a city, a province or state, a nation, a region? Whatever they may wish, are broadcast frequencies available at that level (assuming that they choose to operate legally)? Have they considered carefully the economic and social ramifications of operating at different geographical levels?

THE GEOGRAPHY OF THE ELECTRONIC MEDIA

Ordinarily, when one thinks about ethnic minority media, the tendency is to think of localized services. Certainly, that is the predominant level at which they operate around the world. However, there are cases to be made for various geographical levels of activity, from broadest to smallest.

International

One of the more fascinating aspects of the internet is its capacity for reaching a worldwide audience. Most users are likely to think of this in terms of exchanges of e-mail with family, friends, professional colleagues, and others around the world, but it applies just as readily to Web radio and TV. Some of the traditional international radio broadcast services such as the BBC World Service, the Voice of America, Radio Russia, and many others were quick to realize the value of transmitting their material over Web radio as well as terrestrially: The Web radio transmissions were free of the static and fading that plagued shortwave transmissions. Few domestic radio services used shortwave, but when some of them went on the Web with their AM and FM signals, they were surprised and pleased to see that they received e-mail and snail-mail messages from listeners abroad, even if that was not their target audience. Now, there are hundreds of radio stations in various parts of the world that can be received through the Web, and there are several ethnic minority stations among them.

The internet also has proven useful for ethnic minority international organizations that lack ready access to radio or feel that it is not the only way to reach their members and other sympathizers. For example, there is International Black Women for Wages for Housework, based in the United States, the United Kingdom and the Caribbean. It operates through a Web site (http://allwomen-count.net/EWC%20WoC/IBWWH) owned by a larger organization, All Women Count. It offers news about activities and developments (legislation on welfare benefits, antiwar demonstrations) likely to be of interest not only to Black women, but also to ethnic minority women in general. The Irish-language radio service for Ireland,[11] Raidio na Gaeltachta (www.rng.org), relays its domestic program service to Irish speakers abroad through satellite and the Web. The Women's International News Gathering Service (WINGS; at www.wings.org) acts as a distribution service for taped or satellite-relayed reports on women's activities that it receives from local stations or individual correspondents around the world.

Staff members in many of the ethnic minority electronic media services that I have visited have asked whether there is any ethnic minority organization that brings together and distributes a wide variety of material from similar services in other nations—in other words, a clearinghouse. Although I am not aware of such an organization, the basis for those requests is clear enough: A perceived need to hear and see what other ethnic minority electronic media are presenting, but also a need to share that material with their own audiences. Both needs rest on the assumption that there is something worth learning—perhaps ways in which other minorities have succeeded or failed in dealing with problems faced by themselves, perhaps a celebration of the cultural similarities and differences of ethnic minorities worldwide.

The international radio and television broadcasting services of many of the industrialized nations might furnish at least a bit of programming along those lines, because most of them have ethnic minority groups, some of those groups are sizeable, and listeners and viewers in other nations—the ancestral homelands in particular—probably would be interested in learning more about how their kinfolk and other minorities were faring in the United States, Germany, Australia, and elsewhere. Although some of the international broadcasters do mention the activities of minorities in their nations, none of them devotes a continually scheduled block of airtime to such material.[12] Perhaps that is because many industrialized nations like to think of themselves as fully integrated, but the tendency of most ethnic minority groups living in them seems increasingly to be a desire to express some of their uniqueness (Browne, 1998: 171-179). A few international radio services do carry languages spoken by ethnic minorities. Radio Habana Cuba, for example, broadcasts in two Native American languages, Quechua (spoken largely in Peru and Bolivia) and Guarani (spoken largely in southern Brazil and Paraguay). However, many of its informational programs tend to be quite heavily political and often are tied to a Cold War era dichotomy of the "free" and "communist" world visions—perhaps of less relevance now that there are relatively few communist nations left in the world.

In short, there is some justification for international ethnic minority media services. There are relatively few of them, chiefly because they are difficult to develop and to sustain. Although there are many who would like to have them available, few seem willing to provide the necessary financial and logistical support to establish them, much less to keep them going. When I discussed the value of the sort of international organization just mentioned with one Maori radio station manager, he said that he himself would like his audience to be exposed to the problems, activities, and accomplishments of others like them. However, he really doubted whether most listeners wanted such material very often. Some, he felt, were too insular, and would not bother to listen; others might listen, but would not sense that the experiences of other minorities had much application to their own lives. In either case, he said, there would be little or no support for using any of the station's budget to help maintain such an organization.[13] I do not know how accurate or representative his observation might be, but any international organization that functions as does WINGS probably will receive little financial support from stations that use its material on an occasional basis.

Regional

Although the situation is not all that common, there are cases in which a given ethnic minority will be scattered across a region where electronic media services directed to them often must cross national boundaries. The Kurds are perhaps the most prominent illustration. They are minorities in five proximate nations: Iraq, Iran, Turkey, Syria, and Armenia. In none of them are they particularly welcome, although they may be tolerated. Depending on the political climate, any of those nations may prevent them from broadcasting or publishing anything in their own language,[14] or educating their children in Kurdish.

Some of the international radio services mentioned carry programs in Kurdish. The Voice of America, the BBC World Service, Radio Sweden, Radio Free Europe, and a few others each devote an hour or less per day to the language, but diplomacy influences the sorts of issues they deal with, and neither the United States nor the United Kingdom nor Sweden encourages the creation of a separate Kurdish nation, nor do they ordinarily take sides in the many factional disputes among Kurdish political groups. Both Iran and Iraq (the latter until the 2003 war) offered many hours of Kurdish programming over their national radio services, but neither has been regarded as a very reliable or credible source of information. If Kurds wish to seek out more information on factional disputes and other sensitive topics, they are more likely to turn to the largely unlicensed radio and television services operated by the factions themselves. Because most of Iraq's 3.5 million Kurds live in northern Iraq, it harbors licensed radio, but also the majority of the unlicensed services, which lack sufficient power to reach Kurds in all five nations. As a result, there is some trade in audiocassette recordings of the pronouncements of faction leaders.

Television, too, plays a role here. Medya TV (www.medyatv.com), operated by Kurdish exiles and other from Paris, beams 13 hours per day of television over salellite to the Kurdiareas within the five nations.[15] Although there are no precise figures available, apparently a sizeable number of Kurdish households have satellite dishes. The programming is a mixture of news, interviews commentary, and entertainment (Kurdish dances and songs are prominent, but there also is non but there also is non-Kurdish entertainment, dubbed in the language). Editorial policy forbids any display of factionalism, although not the coverage of disputes among and within factions, and shuns direct advocacy of an independent Kurdish nation.[16] Mesopotamia TV (www.metv.dk) is a similar satellite TV service based in Copenhagen.

There are dozens of Web sites for Kurds, several of them for Kurdish Web radio services from as far away as North America or Australia and two at least for Web TV services. The Web radio services are predominantly entertainment, most of it Kurdish music, although a few also carry newscasts. There are several chat and discussion Web sites, some including languages other than Kurdish. (Several million Kurds live outside the five nation region, and not all of them speak Kurdish.) Most of the Web sites contain some mention of Kurdistan,[17] the usual English title for the as-yet nonexistent Kurdish nation, and some devote considerable time to discussion of its eventual realization.

The Sami ("Lapp") of northern Scandinavia do not have to deal with repressive governments, and the Sami language radio stations in Norway, Sweden, and Finland are operated as part of the public broadcasting systems[18] of each nation (Heatta, 1984; Horn, 1999; Olson, 1984). They broadcast separate programs for their own regions, but also join together for 6 hour's of programming daily (2 hours on weekends). Norway's NRK and Finland's YLE Sami Services contribute the major share, with the Swedish SR Sami Service about 20%. Although Sweden is the most populous of the three nations, and has the second largest Sami population, SR administrators were not all that supportive of a broadcast service in Sami until the late 1990s. That meant a predominance of material about Sami living in Finland and Norway. Now that Sweden has increased its contribution, there is a greater sense of shared participation. The staffs of the three stations confer frequently by telephone, e-mail, and face-to-face (Heatta, 2003).[19]

As different as their situations are, these two electronic media services do have one problem in common: choice of language. Both Kurdish and Sami take several different linguistic forms, and some of those forms are close to being mutually unintelligible. However, if the services wish to emphasize the concept of nationhood, or something like it, it would seem to be important if not essential to include all forms of the language as one element of that concept. Some of those forms may be spoken by no more than a few hundred individuals. How much airtime should the "smaller" forms receive, and are those who speak them ready, willing, and able to broadcast in them?

Another widely diffused ethnic minority population is the Roma ("Gypsies"), who are present in most European nations and in North America but are more prevalent in eastern and central Europe. Because of their wide dispersion, commonalities in language are even more diverse for the Roma than they are for Kurds or Sami. Furthermore, even though many of the Roma have lived in their respective nations of residence for many centuries, almost without exception they have been treated as outcasts. Such mainstream media exposure as they have received often has cast them as thieves (even of mainstream family children), fortune tellers, and generally disreputable, untrustworthy individuals with no sense of civic responsibility.

Not surprisingly, Roma have had little success in bringing mainstream media to reconsider portrayal of their culture, nor were they able to establish their own electronic media voices until quite recently. The end of communist rule in eastern and central Europe served to open the airwaves in many nations to private broadcast services, and the arrival of the internet offered yet another outlet for hitherto "voiceless" communities, including the Roma. National broadcasting services generally were resistant to providing airtime for Roma, but in 1992 Radiozurnal, a Czech FM service, began to carry "O Roma vakeren" ("The

Roma speak") from 8:05 to 9 pm on Fridays, with rebroadcasts on regional stations and on Czech Radio; most material is in Czech, mainly as reports and interviews (www.romove.cz/clanek/18378). Local Roma stations in Macedonia (Radio Cerenja, Stip; 1994), Yugoslavia (Radio Nisava; Nis, 2000), and Hungary (Radio C, Budapest, 2001) all feature Romany music, interviews and features, most of which are broadcast in the national language (Mohacsi, 1999; Russinov, 1999).[20] Hungary and the Czech Republic also have brief (30 minutes or less) television programs about Roma life. In Bulgaria, several local stations began (mid-1990s) to carry small amounts of Roma programming, but their commitment largely disappeared when Roma were unable to pay the stations to continue the broadcasts (Russinov, 1999: 5).

Because most Roma services are local, and much of their output is in national languages rather than Romany, their ability to exchange program material (aside from music) is decidedly limited. The economic status of most Roma makes it unlikely that listener contributions or advertising would be available to help them finance any cooperative efforts that would run across national lines. internet broadcasts in Roma, English and Czech are available through Internet Radio Rota (www.radiorota.cz)—roughly 60% Romany music and 40% talk, news report and commentaries. This should offer better prospects for helping Roma throughout the world to interconnect, as does the RomNews Network Community (www.romnews.com), and a number of Roma make such use of those services, but again, economic status militates against many Roma having ready access to online media.

Regional services for ethnic minorities would seem to have their greatest value in helping to maintain bonds between members of an ethnic group who are divided by national boundaries. As long as those bonds are chiefly cultural, the national governments within whose boundaries the groups live are less likely to be disturbed by the existence of such services. However, the line between cultural and political bonds can be very thin, and whenever a national government decides that the boundaries between the two have been violated, any regional service that happens to be transmitting such material risks being shut down, or, if it is an unauthorized service, hunted down.

There also is the question of whether such services actually do maintain or even strengthen the bonds of identity. When there are several different versions of an ethnic group language, and when regional services attempt to provide programs in most/all of those versions, might that reinforce rather than lessen a sense of separate identity among subgroups? There is little evidence available on that question. When Ireland's Raidio na Gaeltachta (RNG) began its Irish language radio broadcasts in 1970, it operated from three different locations along the west coast of Ireland. Each featured a separate dialect and accent. Complaints about "those awful Kerry/Casla/Donegal accents" (or "odd" word choices) came back to the stations, but they were few in number, and they largely disappeared within a decade. Listeners even observed from time to time that what a given individual had said in a broadcast "made a lot of sense, even if it was in that awful accent."[21] But Irish and Sami speakers do not face the same sorts of internally divisive and/or externally oppressive forces as do the Kurds and the Roma, so the question remains unanswered.

Other regional ethnic minority groups have become sufficiently prominent over the past few decades to warrant being served by a satellite TV broadcaster. There are several million Turkish speakers living in Europe, with nearly 3 million in Germany. There also are a few million Arabic speakers throughout Europe; France alone has roughly 2.5 million Arab residents (I have seen estimates as high as 4 million). Many Turks and Arabs are citizens of European nations, but some are temporary residents, and some are transient. Members of both groups subscribe to Turkish and Arabic TV services from the homelands, which they receive through cable or directly from satellites.[22]

Although there is no Turkish or Arabic television service that exists primarily to provide programming of special relevance to Turks or Arabs living in Europe, one Arab language service at one time reported with some regularity on matters involving or affecting the Arab community in Europe, especially Arabs living in the United Kingdom. The Saudi Arabian-financed Middle Eastern Broadcasting Centre (MBC; at www.mbc1.tv/home) launched its satellite TV channel in 1991. It was a London-based Arabic-language news and information service intended largely for viewers in the Middle East, but could be received in Europe as well, and appeared to be a popular choice among Arabs living there. It remains popular, but when it shifted its base of operation to Dubai in 2002, its modest coverage of the activities of Arabs living in Europe largely vanished.

It may be that, if the Arab population in Europe continues to grow, MBC will find it an attractive business proposition to create a subchannel service with programming of particular relevance to the many different Arab audiences scattered across Europe.[23] If that were to happen, MBC would have to decide which forms of Arabic to use, because much like Kurdish and Sami, Arabic has a host of dialects, some of them difficult for most other Arabs to understand. Substantial numbers of Arabic speakers living in Europe come from North Africa, where the dialects differ quite markedly from the forms of Arabic spoken in the Middle East. The question of what effects a multidialect Arabic service might have on bonds of identity would be relevant here, as well.[24]

The internet also has served the needs of regional audiences and media services in the developing world, and in a few instances has been employed to reach ethnic and linguistic minorities such as Quechua speakers in a number of South American nations: The Pulsar service carries several hours a day of a wide variety of material translated into Quechua, and it can be downloaded by radio stations and other media operations using the language as well as by those relatively few Quechua-speaking and reading individuals who have access to the necessary equipment (Gumicio-Dagron, 2001: 241–246).

National

Most ethnic minority groups lack either sufficiently broad distribution across the nation or a large enough population base to warrant the creation of a national terrestrial radio or television service. Furthermore, where frequency spectrum space is scarce, as it is over much of Europe and in Japan, it is difficult to develop a set of stations that can be melded into a viable network. Cable and satellite radio and TV may not offer infinite numbers of channels, but prospects for minority group national services certainly are brighter through those outlets. Canada's Aboriginal People's Television Network (APTN) provides programming made by Native American and Inuit producers throughout Canada, but also carries programs made in other parts of the Americas (Alia, 1999; Brook, 2000).

There is one major exception among terrestrial services, but it is a qualified exception. Australia's SBS came on air in January 1978 to serve what were at the time ethnic minority groups with ancestral homelands largely in Europe. It took about two decades before the SBS delivery system, aided by satellites, could reach all parts of the nation, and even then not all of the dozens of languages that it was offering by the late 1990s were available nationwide. Most of its radio programming is produced in Sydney, but much of its television material comes from the ancestral homelands, and those programs very seldom deal with émigré experiences in Australia (Davies, 1998; Jakubowicz and Newell, 1995).[25]

There also is an ethnic minority radio service in Cologne, Germany that strives to be nationwide. Funkhaus Europa came into being in 1996 in part because its parent corporation WestDeutsche Rundfunk (WDR), the public broadcasting service for the Rhineland and much of northern Germany, looked to be in a position to lose one of its major radio frequencies unless it could come up with a unique use for the frequency. It helped that top level WDR administrators supported the idea of creating a service for minority groups; it also helped that WDR had been offering limited amounts of airtime for that purpose since the mid-1960s. Drawing upon similar programs being produced at other German public service stations in Berlin and in Stuttgart, it was able to put together a several hour per day schedule which had grown to 24 hours a day by 2002, with nearly total national distribution through a combination of terrestrial and satellite transmission. Its 12 languages are mostly European, but also include Turkish, Arabic, and Kurdish. It uses satellite transmission to supplement its terrestrial distribution.

The United Kingdom has a sizeable South Asian population (roughly 2 million, or slightly more than 3% of the total population, as of 2002), and the BBC's local radio stations in Leicester and Birmingham began in the early 1990s to coordinate the individual programs that each was already producing for Indian and Pakistani audiences. By the end of the 1990s, there was a cohesive schedule of several hours daily. Most of the programs were in English, but some were in Hindi, Urdu, Tamil, and other South Asian languages. It proved popular enough to lead the BBC to designate it as the BBC Asian Network and to put it up on satellite as well as on the Web, so that South Asians throughout the United Kingdom might have some possibility of receiving it. It is a 24-hour daily service, with the early morning hours filled by retransmission of the BBC World Service; it carries a wide mixture of news, sports, light entertainment, as well as large amounts of South Asian popular music, some of it by request (personal interview, Vijay Sharma, BBC Asian Network, Birmingham, U.K., April 2002).

Sunrise Radio, a South Asian 24-hour commercial radio service, broadcasts in English and five South Asia languages and features little else but South Asian popular music. It aspires to be national, at least in the sense that it hopes to establish outlets in those cities where there are large concentrations of South Asians. So far it has an AM station in London, six digital audio (DAB) services in London, the Midlands and Scotland, a second digital-only service (Radio Yarr), and transmission through satellite and on the Web (www.sunriseradio.com). It carries frequent "headline" newscasts, some of which it originates. It also carries ads in English and in the South Asian languages and announcers sometimes intermix South Asian languages with English.[26]

SBS, Funkhaus Europa (FE), and the BBC Asian Network have the benefit of more or less assured financial support, SBS through annual government appropriation and FE and the Asian Network through household annual license fees. None of the services attracts large mainstream audiences. If a national ethnic minority service is to receive financial support through commercial revenues— spot advertising and sponsorship—audience size will be far more important than it is for annual appropriation or fee-supported services.

Population increases among African Americans and Hispanic-Americans in the 1970s[27] contributed to the development of commercially supported national services for each group. African-American radio group owner Radio One, founded in 1980, owns or operates 66 stations in 22 markets and programs five channels on the XM Satellite Radio service (www.radio-one.com). The Black Entertainment Network (BET) and Univision[28] have been in existence for almost 30 years, and their growth has paralleled those increases in population. However, audience size alone would not have brought about their creation. The development of communication satellites capable of distributing program material to local cable television outlets had much to do with that growth, because it permitted national distribution without requiring a set of fully interconnected local TV stations in major cities across the United States. Thus, the national "networks" that were established were far less expensive than they would have been if BET or Univision had attempted to replicate the traditional broadcast networks (CBS, ABC, NBC).

It took several years before either of the services developed much by way of original programming: Univision initially created most of its schedule out of entertainment programs, and particularly *telenovelas* (soap operas), from various Latin American nations—a natural source, given that Univision carried (and still carries) Spanish-language material only. At first, its daily newscasts featured large amounts of news about Latin America and Spain, much of it reported by broadcasters in those nations. BET relied heavily on rock, hiphop, and other popular music videos featuring Black artists, as well as reruns of U.S. sitcoms and dramas with Black actors such as Bill Cosby. It offered newscasts once a week.

As time passed, more of Univision's reporting was done by its own staff and dealt more often with Hispanic-American life, although it has been criticized for devoting too much attention to the viewpoints of various U.S.-based anti-Castro organizations (Rodriguez, 1996). It now offers three national newscasts daily, and a few of its affiliates, notably KMEX-TV (Los Angeles), provide local newscasts. Also, some of the *telenovelas* began to be produced for Univision in Puerto Rico, with story lines that were far more contemporary in the ways they mirrored society. They became more appealing to younger viewers than were the fairy tale story lines of the usual Latin American *telenovelas*. BET began to develop a few of its own entertainment programs (generally variety shows with a host and guests, most of them African-American entertainers), and built up its newscasts to the point where they were running 5 days a week (Monday through Friday) by 2001.[29] Both services are highly popular with their respective target audiences.

Ethnic groups in other nations have found it more difficult to follow in the footsteps of BET and Univision, in part because most of the European industrialized nations were slower to encourage the development of commercial broadcasting than was the United States, but also in part because such groups were fewer in number and of smaller size than were Hispanics and Blacks in the United States. As commercial cable and satellite TV services have taken hold in many parts of Europe, they have served as conduits for the sorts of ancestral homeland television services noted earlier, but the counterparts of BET and Univision have yet to appear, and may not, aside from services for the largest groups: Turks and Arabs.

The chief importance of national ethnic minority services (including the internet, which plays much the same sort of role here as it does at the international and regional levels) lies in the added visibility and prominence they provide for the minority groups themselves—a sense of being a part of national life, but on a group's own terms. The national stage provided by those services also could serve as a way of focusing and even mobilizing Black or Hispanic public opinion, although there is little specific evidence that they do so. There is more evidence along those lines where Black talk radio stations are concerned, but the stations themselves are not part of a national network. Rather, the galvanizing of Black public opinion around such issues as the O.J. Simpson murder trial or the Los Angeles police beating of Rodney King arose more or less spontaneously when Black newspapers and hosts of radio talk shows stressed those aspects of the issues that were not being covered by mainstream media, but were well worth the attention of their local audiences (Jacobs, 2000).

There are some interesting distinctions among the various sorts ethnic minority of national services. From my observations, it seems clear that many of the traditional public service broadcasters are making a more concerted effort to hire ethnic minorities than are their commercial counterparts. The BBC has been especially active in that regard.[30] When public broadcasters provide radio and TV channels specifically for use by minorities, as do Sweden, Norway, and Finland for their Sami radio services, and as does the BBC for its Welsh and Scots Gaelic services, as well as the Asian Network, the manner of program presentation tends to be more formal than it is on ethnic minority commercial channels, and "correctness" of speech more of an issue. There also appears to be greater concern on the part of the ethnic minority public channels for balance in reporting the news, but also in features, commentaries, talk shows, and other informational programs.

Perhaps the greatest advantage of a national service to ethnic minorities is its capacity for reaching members of a minority group wherever they may live, with programming that identifies issues of national concern to the group and reinforces overall group identity. Thus, it may help to overcome tribalism/factionalism/parochialism and to emphasize what can be accomplished by working together. In cases where tribalism, for example, is deeply entrenched and rests on ancient grudges and wrongs, the nationalist message can be a hard sell, as it has been among the Maori in New Zealand.[31]

However, a service such as "Native American Calling," a radio talk program delivered throughout the United States via satellite, shows promise of helping Native Americans to realize that many of the problems they face—Indian land claims, health issues, for example, the prevalence of diabetes and child and spousal abuse—are problems common to virtually all of them, whether on reservations or in cities. Whether that awareness will translate into more effective pressure on government to help them address those problems is another matter, of course, but it is an important step in that direction.[32]

State/Province/Area

Federal systems of government often feature important roles for states, provinces, and areas (subregions). Switzerland, Belgium, Spain, the United Kingdom and Germany all do so, but Germany is the leading example of the prominence of states/provinces/areas where the electronic media are concerned. German broadcast law rests on the foundation of the German States (*Lander*), and there is no national regulation of electronic media services. State governments in the United States often support statewide public radio and television stations through annual appropriations. Ethnic minority electronic media often are not singled out for support, but some of the Australian state governments, Victoria in particular, have appropriated financial support for Aboriginal and other ethnic minority broadcast activities, as have some of Canada's provinces, Quebec leading the way with grants to Native American radio stations.

The United Kingdom, Spain, and France all display considerable electronic media activity in areas (subregions) with their own languages,[33] and a number of other European nations provide at least a modicum of electronic space for that purpose, as does Germany for the Sorbs, or Italy for the German-speaking population of Alto Adige and for Sardinians (Moragas Spa & Garitaonandia, 1999). There even is a commercial TV service for Brittany (Breizh TV), although relatively few of its programs are produced in Breton; far more are subtitled in the language.

Relatively few ethnic groups identify themselves with states, areas, or provinces, thus making a state/province/area ethnic broadcast or internet service a meaningless distinction. Aside from that, the state/province/area governments themselves often prove somewhat unreliable as sources of financial support. Ethnic minority groups usually do not carry a great deal of political clout at that level of government, and appropriations for such groups and their activities can be reduced or eliminated from one year to the next if the economic climate worsens. Recessions in Canada and the United States in the late 1980s and early 1990s saw cutbacks in support for indigenous media by Alaska, Quebec, and Ontario.

Local

The greater part of ethnic minority electronic media activity, aside from the internet,[34] takes place at the local level. Many nations have developed their broadcasting systems on the basis of the licensing of local stations, although many of those stations end up being affiliated with networks or station groups and having limited freedom to produce truly local programming. Some may serve as feeders or relays for program material largely from a single source, and may or may not be permitted to break away from that source in order to produce and broadcast local material. Even in cases where stations belonging to a national commercial group have their own DJs or talk show hosts, the overall program format (play lists, topics to be discussed) probably will be dictated by the group's owners.

Although the radio and television frequency spectrum in most industrialized nations is crowded, it remains possible for minority groups to acquire broadcast licenses. That is particularly true in those nations that have reserved portions of the broadcast spectrum or created specific licensing categories for noncommercial stations in general (United States), for low power stations (United States), for community stations (Australia, New Zealand, Canada), for ethnic minority stations (Australia, New Zealand), and for access stations (New Zealand, United Kingdom, Norway, Sweden, Denmark).

Although many of the ethnic minority local radio stations are noncommercial, a growing number are commercial, at least in North America. One reason is that, in Canada and the United States, AM stations in the larger cities have experienced tremendous losses of audience to FM (UHF). Owners of AM stations often have been increasingly willing to sell them as the competitive picture has worsened, sometimes at an affordable price for would-be ethnic minority owners. For example, during the late 1990s, two AM stations in the Minneapolis-St. Paul metropolitan area (3 million residents) were sold to owners who converted them into Spanish language stations. Nearly every major U.S. city has at least one commercial ethnic minority radio station, and most have two or more. Popular music is the predominant format, but there are talk stations as well; Hispanic and Black national radio news services are carried by most of the stations, few of which have their own local newscasts.

Commercial ethnic minority local stations are becoming more common in Europe, as well. Great Britain has several which serve South Asian listeners, and there have been attempts to establish a commercial network of such stations.[35] There also are a few for African and Caribbean listeners, as well as individual stations for Greeks and for Turks, and a few *rainbow*[36] stations such as Spectrum Radio, a London-based AM station with nearly 20 different blocks of airtime for specific ethnic groups (Sikh, Arabic, Mauritian, etc.). France has a number of commercial ethnic stations, led by Radio Beur (which has developed a small network), which broadcast in Maghreb (North African) Arabic, plus a few Caribbean stations. Germany has Turkish language radio stations. Australia has at least one internet commercial radio station that broadcasts in Arabic. Most of those stations carry large amounts of popular music; few originate newscasts.

Noncommercial local radio stations serving ethnic minorities are likely to be of two sorts. There are rainbow stations, some of them with access radio, where a typical day's schedule consists of 15-, 30- and 60-minute programs produced by ethnic groups and individuals, but also by people with specific cultural interests (e.g., French popular music or heavy metal rock), and a wide variety of others with assorted interests. There also are single-culture stations, with one ethnic group in charge of the entire schedule.[37] The former generally outnumber the latter, if only because many of the ethnic minority groups are too small and/or lack the capital necessary to establish their own radio stations.

Sweden, Norway, and Denmark have taken a somewhat different approach to serving the needs of ethnic minority program producers and others who cannot afford to establish their own local stations or may not wish to do so. All three provide *närradio* ("nearby radio," although in many cases the signal can be heard throughout the city) transmitters that operate at low power and are spread throughout the nation. Any group or association wishing to use those facilities may apply to do so, although the program schedule for any given transmitter may be full in the more popular broadcast hours, so newcomers might have to settle for the early morning hours.

Ethnic minority-run local television stations are far less numerous, primarily because of the high costs of operation. There are Hispanic TV stations in several of the larger U.S. cities, and a few African-American-owned and operated stations. Some of the Hispanic stations serve as terrestrial relays for Univision and Telemundo, and may produce local newscasts, as well, which most of the African-American TV stations do not. When the FCC first proposed the creation of a specific licensing category for low-power TV (LPTV) stations in the late

1970s, one of its hopes was that minority groups might invest in them because they would be less expensive to operate than were conventional stations. The FCC also proposed that the new licenses be issued to noncommercial operations only. By the early 1980s, the FCC was dominated by Reagan administration appointees, and the final version of the LPTV plan opened licensing to any and all applicants, commercial and noncommercial. A few ethnic minority groups did manage to secure LPTV licenses, but most of those that did so either sold their stations to nonminority businesses or entered a partnership with them in which airtime devoted to minority programs was reduced sharply.

There are community television stations where ethnic minority groups have airtime in Australia, Fiji, Venezuela, and other nations. The Australian government issued experimental licenses for six community TV stations in the mid-1990s; four of them remain in operation as of 2003, with a fifth (Adelaide) likely to take the place of a delicensed community TV service by 2004. Although there are no specific requirements that the station provide airtime for ethnic minority groups, the stations in Sydney and Melbourne offer numerous programs made by ethnic minorities (Iranians, Serbs, Croats, etc.), Brisbane carries a few Serbian and Croatian programs, and the station in Perth carries one such program ("Telelatino").[38] A proposed community TV station, MayanTV, in Quetzaltenango, Guatemala (http://mayantv.webcrayon.com), hopes to be entirely Mayan in its program content,[39] whereas Community Television Fiji (ctv@is.com.fj) operates as an access channel, open to anyone who wishes to make a program.

Access cable radio and television, as already noted, offer low cost (and sometimes no cost) opportunities for ethnic minorities to produce programs, and most nations with reasonably well-developed cable TV services require that those services offer access channels; the services also may be responsible for funding the training staffs, studios and equipment necessary to help would-be program producers. Several of the German States (*Länder*) have well-equipped access facilities and good training, thanks to a tax on cable subscriptions that covers most of the costs; cable radio and TV access services in cities with large numbers of ethnic minorities—Hamburg and Berlin, for example—may find a as much as one third to half of the program schedule for both cable radio and TV taken up by ethnic minority productions.

Local radio and TV are popular among most ethnic groups because they are accessible and relatively inexpensive (at least through the access services). Also, many of the groups think of themselves as local, first and foremost. That is particularly true if they live in larger cities, where many of them found themselves settling as migrants, and where Chinatowns and other ethnic neighborhoods still can be found, even if many of their one-time residents have spread to other parts of the city.

Neighborhood

If an ethnic minority group happens to be interested in using electronic media within a neighborhood, there are a few situations where that is possible. The available outlets usually function as access radio or TV services, with studios, equipment and training available at little or no cost to the users. Such services also may provide people lacking any previous production experience with the opportunity to learn in a lower risk environment.

The *närradio* services mentioned earlier sometimes function as neighborhood services in the largest cities, Stockholm in particular. Six low-power FM transmitters serve the Stockholm region, and they are scattered around the city, so groups wishing to make programs for an audience that is concentrated in one particular part of the city may be able to do so, if airtime is available on the appropriate transmitter. Radio Sydvast (Radio Southwest, in the southwestern sector of Stockholm) carries weekly programs in Farsi and more frequent broadcasts in Kurdish and other Middle Eastern/Western Asian languages (Radio Sydvast, 2001), whereas Gothenburg's main *närradio* service, GNP, has sufficient demand for airtime on the part of ethnic minorities and other groups that it provides three channels to carry their broadcasts,[40] some of them at the neighborhood level. Norway's Tellus Radio (initially Radio Immigranten) came on air in Oslo in 1992 as a *närradio* service for ethnic minorities when their numbers were far smaller than they are today, and when it was difficult to induce many of the groups to use the service (Ananthakrishnan, 1994). It broadcasts in eight languages for roughly 50 hours per week on FM and over the internet (www.tellus-radio.no).[41]

A few nations, such as the United Kingdom and New Zealand, have a special category of radio license that is particularly favorable to neighborhood radio, but only if the broadcasts are of limited duration: a few days to as much as a month, and sometimes renewable. *Restricted service licenses* (RSLs) usually are issued by a government communications regulatory authority such as the United Kingdom's Radio Authority (RA), and are for low-power services only.[42] They have become very popular among one particular category of ethnic minority group in the United Kingdom in recent years—devout muslims wishing to broadcast during the holy month of Ramadan. According to the RA's Neil Stock,[43] a few dozen RSLs were issued for that purpose in the 2002 celebrations, which represented a considerable increase over the previous year. The experience gained through a short-term service can be helpful in helping a group to decide whether it has the staying power and the necessary resources to operate a continuous service.

South Africa's communications regulatory authority, ICASA, is considering the establishment of a new licensing category for one-watt radio broadcasting, meaning that such stations would be neighborhood services. However, the distinction between the already-existing community radio services, some of which operate relatively low-power stations at the neighborhood level, and the proposed services was unclear as of February 28, 2003, when the ICASA called for public comment on the proposal (ICASA, 2003[44]; Mabuza, 2003).

Unlicensed radio services operate almost exclusively at the neighborhood level, in part because they operate at low power, but also because a close association with the neighborhood helps to ensure that there will be a ready supply of hideouts and of informants who will warn the service operators of the presence of government officials seeking to shut down the services. A few of them are or have been run by ethnic minorities, most notably by African Americans[45] and Hispanic-Americans (Elizade, 1996) in the United States and by Afro-Caribbeans and South Asians in Great Britain (Hind & Moss, 1985).

Neighborhood TV is quite rare, but there are a few examples. The city of Barcelona is divided into 10 districts, and its cable television service devotes a channel, Barcelona Televisio, to the programs made by them (Moragas Spa & Garitaonandia, 1999: 361–362; Rodriguez, 2001: 83–108). Each district maintains a small production studio and provides training for users. The city government helps to offset those costs, and coordinates the channel schedule through a contracted organization, ICB SA.

CLOT-TV, in the "working-class" Clot district, is one of the more active users in terms of the number and diverse character of programs it contributes to the district channel (CLOT-TV, 2002; Mayugo, 2002). Sizable numbers of ethnic minorities are a recent phenomenon for the city in general, but the Clot district has a few thousand Pakistanis, some of whom have become active in producing programs.[46] Also, the service has produced a promotional video for an association ("Diakha Medina") which supports the Mandinga people (Senegal) living in the district (CLOT-TV, 2002).

Caracas, Venezuela had a neighborhood TV station, Catia TV, which served one of the city's low-income areas (East Caracas) until mid-2003, when it was raided and closed by the municipal authorities. It had been operated largely by the residents of the neighborhood, in conjunction with the National Community Media School, which was inaugurated in April 2003. The latter already had begun to train ethnic minority children ("afro-colombo-venezolanos") as journalists (Contreras, 2003). The shutdown was temporary: Pressure from several citizens' groups and media activists inside and outside of Venezuela soon led to its reopening (Gomez, 2003).

The concept of neighborhood services for ethnic minority groups is sound enough in principle because it is quite common for members of newly arrived groups to cluster together in cities. How much long-term utility it may have is another question. Newly arrived groups may begin to spread out within 5 or 10 years, at which point a local radio or TV service may make better sense if group members who are active in media production want to continue to reach as many of the group's members as possible. Because most large cities in the industrialized nations seem to attract new ethnic groups every year or two, there always should be at least a few of them who will benefit from neighborhood electronic media services, but those services should not be considered as substitutes for more broadly local services.

SUMMARY

There certainly is no shortage of *potential* electronic media outlets available to ethnic minorities, and there are numerous examples of ethnic minority use of every type of outlet covered here. Furthermore, no level of geography is without some degree of ethnic minority electronic media activity: Even at the international and regional levels, groups such as the Kurds have managed to create radio and television services to reach their often widely scattered members. At the same time, no types or levels of service are set aside for ethnic minorities to use, and because most services came into existence long before ethnic minorities became involved in them, the minorities have found themselves in the usual position of someone who arrives late for the feast: They seem often to get whatever is left over, whatever no one else wants (or at least prefers).

Where late arrival has meant poorer equipment and little or no training—nd that certainly is not always the case—some of the programs made by minority groups can seem quite plain at best, and comical at worst. There is quite a difference between an access TV program made by a minority group working with the excellent facilities and training available at Berlin's Offener Kanal-e and a program made with second- or third-hand equipment and training that consists of little more than "This is the lens and here's how you look through it. Here's the button you press to start recording. Now you're all set." Most of us can barely tolerate poorly made home movies or videos, even when our friends and family have made them. Are we likely to be any better disposed toward similar programs made by minorities, especially if it is so easy to dismiss them by switching to another channel or turning off the set? What is more, the fact that we receive such material over the very same equipment whose speakers and screens bring us a plethora of professionally produced entertainment and information may reduce our receptiveness to material of lesser quality. (Conversely, its plain and "genuine" character may come as a relief to a heavy diet of slickly produced material.)

Still, the predominant share of ethnic minority programming that I have seen and heard is not intended primarily (if at all) for the mainstream majority. Are minority audiences more tolerant of less than professional production standards when they appear in minority-made programs? And if that should prove to be the case, does the degree of tolerance vary according to the specific minority group producing the program? Might there be greater tolerance for subprofessional production when it is not made by members of the viewer's own group, perhaps on the grounds that it provides nongroup viewers with one more negative image of that group? We lack hard evidence on such issues; like many similar issues in ethnic minority electronic media activity, this would be an excellent research topic.

Certainly, the ethnic minority services available at each geographic level feature some important advantages and disadvantages; it would be worth the time of any group to consider them carefully when developing or revising a media plan, if there is one. And of course advantages and disadvantages do not mean as much when a group lacks a range of choices, although it remains worthwhile to consider how to make the most efficient use of the only choice available. However, another pair of elements—policies and financing—has important effects on not just the range of choices, but also what can be accomplished with the choices made. They are the subject of the next chapter.

NOTES

1. In Te Upoko O Te Ika, a Maori radio station in Wellington, New Zealand. The "studio" was discarded when the station moved to more spacious quarters in the 1990s. Some of the staff felt that it should have been preserved as a monument to the station's humble beginnings!

2. In CKHQ, a Canadian Mohawk radio station in Kahnasetake, northwest of Montreal, Quebec; Radio Zibonele, a Black township radio station in Kayelitsha (just east of Cape Town, South Africa) has a large cargo container that has been fitted out for that purpose.

3. One of New Zealand's access radio stations, in Wellington, operates at 10 KW, so it certainly is not low-power.

4. Professor Everitt (2003) also prepared a report for the authority that sums up the experiences of the stations over their initial year of operation; on the whole, the experiences appear to have been very positive.

5. Molnar (1993), Meadows (1992), and Molnar and Meadows (2001) offer detailed accounts of Imparja. I provide brief coverage of those earlier ventures in Browne (1996: 42-48).

6. Alia (1999) provides an extensive account of APTN, and indicates that there has been widespread resistance on the part of Canadian cable service operators to the requirement that it be carried as a national service; some of the operators have sought to avoid doing so. See also Clarity (1994).

7. Molnar and Meadows (2001: 43). The authors dedicate two major sections of the book to satellites and their uses by indigenous groups in Australia and Canada.

8. Myria Georgiu noted in the course of a personal discussion with me (London, April 2003) that the online activities of diaspora groups often take the forms of online publishing and use of search engines, in addition to the maintenance of personal contacts. She also noted that online publishing often is bilingual (presumably in recognition of the likelihood that many primary users of diaspora Web sites will be more fluent in the "new homelands" languages). Aksoy and Robins (2003) observe that Turkish émigrés sometimes maintain two or three homes, each in a different nation (e.g., United Kingdom., Germany, and Turkey), and use the internet to maintain contacts with and within all three, thus supporting a simultaneous co-existence. They see this as departing from the traditional notion of the diaspora as a strictly "old homeland-new homeland" relationship.

9.   Karim (2003) includes several chapters dealing with ethnic minority usage of the internet, ranging from activities of a Free Tibet movement to those of Ghanaian Seventh Day Adventists in London and North America. The development of independent media centers is covered in some detail by Downing (2002, 2003). Hughes (2003) covers two such centers, in Sri Lanka and in Mali, and indicates some of the problems that can arise, as well as some of the solutions that are developed.

10.   Statistic from "Media Pack: Black Britain" (2002). See Gibson (2002) for a brief history of the development of Black and other minority Web sites in Great Britain.

11.   Although Irish is one of the two official languages for the Republic of Ireland, less than 10% of the population speaks it with reasonable fluency, so it certainly qualifies as a minority language.

12.   The BBC World Service did produce a series of radio programs entitled "The Right to Refuge" in 2001 (www.bbc.co.uk/refugees). The series, in nine languages, examined various aspects of global and local experiences of refugees, and was intended particularly for regions where the presence of refugees had become a major issue.

13.   The manager did not wish to be identified as the source of this observation.

14.   Turkey has been particularly strict with respect to broadcasts in Kurdish, claiming that they are used to incite the Turkish Kurds—there are roughly 12 million of them living in Turkey—to work for a separate Kurdish nation. In late November 2002, the government agreed to authorize broadcasting in Kurdish (which it had done sporadically in the past), with one radio service run through the national system (TRT) for no more than 45 minutes daily and a total of 4 hours per week; television was limited to 30 minutes per day and 2 hours per week, also through TRT. Furthermore, it was pressure from the EU, which Turkey hoped to join, that was largely responsible for even that much of a concession ("Turkey," 2002: A5).

15.   Medya TV started life as Med-TV, a satellite service operating from London. As Hasssanpour (2003: 81-86) indicates, the Turkish government soon applied pressure on the British government to cancel its license (it was legally licensed to operate from the United Kingdom), or failing that, to punish it for (allegedly) encouraging acts of violence. This was part of a larger Turkish campaign to discourage media activities on the part of the Kurds living in Europe. In June 1999, the British TV licensing authority, the Independent Television Commission, withdrew Med-TV's license, but in late July it came back on air from Paris as Medya TV.

16.   This apparently was part of the service's agreement with French authorities that it would limit itself to programming that was sensitive to the European standards of impartiality (Hassanpour, 2003: 86).

17.   As do many of the broadcast services, especially given the increasing use of the term by Kurdish officials in Iraq, who often employ the term *Kurdistan* when discussing the Kurdish region's right to semi-autonomous (at the least) status in a reconstituted Iraq.

18.   Sveriges Radio (SR—Sweden); Norsk Rikskringkasting (NRK—Norway); Yleisradio (YLE—Finland).

19.   I also draw upon my visits to the three Sami stations in June 1993, and to my visits to the NRK and YLE Sami stations in September 1994 and November 1995.

20.   For Radio Cerenja, see http://medienhilfe.ch/Projekte/MAC/RCERENJA; for Radio Nisava, see www.bahtaldrom.org.yu./eng/radioe; for Radio C, see www.inthesetimes.com/issue/25/12/weselowsky2512; for Bulgaria, see www.mul-

ticultural.net/newsletter/article/issue5-angelova. There are two interesting personal narrations by Roma individuals working for and with mainstream broadcast services (see also Mohacsi, 1995: 5 and Russinov, 1995: 5). See Media and the Roma (1996) for a detailed report on a conference held in Prague in 1996 at which Roma media staff and others discussed the difficulties (monetary, societal, and educational) faced by Roma attempting to express themselves through mainstream media and through their own (very few) media outlets.

21.   Those observations were made by several RNG staff members in the course of my three visits (1990, 1991, 1994) to the stations. They felt strongly that the provision of a schedule made up of program in different regional accents was instrumental in breaking down some of the existing insularity in the region.

22.   Askoy and Robins (2003: 95) contend that the banality of everyday life in Turkey as displayed through those cable and satellite services "disturbs the imagination of a 'there and then' Turkey—thereby working against the romance of diaspora-as-exile, against a tendency to false idealization of the 'homeland'."

23.   For example, North African Arabs predominate in France, whereas the U.K. Arabic population is mainly from the Middle East.

24.   MBC could broadcast to Europe in modern classical Arabic, which more highly educated Arabs understand.

25.   I have also drawn on my visits to SBS in September 1987, February 1996, and March 2001.

26.   Gillespie (1995), in her survey of Punjabis living in London's Southall district, notes (98-100) that Sunrise Radio was perceived as more of an "older adult" service that did not play much "progressive" music, such as Bangra, and thus attracted relatively few young listeners. However, it appears to be quite popular with older listeners. Tsagarousiano (2002: 219-220) indicates that it has a heavily commercial orientation, despite what station management says about the "community" nature of the service. Its share of audience in the June-September 2003 period for the London region was 1.2%, whereas the BBC Asian Network had a share of 0.4% for the entire nation, but 1.9% for the Midlands, where it has a number of AM radio outlets (figures from the RAJAR 1Web site www.rajar.co.uk).

27.   U.S. Census Bureau data from the 2000 census indicate that each group makes up roughly 13% of the U.S. population, with Hispanic-Americans holding a slight lead over African Americans.

28.   Another Hispanic-American TV service, Telemundo, was formed to compete with Univision, but the latter has always held a wide lead, and has developed two additional Spanish language channels, Galavision (for adults in the 21-49 range) and TeleFutura (A "general" service). Telemundo was purchased by General Electric, NBC's parent corporation, in October 2001. Several Hispanic-American groups protested the merger; one of them, the League of United Latin American citizens (LULAC), passed a resolution in December 2000 stating *inter alia* that "NBC and Telemundo have refused to allow Latino organizations to participate in the formulation of decisions affecting the future of Latinos with their network and for the Latino community at large." The resolution supported a petition filed by the National Latino Media Council to deny FCC approval of the merger. However, it received final FCC approval in April 2002 ("Resolution," 2001; "Telemundo," 2002).

29.   The purchae of BET by Viacom, a U.S. media mega corporation that includes com-
        mercial network CBS, has meant that CBS now advises BET on the production of
        newscasts. (For a broad if uncritical picture of BET and its many media enterprises,
        see Barber & Tait, 2001: 111-126.)
30.   The BBC approach to minority employment programs also includes the provision
        of training programs such as "Ascend" specifically for ethnic minorities.
31.   Derek Fox, who served as the director of Mana Maori Media (a national Maori
        news-gathering and dissemination service) for several years, noted that he had
        made numerous attempts to get the Maori National Congress to support Mana
        Maori's efforts more vigorously and concretely, especially through financial sup-
        port. Members of the Congress expressed their support in public, but the Congress
        did not approve financial support. He attributed this to the strong tribalist feelings
        of key members of the Congress, and said that he had been told by some of those
        members that it was fine to talk about national concerns of the Maori, but what
        really mattered took place at the tribal (*iwi*) level. The Tainui, probably the most
        powerful of the tribes, refused to broadcast Mana Maori's national newscast because
        the anchors and reporters did not have Tainui accents and did not include enough
        news about Tainui acitivities (personal interview with Fox, Ruatoria, New Zealand,
        October 1993).
32   In my examination of the "Archives" section of the program's Web site
        (www.nativeamericacalling.org), all of those subjects were common throughout the
        period 1995-2003, but that programs on "intra-Indian" relations, such as tribal fraud,
        resolving disputes through mediation, tribal infighting, also appeared frequently.
33   Wales, Scotland, and Northern Ireland for the United Kingdom; Catalonia, the
        Basque country, and Galicia for Spain; Brittany, Alsace-Lorraine, Corsica,
        Provence,. and Aquitaine for France.
34.   However, cities and counties sometimes do feature ethnic minority Web sites, such
        as the Los Angeles County Filipino American Employees Association (LACFAEA;
        at www.lacfaea.org). Such sites generally are operated by and for specific groups
        within ethnic minority communities, and tend to be heavily informational.
35.   When the BBC announced that it would be expanding the BBC Asian Network
        into a 24-hour operation, some of the local commercial stations serving Asian com-
        munities protested, in part on the grounds that this move made it nearly impossible
        for them to go ahead with their plans to establish a nationwide commercial Asian
        network because the BBC service presumably would draw too many listeners to
        allow the commercial service to be financially viable (Ali, 2001).
36.   A U.S. term designating those stations (usually community radio) with a wide
        diversity in program content, divided into generally small segments of airtime.
37.   Some ethnic stations may fall somewhere in between rainbow and single-culture
        services. For example, New Zealand radio stations operated by groups from the
        Pacific Island (PI) nations provide programming intended chiefly for Pacific
        Islanders and in several of the PI languages, although English also is commonly
        used. The manager of Auckland-based Radio 531PI, Sef Hao'uli, told me in the
        course of my March 1996 visit that he encouraged announcers to use a mix of
        English and the PI languages, in hopes that that would encourage younger English-
        speaking Pacific Islanders to learn their "old homeland" languages. He also
        observed that he received a great deal of criticism from older listeners for doing so,
        because it compromised the purity of the languages.

38. Personal visits to community TV stations in Sydney, Melbourne, Brisbane, Adelaide and Perth in March 2001.

39. According to a May 30, 2003 e-mail to the author from Professor Brian Stross (coordinator for the MayanTV project), anticipated funding for the service had not materialized, but a media training program already was in place.

40. According to GNP's manager, Hans Hirschi (personal interview, Gothenburg, May 2001), the service has had strong support from the city government in part because Gothenburg has a quite rapidly growing émigré population. The city also became aware of the important role that the service could play when a disastrous fire at a local disco in October 1998 resulted in more than 60 deaths, most of them Macedonians. The station served as a reliable source of information on the disaster and the investigation that followed; it also served in the days immediately following the fire as clearinghouse for names of those who had survived.

41. I also draw upon my visit to the station in November 1995.

42. See Gordon (2000) for a detailed presentation of RSLs. ICASA (2003: 13-18) offers a summary of regulatory practices in the United States, United Kingdom, Australia and Canada where low-power broadcast licensing, some of it through RSLs, is concerned.

43. Personal interview, Radio Authority, London, April 2003.

44. The ICASA Report did raise a number of questions on the issue of distinction, including "What should the differentiating feature be between a community broadcasting service and a low power sound broadcasting service, if any?" (Q.2.d, p. 6).The report specifically solicited public comment.

45. Those unlicensed activities appear to have begun in the mid-1980s, with Black Magic Liberation Radio in Fresno, California and somewhat later with West Tampa Delight in Tampa, Florida. In the latter case, the station's founder, "Blackbeard," sometimes broadcast the work of local groups; he also drew criticism for airing music with lyrics that denigrated women (Soley, 1999: 66-67). See also the section on M'banna Kantako and his Zoom Black Magic Liberation Radio in Chapter 4.

46. CLOT-TV staff members indicated to me in the course of a discussion (Barcelona, July 2002) that, although they welcomed ethnic minorities, those individuals were expected to work with the service in general, and not to confine their efforts to programs highlighting their own groups.

Policies and Policymaking

Rarely does anyone question the assumption that it is essential to consider policymaking when seeking to understand how and why media systems work as they do. However, it often seems to be regarded as among the driest, least interesting aspects of the subject—something like the least favorite vegetables that we are told to eat because they make us stronger. Perhaps that is because so much of each activity goes on behind closed doors, leaving the public with access to the laws, mission statements, and other documents that represent the final fruits of the process, but tell us little of the dynamics of their creation: the "horse-trading," tugs of war, convincing and unconvincing arguments, and other elements that enter into the decision-making process.

Happily for our purposes, policymaking often is quite transparent and accessible where ethnic minority electronic media activity is concerned.[1] That may be due in part to the relatively late arrival of such activity on the media scene. People who have been provided with little opportunity to express themselves through the media may work harder to discover what is going on when media policymaking finally shows signs of acknowledging their presence.

THE NATURE OF POLICYMAKING

There are several ways in which to consider policymaking by governments.[2] If we think in terms of its *purposes*, Portney's set of typologies covers the range of choices quite well. He includes *distributive*, *regulatory*, *redistributive*, and a fourth concept, *structural*, which he does not define and which in any case does not seem to apply to what we examine here. *Distributive* covers the passage of legislation, rules, and regulations that will lead to private activities (those *not* undertaken by the government) that should be useful/desirable to society. *Regulatory* relates to legislation needed to enable users to develop and share a scarce resource (such as the broadcast frequency spectrum) and/or to protect the public from harm through the actions ("obscene" programs, inflated rates for using the service) of those users. *Redistributive* acknowledges the (frequent) need to revisit (and perhaps amend or revise) legislation that has not worked as well as it should have (Portney, 1986: 6-7).[3] All three are present for policymaking that affects the electronic media—and often present in the self-same policymaking venture, as seen later in the chapter in the case study of the FCC and its development of a preference policy to encourage ethnic minority ownership of broadcast stations.

To approach the admittedly complex *process* of policymaking,[4] we first consider it in terms of its least controversial characteristics: *geography*, including international, regional, national, state/provincial, local, and *institutions*, including governmental, nongovernmental (media services), and nongovernmental (lobbyists, including "watchdogs" and "helpers").

Geography

International and Regional. In theory, international and regional government policymaking could (and perhaps should) be quite important to ethnic minority media. Left to their own devices, national governments may prefer to ignore the presence of ethnic minorities, and in worst-case scenarios may forbid or actively discourage them from speaking their own languages and honoring their own cultures. They even may coerce minority groups into total assimilation with the majority culture. Many governments followed one or another of those policies in the not-too-distant past. Pressure from regional and international governments and quasi-governments might persuade the national government to ease up or to abandon an anti-minority policy.

The same could be said of nongovernmental organizations (NGOs) at this level. Such bodies often lack the formal links with national governments enjoyed by international and regional governments, and for the most part they are not policymakers. However, the watchdogs can apply a certain degree of moral pressure, and often work closely with the mainstream media (especially print) to publicize what they regard as biased media portrayals of minorities (on TV in particular), censorship of ethnic minority views, restrictions on ethnic minority use of the electronic media, and so on. The helpers often assist the media services in responding to watchdog complaints, and may lobby legislators on behalf of the media, occasionally to the point of suggesting what should be covered in policies, regulations and rules and how it might be phrased.

Watchdogs and helpers are not very active at the international or regional levels, in large part because media services rarely operate at those levels. However, a more globalized economy could spur the growth of international and regional networks. Already there is considerable investment in international and regional corporations owning media services in a number of countries, but at present most of those services produce their own programs and/or purchase them from a variety of suppliers. It is quite likely that international and regional networks with a single program schedule but with skillfully dubbed audio tracks for the major languages in a given region will begin to appear in the near future, which may bring increased activity on the part of nongovernmental watchdogs, if not helpers. Whether any of those networks would serve ethnic minority audiences is another question, because the "economy of scale" approach that they are most likely to feature will favor mainstream audiences.

National. Most government-created media policy is national, in part because domestic broadcast signals often travel beyond national boundaries. That may not be very evident to a U.S. citizen, but it certainly is to most Europeans, whose many nations are packed into a far smaller space than the United States occupies. When signals from one nation cross borders and interfere with signals in another, it is expected that the national governments will sort things out. Even if national governments did not have to concern themselves about signal interference, they still would be certain to claim an interest in protecting the public (some segments of it, e.g., young children, more than others) from possibly harmful effects of inaccurate, inappropriate, unreliable media messages. Less often will they seek to protect ethnic minority groups from racist language or ethnically biased visual depictions. A few have insisted that the government itself provide some or even all of the media content, on the grounds that only the government knows what "the people" should have, regardless of what they might want.

Nongovernmental media organizations operating at the national level are of the sorts already described: national providers of electronic media services, such as networks; and critics (watchdogs) or supporters (helpers) of those services. The national providers certainly are involved in policymaking; the groups and associations often attempt to influence policymaking on the part of both the government and the media services.

State/Provincial, Local and Neighborhood. Policymaking by government at these levels is quite rare, with Germany as the major exception. Most state and local governments do not operate their own radio and television services, although many of them do have their own Web sites. Neighborhoods rarely have their own governments. NGOs, providers in particular, usually are more numerous and active at the local level than they are at the state/provincial level; and far more ethnic minority media service providers operate at the local level than at any other. Many of the mainstream local media services, public and commercial alike, are affiliated with national services, and as a result have little or no policymaking power, whereas ethnic service providers are far more apt to be on their own, and must take responsibility for setting goals, if not creating policy.

Institutions

International and Regional. Several policymaking institutions are active at the international and regional levels, but media policy is not one of their primary concerns.[5] The United Nations, an international quasi-government, has fashioned a Declaration of Human Rights, and some of its provisions certainly could be applied to ethnic minority involvement in the electronic media. Article 19 states that "Everyone has the right to freedom of opinion and expression; this right includes freedom . . . to seek, receive and impart information and ideas through *any media* and regardless of frontiers" (italics added). Article 27— "Everyone has the right freely to participate in the cultural life of the community"—sounds very much like Habermas' public sphere.

However, the United Nations tend to follow a hands-off policy where the specific practices of any single nation are concerned, unless it can be shown that they pose a clear and present physical danger to either neighbor states or to a significant (prominent, populous) group within the nation. Ethnic minority rights rarely qualify. It appears to require something close to genocide to stir the UN into issuing anything more than a declaration supporting ethnic minority rights. One UN administrative body—the International Telecommunications Union (ITU)—deals with the electronic media. However, the ITU very rarely concerns itself with issues of media portrayal or access, and in any case limits itself to problems arising between nations rather than within them. Another UN body, UNESCO, collects and publicizes information about media usage in a wide variety of situations, but seldom are ethnic minority experiences among them.

International helper/watchdog organizations dealing with ethnic minority electronic media are rare, but one—the World Association of Community Broadcasters (AMARC, from its French title)—assists ethnic minority efforts as part of its overall mission of supporting community broadcasting. That support takes several forms, including exchange of information on experiences, guidance on starting a community-based station, promoting and assisting with training programs, and making its members aware of the suppression of community stations by national governments and the need for members to bring pressure to bear on those governments to relent. That final category of activity is the closest that AMARC comes to being involved in policymaking. There also are regional offices of AMARC for Europe and for Africa.

Regional governments such as the European Community/Union and the African Union seem similarly reluctant to become involved in ethnic media policymaking, although the European Community/Union Parliament has considered resolutions supporting ethnic minority media activity on several occasions. As far back as 1981, the European (Community) Parliament adopted Resolution 0.4.3.1

(on a charter of regional languages and cultures and on rights of ethnic minorities) urging members "to allow and take steps to ensure access to local radio and television in a way that guarantees consistent and effective community communication . . . [and] to ensure that minority groups receive organizational and financial assistance for their cultural events equivalent to that received by the majority groups." In 1994, the Parliament approved Resolution 0.4.3.6. (on linguistic minorities in the European Community), where Provision 10 calls on the Commission of the European Community to "encourage the use of lesser used languages in the Community's audiovisual policy . . . and assist lesser used language producers and broadcasters to produce new programmes in a 16:9 [HDTV] format" as well as to "ensure that modern digital technology . . . is used for carrying a greater number of minority languages."[6]

Neither resolution has led to actual support of ethnic minority media enterprises, although the Commission has provided modest financial support for such activities as the radio service Voices Without Frontiers (VWF), which gathers stories about racial discrimination and steps being taken to combat it, then distributes them to community radio stations around the world. VWF also is attempting to reactivate an online discussion forum on anti-racism and other ethnic minority issues. The Commission has budgeted just under 100,000 Euros (just over U.S.$115,000 as of late 2003) for the support of VWF over the period 2000-2003 (Wajid, 2000).[7]

The Council of Europe, although not a regional government, serves as what might be termed "the conscience of Europe." As such, it discusses a wide variety of societal issues, including the place of ethnic minorities in European nations. It also holds annual meetings of the member government "offices for national minorities" (www.humanrights.coe.int/Minorities). The meetings feature considerable discussion and result in annual reports[8] filled with suggestions of ways in which the offices could improve the quality of their individual reports to the Council. Sometimes the annual reports draw upon the individual reports to provide examples of good and bad practices concerning the treatment of ethnic minorities. That can serve as a catalyst for action, but only when individual nations become motivated to take it.

One interesting example of a regional nongovernmental institution that plays a helper/watchdog role for ethnic minority services is the European Ethnic Broadcasting Association (www.european-journalists.org/eeba), founded in 1996. It deals primarily with exchanges of programming among its members—ethnic minority radio stations in Europe. It also attempts to influence governments and mainstream media services to assist the ethnic media in setting up training programs for young ethnic journalists. The Association sometimes presses national governments to help in supporting ethnic media services themselves. It hopes to develop a World Ethnic Broadcasting Association, as well. It could attempt to influence government policymaking more directly at any or all levels, but has not done so thus far, perhaps because the program exchanges and training programs have higher priority and funds are in short supply.

Other nongovernmental watchdog or helper international and regional organizations involved with ethnic minority media activity could include the International Federation of Journalists and the European Federation of Journalists (both at www.ifj.org), as well as Article 19 (www.article19.org). All three deal with issues related to censorship and the maltreatment of journalists, press governments to ease restrictions on reporters (some of them ethnic minorities) at times, and occasionally seek to influence national government policies toward journalists. As an examination of their Web sites will reveal, ethnic minority media activity is not a major concern of any of those organizations. Article 19 did issue a statement on February 12, 2003 affirming the "right of every individual or community to have its stories and views heard" as well as the "right to practice and express one's culture" (www.article19.org).

A number of nationally based citizen's organizations concerned about ethnic minority media services in Europe, such as the U.K. Community Media Association, have developed a "European Manifesto to support and to underline the importance of minority community media."[9] They are enlisting the endorsement of minority community media services and other supportive organizations, and presented the Manifesto to the president of the European Parliament during the 2004 elections to the Parliament. The Manifesto presents a strong justification for the strengthening of ethnic media, and requests financial support from the Parliament. However, given the relatively low levels of EU support for such activity up to this point, this is likely to be a tough sell.

Because government policymaking for ethnic minority media takes place primarily at the *national* level, there are many institutions to consider. Certainly, the various national legislative bodies—parliaments, congresses, and the like—are of paramount importance, with the courts and cabinets close behind, although that varies between nations. For example, media-related disputes seldom come before the courts in most European nations. They do so frequently in the United States—probably the world's most litigious nation—and their presence in British, Canadian, and Australian courts seems to be increasing. Although courts do not make policy, they certainly can shape it through their decisions on cases in which it is challenged.

Just as important as the legislatures are the regulatory agencies, such as the FCC, the Canadian Radio-Television and Telecommunications Commission (CRTC), the Australian Broadcasting Authority (ABA), the French Conseil Superieure de l'Audiovisuel (CSA), South Africa's ICASA, and the U.K. Office of Communications (Ofcom), which consolidated the operations of several electronic media regulatory agencies in December 2003. In fact, those agencies tend to be more frequently involved as policymakers where ethnic minority electronic media are concerned than are legislatures: The latter develop broad policies for electronic media activity, whereas the former often must develop rules and regulations for specific (not to mention more rapidly changing) facets of media performance.

Most of the regulatory agencies have not emphasized the ethnic minority sector in their policymaking. The case studies in Chapter 4 include examples of notable efforts along those lines on the part of the FCC and South Africa's ICASA, but the FCC initiatives soon tapered off and then vanished. ICASA has existed for just over a decade (it was founded in 1993); time will tell whether it sustains its support of the community radio sector, where Zulu, Xhosa, and other groups are most active. Several other regulatory agencies have issued public pronouncements in support of ethnic minority media services, but specific and tangible manifestations of that support may not be as evident. A report on the French CSA casts doubt on the sincerity of that body:

> The Conseil declares itself attentive to the efforts of the public and private channels, and congratulates itself in particular about the new agreement [on increasing minority representation] with Canal Plus in May 2000, cited above.
>
> Of a total of 221 pages [in the CSA Annual Report for 2000], the question of the representation of minorities occupies barely half a page, and the CSA seems to think that it has played its regulatory role, and that it is now up to the channels to do what is necessary to apply the decree.
>
> In a telephone contact with the press service of the CSA in January 2002, we hear that *"the subject doesn't interest anyone anymore."* (Grrem [*sic*], in *Tuning into Diversity*, 2002: 335)[10]

A few nations have created watchdog agencies that are supported through government appropriations but are independent of the government. They are not regulatory agencies, and thus have no authority to penalize electronic media services, but they can and do issue statements once they have investigated allegations of erroneous or biased programs. The statements often appear in newspapers, magazines, radio, and television, and in Great Britain they *must* appear in broadcasts of the service named in the allegation. Great Britain's Broadcasting Standards Commission (BSC) was created in the late 1980s, and similar agencies have appeared in Ireland, South Africa, and Canada during the 1990s.[11] The BSC often has considered portrayals of ethnic minorities through radio and TV, and has commissioned audience research on the subject.[12] However, it has done very little that relates directly to ethnic minority media services. It certainly can affect broadcast programming policies, but it appears to have little impact on government policymaking.

Nongovernmental media services are very active at the national level, and their policies sometimes have a major effect on ethnic minority activity. That is particularly true where there is a national PSB in place, as there is in most industrialized nations. The PSBs in Europe often were slow to recognize that they were not serving the growing ethnic minority population, although a few of the PSBs in Germany began in the early 1960s to provide brief radio newscasts in Turkish, Italian, Serbo-Croatian, North African Arabic, and other languages spoken by the guest workers employed in the country at that time. Some PSBs were a bit quicker to create or expand services for indigenous ethnic minority groups[13] such as the Sami ("Lapps") in northern Scandinavia, Native Americans in Canada, Welsh and Scots Gaelic speakers in Great Britain, and Basque, Breton, Alsatian, and Provençal speakers in France.

When some of the PSBs began to develop local radio stations in the 1970s and 1980s, they often appear to have made conscious policy decisions to include some airtime for locally prominent ethnic minority groups. Most of those services were operated *for* the minority groups but not administered by them, and hours of broadcast, for TV in particular, generally were limited. They did serve to whet the appetites of their listeners and viewers for more such broadcasts, and they also served as a training ground for some of the ethnic minority individuals who went on to develop independent ethnic stations.

Most of the mainstream commercial broadcast services have been less active than the PSBs in developing program policies that include provision of airtime for ethnic minority programs.[14] The chief exception is Great Britain's Independent Local Radio (ILR) system, where ILR stations were encouraged by ILR central administration to make efforts along those lines. The policy consideration here appeared to be based at least in part on a desire to show the public (and possibly the government) that ILR was interested in reaching more than just mainstream listeners who would be attractive to advertisers; it saw itself performing a public service as well, and doing at least as much as were the BBC local radio stations to reach ethnic minorities.[15]

Watchdog and helper organizations at the national level often are quite active in working with ethnic minority media services, although for different reasons: Watchdogs tend to support the creation of ethnic services that can operate independently, whereas helpers tend to support mainstream media efforts to assist ethnic minorities working *within* the mainstream system. Both policies can be beneficial to ethnic minorities, but independent services are far more likely to result in programming that permits minorities to speak for themselves and perhaps *to* themselves, albeit on a very tight budget; mainstream services are more likely to expect ethnic minorities to adapt themselves to mainstream tastes and to bear in mind that the mainstream audience is at least as important as ethnic minority audiences—and usually *more* important.

Watchdogs and helpers often differ in yet another respect: where they exert their greatest efforts. Watchdogs are likely to spend considerable time in lobbying the national government (especially the regulatory agencies) to be more supportive of ethnic minority media activity; they also may try to get mainstream media to provide more coverage of that activity. Groups such as Great Britain's Community Media Association, The Netherlands' Organization for Local Radio (OLON), South Africa's National Community Radio Forum, Sweden's Närradio Foerbund, and the U.S. National Community Radio Federation deal with community radio in general, and ethnic minority activity is one facet of that involvement. Australia's National Indigenous Media Association of Australia (NIMAA) and The Netherlands' STOA (since 2002, Miramedia)[16] are among the few watchdog organizations to work solely with ethnic minority media, although there are several associations of ethnic minority journalists in the United States: The National Association of Hispanic Journalists, the Native American Journalist's Association and others. Helpers such as the U.S. National Association of Broadcasters (NAB) and the Canadian Association of Broadcasters are more likely to prompt mainstream commercial broadcasters to develop training programs for minorities and to help publicize the positive steps that those broadcasters already are taking to serve ethnic minority audiences as well as to assist ethnic minority media services.

There is a good illustration of those differences in approach in the policies pursued by watchdogs and helpers in the United States during the 1970s. The watchdogs, including such organizations as Black Efforts for Soul in Television (BEST), the Citizen's Communication Center (CCC), and La Raza (a Hispanic-American organization), devoted the bulk of their effort to helping ethnic minorities and other groups as they filed petitions with the FCC to deny license renewals. Most of those filings singled out mainstream stations that failed to cover the activities of ethnic minority communities, provided racially biased coverage of those communities, and employed few if any ethnic minorities (rarely in positions involving program content). The helpers, chiefly the NAB, directed most of their efforts toward assisting stations in reaching settlements with minorities *before* the FCC held hearings on the petitions to deny license renewals and to working with mainstream broadcasters to establish training programs, internships and mentoring services (the latter for minority station administrators).[17] (Again, both approaches were beneficial, but in quite different ways.

State/Provincial, Local and Neighborhood. Governments at these levels, as I have noted, rarely become involved in media policymaking. However, some of the Canadian provincial and Australian and U.S. state governments have adopted policies of providing financial support for electronic media activities serving ethnic minorities. The Canadian provinces of Quebec, Ontario, and British Columbia all have approved annual appropriations for the (partial) support of Aboriginal (Native American and Inuit) radio and TV stations and networks, as has the Australian state of Victoria (through the Community Broadcasting Foundation) and the U.S. state of Alaska (appropriations to Native American and Inuit stations). Economic ups and downs have affected the amount of money available in any given year, but the policy commitment to financial support generally has remained in place.[18]

Germany stands as the one great exception where state government involvement in policymaking is concerned. The German Constitution gives the German states (*Länder*), and not the federal government, the power to license and regulate the broadcast media within their borders.[19] Most states have media councils (*Medienanstalten*) to carry out this responsibility. Whereas the state legislatures enact and amend the media laws, the councils often take the initiative in suggesting provisions and amendments. Most of the councils are made up of "representatives of society": one member to represent trade unions, another from the Protestant churches, and so on. The organizations themselves, such as the trade unions, choose their own representatives.[20]

Ideally, the result should be that programming will more accurately mirror society in each state because the organizations and the councils can bring pressure on the media services to do just that. As most German states have sizable ethnic minority populations, ethnic minorities should stand a good chance of being accurately portrayed (and perhaps portraying themselves) through each state's electronic media services. However, the concept of the media council first appeared in the late 1940s, when there were very few ethnic minorities in *any* of the states. It has been only during the past two decades that some (but not all) of the councils have made room for representatives of the ethnic minority groups. And finally, since the councils usually meet just four to six times a year, hold 1-day sessions, and frequently are large (25-50 or more members), there are limits to their impact on programming of any sort.

Some of the Australian states and cities have indigenous (Aboriginal) media production centers, where broadcasting usually is the major activity, but with independent video production and in some cases, productions for internet Web sites. Some of the associations have pooled their resources by exchanges of productions through Australia's remote areas satellite service, BRACS. Management of the associations sometimes has proven difficult, chiefly because financial resources are quite limited, but also because the associations may become caught up in power struggles within ethnic communities.[21]

Watchdog groups sometimes operate at the *local* level, and at one time there were many of them, especially in the United States and in Canada, and to a lesser extent in Australia, Great Britain, and Germany. As public and commercial broadcast networks became dominant in so many nations, local stations often became far less local, serving as little more than relays for national services or fitting into a mold that the networks dictated. As a result, the groups had very little truly local programming to praise or criticize, and listener/viewer councils, associations and other groups in Montreal, Melbourne, Minneapolis, Manchester, and Munich and other cities withered on the vine. There still are instances of local activism on the part of citizens who band together to protest or support local media activities—Jesse Jackson's "Operation Push" has mobilized Chicagoans to campaign for more employment of ethnic minority station managers and newscast anchorpersons—but such efforts tend to be sporadic, and their effects on long-term policy minimal.

Summarizing Geography

Where ethnic minority media services are concerned, governmental policymaking is highly concentrated at the *national* level. That also is where one finds the greatest variety of institutions active in creating or influencing policies that affect minority services. The relative absence of such institutions at other levels should not be all that surprising, since national governments and their institutions generally are leery of allowing governments and institutions at other levels to usurp their policymaking functions; nor are those other governments and institutions all that anxious to take responsibility for media policymaking, which often can seem a burdensome and thankless task. And finally, some national governments are sensitive about "outsiders" calling attention to (alleged) mistreatment of ethnic minorities or encouraging them to speak for themselves—one more reason for those governments to justify retention of control over media policy.

I also have indicated that the watchdogs are quite active at the *local* level, but some of the national operations have been prominent, as well. In both cases, it is rare to find watchdogs specializing in situations involving ethnic minorities; that is far more likely to be one of several concerns they embrace. Part of the problem here is available resources: Watchdogs usually are not well funded, and rely heavily on volunteers to carry on their work. The more narrowly a watchdog group defines itself, the more difficult it is likely to be to attract a sizable number of volunteers in the first place, and to keep them interested over the long haul. The U.S. National Black Media Coalition (NMBC), for example, is an amalgam of three watchdog groups that found it difficult to sustain themselves as individual bodies. As we move on to consider how governmental policymaking actually works, it should become clear that trying to influence the process from outside can be a lengthy and frustrating, if sometimes rewarding, process.

POLICYMAKING IN THE REAL WORLD

An old adage holds that there are two things that no one would want to see while they are being made if one expects to maintain an appetite for either of them: sausages and policies. The ingredients of each allegedly are of such dubious quality that the end product will be unpalatable and unhealthy. It is true that more ingredients go into the making of both than most consumers realize. But if we are to understand how policies affecting ethnic minority media come to be shaped as they are and how we might improve them, we must first dissect them in order to have a better idea of their component parts and how they interrelate.

When we considered the various policymaking institutions, we saw that there were many forces that might be at work. Although legislative bodies are responsible for policymaking through the passage of laws, they have several other interested parties to help them along the way (see Table 3.1). A number of them are full (F) partners, engaged in the daily business of running the government. A few, such as the courts, are silent (S) partners, but legislatures feel their presence because many lawmakers are aware of judicial precedent: past rulings by the courts that have overturned parts or all of previously enacted legislation. Some,

Table 1. Political, Economic, Social and Technological Climates (C)

Government	Primary Outsiders	Secondary Outsiders
Courts(S)	Lobbyists[b]/Donors (I)	The Broader Public (C)
Legislature (F)	Political Parties (F)	
Chief Executive/Cabinet[a] (F)	Broadcasters (I)	
Regulatory Agencies (J)		

[a]including Government Departments (Media, Culture)
[b]including Watchdogs/Helpers
(F) full partners (S) silent partners (I) invisible partners (J) junior partners (C) context

such as lobbyists and broadcasters, are invisible (I) partners, in that ordinarily they will not be perceptible during legislative sessions, will not be referred to when lawmakers speak or when discussions and debates are transcribed, and may not even visit lawmakers in their offices; their work goes on behind the scenes. Others, such as regulatory agencies, are junior (J) partners, created by legislatures and receiving annual appropriations from them; lawmakers *may* listen to them, but are much more apt to direct them. Finally, some are not partners at all, but form part of the broader context (C) in which everyone functions; they would include the national (and sometimes international) political, economic, social, and technological climates as well as the broader public.

To illustrate more clearly how the policymaking process works, I present four case studies of quite different situations: the Australian government's decision to establish a national ethnic minority broadcasting service; The FCC's decision to provide incentives for ethnic minority ownership of broadcast stations; the South African government's decision to include a specified category for community radio services (including ethnic minority services) in the nation's 1993 Broadcasting Act; and the creation of SFB4—Radio MultiKulti in Berlin, Germany.

Australia and the Special Broadcasting Service

Since the early part of the 19th century, Australia has been receiving émigrés from Europe.[22] However, it opened its borders to them in a major way just after World War II, when large numbers of Europeans either were dispossessed from their homelands or were seeking a new life far away from Europe. Australia needed to augment its labor force, predominantly in manual labor but also for highly skilled professionals such as doctors and dentists. While some of the fresh blood came from Great Britain, far more of it came from southern and eastern Europe. Many of the latter did not speak (much less read or write) English and many of the manual laborers had little or no formal education. The government provided some instruction in speaking, reading and writing English; however, as instructors generally operated on the assumption that the students already were literate in their homeland languages, illiterate or near-illiterate émigrés found them of little use.[23]

Over the next three decades or so, émigrés continued to arrive. After the elimination in 1973 of the government's "White Australia" policy (no non-Caucasian émigrés), they began to include Asians. Again, English-language classes were helpful to some, but virtually useless to others. The Australian mass media served an almost exclusively English-listening and reading public; there were a few foreign language newspapers, most of them weeklies, in the largest cities, and no broadcast services in foreign languages, aside from minuscule bits of airtime on local radio stations here and there.[24]

Citizen activism, fueled in part by protests opposing the involvement of Australian armed forces in the Vietnam War and pressuring the government to grant civil rights to Aboriginals, brought a Labor government to power in 1972. Some of the protestors had discovered that radio and TV could be useful in bringing their demands to the attention of a broader public, but they also learned that the stations themselves decided who, where, and what would receive coverage. That led some of them to push the government to create a third sector[25] in Australian broadcasting: noncommercial, community-based radio stations through which the "voice of the people" could be heard. The 1972 Migrant Workers Conference issued a demand for the creation of an ethnic minority broadcast service;[26] the 1973 Migrant Education Action Conference repeated the demand.

Australian media activists found three kindred spirits in the new Labor government—Moss Cass (Department of the Media; in mid-1975, Minister of the Media); Cass' assistant, Geoff Evans; and Al Grassby (Minister for Immigration and Ethnic Affairs; after 1974, Commissioner for Community Relations). Prime Minister Gough Whitlam was sympathetic to the idea, and because the stations would be noncommercial and for the most part self-supporting, the government might not risk antagonizing the commercial broadcast sector or the guardians of the federal budget.[27] It also seemed a good way to reward Australia's ethnic minority communities for their strong support of the Labor Party in the 1972 election (Davies, 1998: 3). Although the ABC in general seemed indifferent to community-based noncommercial radio, one of its former staff members—Director of Science Programs Dr. Peter Pockley—was a strong supporter of the concept and lobbied on its behalf.[28] And finally, the 1974 report by the McLean Committee on the allocation of FM frequencies had shown that there were sufficient FM *and* AM frequencies available for some expansion of services the Committee specifically recommended consideration of community radio (Government of Australia, 1974).

The first of the community stations, 5UV in Adelaide, came on air in 1975, and others soon followed. Some of them provided airtime for foreign-language broadcasts. Almost simultaneously, the license fee-supported ABC established two new stations, in part to show that it was willing to experiment with serving hitherto underserved audiences. Station 2JJ (Sydney, 1975) was to provide young people with something more contemporary than the relatively tradition-bound ABC had ever furnished its listeners; Station 3ZZ (Melbourne, 1975) was to include a wide variety of programs for, and sometimes by, Melbourne's many cultural and ethnic communities, and was to be more of an "access" station than were the ABC or the commercial stations.[29]

In 1975, the government launched a new nationwide health care plan: Medicare. It was sufficiently different from existing health plans, as well as sufficiently complex, to warrant a campaign designed to help people understand their rights and privileges under the new plan, as well as how to use it. Realizing that a fair share of the nation's residents—perhaps as many as 15%—lacked sufficient command of English to be able to understand the campaign messages, the government set up two temporary radio services. Melbourne (station 3EA) and Sydney (station 2EA) had the nation's largest concentrations of non-English speakers—possibly 2.5 million between them—so they were logical choices. The government also contracted for airtime in other parts of Australia, and then developed sets of messages in a variety of languages. The target audiences reported being greatly helped by the new service, and some among them began to ask the government to keep it going after the campaign was over.

A bill proposing continuation came before the Australian Parliament in 1977, where the Liberal-Country Party coalition had been in power since the end of 1975. There already were a few members of the national legislature who came from ethnic communities—Greek, Italian, Cypriot, and others—and they were in a good position to argue for permanent status. However, the development of what would be in effect a new and unprecedented[30] national broadcast service for ethnic minorities led to prolonged discussion and debate in parliament. Some of the points that arose had to do with program content, particularly in terms of "how do we know that *they* aren't saying subversive things about [God, Motherhood, the Flag] when they speak in languages that *we* (mainstream whites) can't understand?" Others concerned a related issue—supervision of the ethnic minority staff—where arguments were over"too much" as well as "too little."

Despite the differences of opinion, most of the lawmakers could agree on one thing, even if not all of them welcomed the change: Australia was becoming a more multicultural nation. Furthermore, ethnic minorities voted, and their growing numbers meant that those votes were increasingly important. The new service was not likely to cost all that much, radio being much less expensive than television and volunteer or low-cost labor on the part of ethnic minority broadcasters being quite likely. As for worries about "subversive" programming, an administrative system that made it easy to transfer "troublemakers" to nonbroadcasting positions would keep things under control. In November 1977, the bill passed and the new service, with the innocuous title of Special Broadcasting Service, made its debut in January 1978.

At the beginning of the 1970s, few people would have thought it possible that anything remotely resembling SBS would ever materialize, never mind in less than 8 years. What made it happen?

Social Climate. The willingness of more and more Australians, politicians among them, to recognize that the nation was becoming more multicultural, and that this was a necessary and beneficial (with some doubters on that score) development, was vital in setting the stage. Once the community and ethnic stations, along with 3ZZ, began to exhibit what could be done by ethnic groups through radio, people had a more concrete notion of what such services could contribute to society.

Cabinet and Legislature. The 1972 election brought the Labor Party into power. Many members of parliament (MPs) and of the cabinet were young, progressive and generally positive toward the notion of a multicultural Australia. Two of them—Cass and Grassby—were in key positions to effect changes in media policy for ethnic minorities. Several MPs themselves *were* ethnic minorities. Ethnic minority voters had been important in bringing about the Labor Party victory.[31]

Technology. The McLean Committee's disclosure that there was more frequency spectrum space available than had been supposed discredited the longstanding argument that there was not enough airspace available to accommodate new broadcast services. Also, radio equipment was becoming less expensive.

Lobbyists. The émigrés themselves had declared their interest in an ethnic broadcast service even before the Labor government began to work on similar proposals. The 1972 Migrant Workers Conference and the 1973 Migrant Education Action Conference made that interest clear, and appeared to represent the general feelings of émigrés. Some of the mainstream media publicized the demands of the two conferences, thus making the issue more visible and the political clout of the émigrés more obvious.

The FCC and Minority Preference Policies

Recall the WLBT-TV case that was presented in chapter 1. It is crucial to understanding why in the 1970s the FCC, with some prodding from other "partners," provided preferential consideration for ethnic minorities seeking to own radio and television stations—a remarkable step in view of the FCC's overall conservatism. The FCC has been a cautious regulatory agency throughout most of its history, rarely challenging the status quo and sometimes actively upholding it, as it did from the mid-1960s through the early 1970s when terrestrial broadcasting faced competition from cable television. Several authors have noted its positive disposition toward mainstream commercial broadcasting (Baughman, 1985;

McChesney, 1993; Ray, 1990) and by implication toward a dominant private enterprise model, with minimal control over program content or concern over ethnic ownership.

The reasons are many, but three stand out in any consideration of what shapes policy where electronic media regulation is concerned: freedom of speech as proclaimed in the First Amendment to the U.S. Constitution; the desire of a well-nigh constant majority of Congress to maintain the private enterprise model; and the highly effective lobbying efforts on behalf of that model by the National Association of [Commercial] Broadcasters and, more recently, the National Cable Television Association.

The maintenance of the private enterprise model was part of the FCC's motivation to renew WLBT-TV's license. It did so despite a well-organized and carefully documented effort by leaders of Jackson, Mississippi's African-American community[32] to persuade the FCC that the station was not worthy of relicensing, as well as a negative decision by the U.S. District of Columbia Court of Appeals (1996) on the FCC's handling of the case. That Court's second decision (U.S. Court of Appeals, 1969) was even harsher in its language, in essence accusing the FCC of having neglected its obligation to act in the public interest because it was so wedded to the private enterprise model. As noted in chapter 1, the decision also forced the FCC to recognize and to honor the rights of citizens to challenge the renewal of a station's license, whether or not they themselves wanted the license. That led to hundreds of such challenges.

At the same time, the Civil Rights Movement and several violent and disruptive demonstrations in urban areas (Detroit, Newark, Los Angeles) were increasing public awareness of the appalling conditions in many of America's ethnic minority-dominated inner cities. Ironically, television was blamed for having contributed to the public's *un*awareness of those conditions by not portraying them until the demonstrations started, at which point the medium began to serve as the nation's chief source of information on what was occurring (but seldom *why*). One frequently offered explanation for television's "color-blindness" was that the major TV networks and local stations employed very few people of color as journalists, camerapersons, news editors, program directors or station managers, and thus had little or no sense of what life was like for African Americans and other ethnic minorities.

Given the aversion of Congress to having the FCC interfere with the programming practices of individual stations (the FCC has no direct control over the networks because it does not license them), the agency had a very limited set of options that it could exercise if it chose to correct the imbalance. The Equal Employment Opportunity (EEO) Act of 1965 gave it the power—indeed, obligation—to require stations to at least seek to employ more minorities, and to employ them in meaningful positions. That could help, and eventually it did, to a modest degree.[33] The FCC was slow to apply it, not issuing its first requirement that stations file annual employment reports on ethnic minority employment until 1970; female employment was added as a requirement in 1971. Still, it would mean that those minorities would be working in a mainstream environment, and would not necessarily be able to "speak in their own voices." The second option was finding ways to increase ethnic minority *ownership* of stations.

The FCC never had undertaken anything along those lines. It had reserved some FM frequencies for noncommercial stations starting in 1945, and it did the same for non-commercial television in 1949, but in neither case did that involve "social engineering." Its licensing procedure did contain several *comparative hearing preferences*—that is, qualifications for which the FCC would award points when deciding between two or more competing applicants for a license. However, those qualifications had nothing to do with a potential owner's gender or ethnicity; they included such relatively noncontroversial items as local ownership and previous experience in broadcasting. Adding ethnicity to the list (gender came along slightly later) was an excursion into uncharted waters.

Although the FCC at the time was dominated by conservative commissioners who upheld the free enterprise model, it also had two of the most "activist" commissioners who had ever served on it: Kenneth Cox and Nicholas Johnson. Both had opposed the decision to renew WLBT-TV's license. (Following that decision, Johnson remarked that he thought the only way a station could lose its license now would be if someone broke in and stole it off the wall.) The FCC also had a very talented and socially conscious General Counsel, Henry Geller. Geller noted[34] that he, Cox, and Johnson worked together to persuade their colleagues, Chairman Rosel Hyde in particular, to accept the need for policies that provided ethnic minority investors with better prospects for owning radio and television stations.

As they did so, they enjoyed a considerable moral advantage. They had opposed the majority decision in the WLBT-TV case, which was twice rejected by the second highest court in the land. The new EEO law did not provide preferences for ethnic minority broadcasters, but it did indicate government support for assisting minorities as they sought more meaningful employment in stations. It was not a very long step from that position to the introduction of a preference that would not deny opportunities to nonminority applicants—an important distinction for those on the FCC who thought that licensing itself should be open to the widest possible range of applicants. Rather, it would provide a preference "point" in comparative hearings for a broadcast license—that is, where more than one party had applied for a given license. If an applicant could show that ethnic minority ownership would constitute at least 25% of the total investment in a station, and provided that the applicant met the FCC's minimum qualifications for a license holder, that was worth a point, which could, and sometimes did, tip the balance in favor of the ethnic minority applicant. It was first applied in the licensing of Channel 9 (Orlando, Florida) in 1972, when the FCC ruled in favor of an applicant with ethnic minority stockholders who resided in the community and would participate in the station's operation. More importantly, the U.S. District of Columbia Court of Appeals not only upheld the FCC's verdict, but stated that it was "consistent with the primary objective of maximum diversifica-

tion of ownership of mass communications media for the Commission in a comparative license hearing to afford favorable consideration to an applicant who,
not as a mere token, but in good faith as broadening community representation,
gives a local minority group media entrepreneurship" (Wilson, 1988: 100).

The FCC followed up on that decision by requiring that a minority applicant
who requested enhancement (consideration for preference) must indicate that
minority ownership would affect programming content (Wilson, 1988: 100). The
U.S. District of Columbia Court of Appeals invalidated that requirement in
Garrett vs. FCC (1975), where a Black Huntsville, Alabama businessman who
had been denied preference in a license application argued that he should not be
required to show that his status as a Black business owner would have such an
effect.[35] The Court upheld his argument, stating that "black ownership and participation together are themselves likely to bring about programming that is
responsive to the needs of the black citizenry" (Wilson, 1988: 100-101).

Later in the decade, FCC policy to enhance minority ownership was applied
to unusual, infrequent situations. One involved the "distress sale" of a station,
where a broadcaster whose license had been designated for a revocation hearing
(meaning that the broadcaster would almost certainly lose the license, and the
sale value of the station would be sharply reduced) could avoid revocation by
assigning (selling) his station to an ethnic minority organization that had been
approved by the FCC. Interestingly, the NAB, and notably its General Counsel,
Erwin G. Krasnow, had prompted the FCC to make that rule (Krasnow, 1997:
80).[36] Another rule provided a tax certificate to the owner of a broadcast property
not under threat of revocation who sold it to an organization with an ethnic
minority ownership share of more than 50%; the tax certificate allowed the seller
to defer capital gains taxation on the sale.

Those two proposals were approved by the FCC, with strong leadership from
then Chair Richard Wiley, and were codified in the FCC's 1978 Statement of
Policy on Minority Ownership of Broadcast Facilities (Federal Communications
Commission, 1978). A fourth preference was added by the FCC in 1981, when it
instituted a lottery-based system of awarding LPTV licenses: It provided qualified ethnic minority applicants with *two* numbers per lottery drawing, thus dou-
bling their chances for being selected (Federal Communications Commission,
1983). Over the period from 1978 to 1995, ethnic minority ownership had
increased from less than 1% of 8,500 stations to 3% of about 16,000 stations.[37]

Much like the Australian government's decision to create the SBS, few of
those who followed the FCC's handling of the WLBT-TV case would have
expected the FCC to approve and implement ethnically based preference policies. Why did it do so? Several factors contributed to this change.

Social Climate. The late 1960s saw many changes in U.S. society, and a number
of them had to do with civil rights. The EEO Act was a major change. So were
the community radio stations that blossomed in part because community activists
had discovered the value of radio in promoting alternative visions of society, but

wanted to speak out in ways that mainstream broadcasting did not always care to represent.

The Courts. The U.S. District of Columbia Court of Appeals decisions on the WLBT-TV license renewal were far less prominent than EEO, but they led to a significant shift in the FCC's procedure for holding hearings on renewals, and they opened the gates to much greater citizen involvement in the process. They also weakened the hands of those commissioners who otherwise might have fought tooth and nail against the creation of ethnic minority preferences, because they challenged the private enterprise model that had dominated FCC policies and procedures for so long. The Court's decisions on the TV 9 and Garrett cases served to reaffirm the FCC's right to apply the ethnic preference criterion in awarding a license, and in Garrett even relaxed the FCC's requirement that those claiming that preference would have to demonstrate how programming policy would be affected by minority ownership.

Regulatory Agency. Luckily for those who welcomed the ethnic minority preference policies, there were a few well-placed individuals on the FCC who were willing to attempt to turn it in a new direction after the Circuit Court's 1969 ruling on WLBT. Commissioners Nicholas Johnson and Kenneth Cox, as well as Geller, had opposed WLBT-TV's license renewal, and were ready to take on a new and redemptive (for supporters of ethnic minority rights) challenge to the status quo. Richard Wylie exercised similar leadership in the mid-1970s.

Broadcasters. Starting in the late 1960s, the commercial broadcast industry became the target of a great deal of criticism for its neglect of ethnic minorities, both in employment and in portrayal. It might have opposed the new ethnic minority preferences more vigorously if it had had a better record of treating ethnic minorities.

Lobbyists. Black Efforts for Soul in Television, and later, the National Black Media Coalition (with BEST as a member), pushed the FCC to take action to improve both ethnic minority depiction and ownership throughout the 1970s. The NAB petitioned the FCC to make a rule that would permit ethnic minorities to purchase a station under "tax certificate" terms.

Community Radio in the New South Africa

Anyone familiar with the situation in South Africa under the *apartheid* government would not have expected that government to provide a radio service for black audiences. As noted in chapter 1 (footnote 45), it did, but under highly restrictive conditions. I also pointed out that the African National Congress created its own radio station, Radio Freedom. It is little wonder, then, that the architects of the power-sharing agreement that made Nelson Mandela and Frederick W. de Klerk the nation's co-presidents in 1993 also would see the need for a new communications act to establish a broadcast service more in keeping with the new South Africa.

In fact, the process of crafting a new act already had been under way for some time. The *apartheid* government already had appointed a Task Force on Broadcasting in 1990, whereas the anti-*apartheid* organizations working through the Mass Democratic Movement (which included broadcasters) began to draw up a plan for the future broadcasting system. The Task Force soon was criticized for being insufficiently representative and for holding its meetings in secret. Two organizations—the Campaign for Open Media and the Film and Allied Workers Organization (FEWA)—protested, there was an antigovernment demonstration outside the headquarters of the SABC, and a number of conferences and workshops took place to help solidify an anti-apartheid position on the future of broadcasting.

The Task Force, chastened by the negative reaction, and the Mass Democratic Movement presented their proposals at the Jabulani-Freedom of the Airwaves power-sharing conference arranged by the Council for a Democratic South Africa (CODESA) and held in Amsterdam in August 1991. CODESA formed a broadcast negotiating forum, which developed a draft of a new communications bill and also supported the establishment of a new broadcast regulatory authority.

In the course of those negotiations, which also were attended by the African National Congress (ANC; with some of the Radio Freedom staff, as well), FEWA, and a number of Western governments, NGOs, public broadcasters, training organizations, community broadcasting emerged as a proposal, and met with general support. However, although the negotiations were proceeding, the *apartheid* government began to license community broadcasters through its Ministry of Home Affairs and without consulting the other negotiating parties. Furthermore, the stations licensed tended to be those operated by various right-wing Afrikaner groups.[38]

The anti-*apartheid* groups were infuriated, and soon proposed a democratically accountable commission of inquiry into broadcasting that would be appointed by an all-Party conference, as well as a media monitoring commission. That, they felt, would help to guarantee open and accurate reporting in the transition from the *apartheid* government to the new government. They also were all the more determined to draw up a new communications act and to create a new regulatory commission that would guarantee a more democratic broadcasting system—one with specific provision for community broadcasting. They also sought to insure that the new regulatory authority would be in place before the next national elections (1994).[39]

Two more conferences followed in late 1991—one in Bophuthatswana, the other in Cape Town. Both resulted in pressure on CODESA to ensure that the *apartheid* government not be given the opportunity to create a "new" system that remained under government control. Nevertheless, the government continued its attempts to control the SABC. That led to the establishment of yet another anti-

apartheid group: the Campaign for Independent Broadcasting (CIB). The CIB was a coalition that included some very powerful organizations, among them the ANC, the South African Communist Party, the South African Council of Churches, and Confederation of South African Trade Unions (COSATU). It called for the appointment of a new board to supervise the SABC—one that would be far more representative of the entire nation than was the present White-dominated board. The new board—the Independent Broadcasting Authority (IBA)—was appointed in May 1993, at roughly the same time as CODESA was drawing up the IBA Act. In 1994, President de Klerk approved the appointment of the IBA, shortly before the national elections that ended *apartheid* and brought a black majority government to power.

The IBA Act of 1994 contained a phrase familiar to anyone who has studied broadcasting in the United States: "to regulate broadcasting in the public interest." The Act established a tripartite system, with *public, commercial,* and *community* radio and TV stations throughout the nation. Realizing that the term community was open to numerous interpretations, the IBA defined the categories of activity that it would license as community stations: *geographic* (services for a specific location) and *community of interest.* The latter included institutional (colleges and universities, activity-oriented clubs and associations, trade unions, etc.), religious, and cultural (specific language services, groups with strong cultural affinities). Applicants were required to specify *one* of those categories and to spell out in some detail what the station would present along those lines. And finally, the station would have to be largely local in its programming.

There are few electronic media regulatory systems in the world that have made specific provision for licensing community radio, or that have gone to such lengths to define what is required of licensees. Clearly, the various groups that fought for its inclusion within the new system wanted to make sure that it was both protected and made responsible in its role as a community service. Just as clearly, the *apartheid* government did not want to see anything of the sort created. Why did the supporters prevail in the policymaking battle, and did they get what they wanted/hoped for? Three aspects contributed to a response to this question.

Social Climate. By 1990, it was clear that there would be a new South Africa in the near future. The chief bone of contention during the early 1990s was the extent to which the *apartheid* government would be able to preserve the privileged status enjoyed by white people. Black South Africans proved to be very adept at organizing opposition to a continuation of that status.

Chief Executive and Cabinet. The *apartheid* government virtually ensured that the new broadcasting system would be very different by virtue of its obvious reluctance to lose its influence over the SABC and its readiness to issue new licenses to its followers.

Lobbyists. Many groups and organizations, national and international, played an influential role in ensuring that community radio would emerge as a specified part of the new broadcasting system. Various South African groups also engaged in that struggle, as did some of the nation's leading political, social and cultural organizations opposing the *apartheid* government. Furthermore, the groups and organizations for the most part worked well together, and developed new organizational forms as need dictated.

There seemed to be a widely shared perception that community empowerment was vital to the nation's future, and that community radio would be the ideal medium to support that empowerment: it could reach literate and illiterate alike, was inexpensive, easy to use, and well suited to a largely oral culture. That made it worthwhile to invest the time, money and effort in blocking the *apartheid* government's frequent efforts retain as much of the old system as possible, and for Bush Radio to directly confront that government's co-optation of the community radio concept by claiming the right to a license, as well.

The first ICA-licensed community radio station came on air in 1995. By 2003, there were more than 80 licensed community stations, although not all of them had yet come on air. Those who regarded the stations as significant players in the development of community empowerment could point to a number of specific examples. Bush Radio and Radio Zibonele in the Western Cape, Radio ALX in Alexandra and other Black township stations have established themselves as forces for the empowerment of their communities. But there are relatively few such stations in the country, and those that do exist generally live a hand-to-mouth existence. Reliable sources of continuous funding are in short supply, and the national budget very tight. It has proven far easier to create an empowerment-oriented community radio sector than to support it.

Multicultural Radio for Berlin: SFB4 Radio MultiKulti[40]

During the 1960s, West Germany became an increasingly multicultural nation, as guest workers from southern Europe, Spain, and Turkey began to serve the nation's needs, largely as garbage collectors, road repair crew members, and in other low-paying types of manual labor. West Berlin was a particularly powerful magnet, in part because it was regarded by many of the newcomers as somewhat less prejudiced against *Ausländer*[41] ("foreigners"). However, they found very little mass media material available in the languages of their homelands, aside from a few imported (and expensive) newspapers and the very brief radio programs in Serbian, Croatian, and Turkish offered by Sender Freies Berlin (SFB), one of the West German public radio stations. That situation remained much the same until the 1990s, even as the numbers of *Ausländer* were increasing.

The West German public radio stations had begun discussing the creation of a nationally available *Ausländer* radio service with more languages and longer hours in the 1980s, but there were three difficult issues: Where would the money for such a service come from? Where would the additional airtime come from? Who would coordinate the effort? Money was tight because the West German public broadcasters relied almost totally on the income from annual license fees, and that income had increased very little during the 1980s. Airtime was a problem because newly licensed commercial radio services had claimed most of the unused frequency spectrum space, and putting pressure on the governments of the *Länder* (States) to force the public stations to give up some of their frequencies, or at least ensure that they not be awarded any more. Coordination was a problem because many of the public stations were suspicious of the largest (by far) station: WestDeutsche Rundfunk (WDR); they did not wish to see WDR acquire yet more power.[42]

SFB, which served the city with the largest *Ausländer* population in Germany, participated in the talks, but did not play a particularly active role. The station already had four distinct radio services, but little *Ausländer*-oriented programming: one weekly program for Turks, another for Serbs and Croats.[43] Unification with the former German Democratic Republic (GDR) in October 1990 posed a potential threat for SFB, because East Berlin (capital of the GDR) was home to the nation's largest broadcasting service; now that the two Germanies were united, so was Berlin, which raised the question of what to do with two public broadcast services for the re-unified city. The ultimate solution left SFB intact and folded the GDR service into other existing West German services, but placed further pressure on an already-strained SFB budget.

Given the budget situation and SFB's reputation for being a conservative organization[44] without much interest in serving the *Ausländer*, it was surprising that the station was willing to consider the creation of a new service, much less a service that had no counterpart in German broadcasting. Yet early in 1993, SFB Director of Radio Jens Wendland suggested the possibility of creating a dedicated multicultural service for Berlin's roughly 430,000 ethnic minority residents that would at the same time be accessible to the mainstream population because there would be a substantial amount of programming produced by German-speaking *Ausländer*.

Eighteen months passed before that service came on air. Even as it did, some (including certain SFB staff members) were criticizing it as a Social Democrat/Buendnis 90/Green Party-supported venture that was just another instance of seeking *Ausländer* support at election time, and with hints that it probably would not amount to anything (Buenger, 1995: 46; Hoege, 1994). However, it quickly attracted critical praise from the German media, as well as sizable audiences of *Ausländer* and mainstream ("native") Germans. What led to the realization of the proposal?

Internal Leadership. A few key senior staff members within SFB were strongly supportive of a new multicultural service. Jens Wendland was anxious to show that the station was ready to play a more important role in serving Berlin's large *Ausländer* population.[45] Because Berlin now was to serve as capital of a united

Germany, and already was considered to be the nation's most multicultural city, SFB could display its relevance and reinforce its right to exist in Germany's changing mediascape. His enthusiasm was matched, if not exceeded, by that of Dr. Friedrich Voss, who was an accomplished scholar in Asian studies, had served as ARD (Association of German Public Broadcasters) correspondent in Tokyo, and was in charge of SFB's Cultural Division. He was well aware both of the ways in which the presence of a large *Ausländer* population had enriched the cultural life of Berlin and of the tensions that existed between the mainstream population of Berlin and the various *Ausländer* groups. Although he and Wendland could not persuade all of their senior colleagues that the proposal was appropriate, workable and affordable, they did manage to win enough support to gain approval for a pilot project.

Political Parties. The Green Party enjoys considerable influence in Berlin's political circles. It was strongly supportive of an SFB multicultural radio service, and one of its members, Alice Stroever, was a member of the station's governing council (*Rundfunkrat*). Shortly after the 1992 and 1993 murders of Turks in the German cities of Moelln and Solingen, Stroever pushed the council to move ahead with the multicultural service, later saying that "It seemed so macabre, after the murders of the Turks . . . to see the opposition of SFB administration to a multicultural radio broken" (Schneckener, 1994).

Lobbyists. Several of the *Ausländer* groups had been putting pressure on SFB to provide more broadcasts in their languages, but one group in particular—the Turks—was especially persistent in that regard. The Bund der Einwanderer aus der Turkei in Berlin-Brandenburg e. V. (BETB; the Federation of Turkish Emigres in Berlin-Brandenburg) protested the shifting of SFB's Turkish program to the less desirable medium wave (AM) band and called for it to be put back on UHF (FM). Then in a hearing held by the Berlin parliament in February 1992, they recited a list of actions taken in Berlin and elsewhere in the nation that showed decreasing support on the part of public broadcasters for services to the *Ausländer.* BETB pointed out that they had enriched the cultural and social life of the city and its surrounding area, that they paid license fees, and that they deserved better treatment than they were getting (Buenger, 1995).

Social Climate. The 1993 murders of the Turks were only one manifestation of what appeared to be a growing resentment on the part of mainstream Germans, particularly those in the former East Germany (where unemployment was high), at the presence of the *Ausländer* groups (particularly those from outside Europe). The creation of a media service that could reach both the *Ausländer* and the mainstream population with programming that could serve as a bridge between the two appeared very attractive, and helped to persuade the Berlin/Brandenburg Media Council to set aside an FM frequency for the purpose, but also to provide a grant of two million Marks (about US$1.3 million) in support of the new service during its 18-month trial period.

POLICYMAKING: A SUMMARY OF EXPERIENCES

The four case studies presented here do not cover the full range of policymaking practices, but they do illustrate how the confluence of forces at work can vary in terms of their importance to the shaping of policy. Clearly *social climate* is an important element, although we have no way of knowing just *how* important. It is worth noting that most societies have experienced periods of intense social activism, especially in the final decades of the 20th century, yet that activism has not always translated into policymaking. Even when it has, the policies themselves occasionally have been regressive rather than progressive, at least to the causes supported by the activists.

Involvement by *lobbyists*, and by watchdog groups in particular, clearly was of paramount importance in South Africa, and of some importance in the United States, Australia, and Berlin. None of the three nations had a long tradition of social activism where broadcast policymaking was concerned,[46] nor did Berlin, and many of the activist groups I have mentioned were created on the spot or had existed for a very short time. It may be that such groups flourish in situations where their members can see an immediate problem that is meaningful to them, and also feel that they can make a difference if they apply themselves fully to addressing it. It is difficult to sustain such an effort, which may be why those groups often disband after a few years or even months whether they have been successful or not. Still, we have seen that their involvement *can* make a difference.

Involvement by other official institutions is more difficult to assess, at least on the basis of the case studies. The *courts* certainly made a difference in the United States, but not in South Africa, Berlin or Australia. That probably has a lot to do with the readiness of U.S. courts to hear cases involving the electronic media. The *legislature* was significant in Australia, where it and the chief executive and cabinet of one *political party* laid the groundwork for the eventual creation of SBS; the *political parties* (the Socialist/Buendnis 90/Green Party coalition) assisted in supporting the case for creation of SFB4. However, those actors had negligible impact on the FCC's development of preference policies, and little to do with the creation of a constitutionally guaranteed community radio sector in South Africa (except for the *apartheid* government's attempts to retain some power, which ended up harming its cause, and the general support of the ANC). Obviously, it is possible to create media policy without major involvement on the part of the government's chief lawmaking body.

A *regulatory agency* also can make a difference. The FCC did during the 1970s, but often with pushes and shoves from the courts and watchdogs. That may be just what one should expect from such an agency, which is supposed to be responsive to various forces in society. However, regulatory agencies also are supposed to protect the public interest, and that is where they often fall short. Why? Because governments, and particularly politicians and their parties, usually have a fair degree of influence over them, and sometimes use them to protect the interests of their major financial supporters rather than the public. Also, legislatures rarely seem willing to appropriate the budgetary support that would be necessary if the agencies are to have sufficient staff to carry out the investigative work required to maintain performance standards. Bodies such as Great Britain's Broadcasting Standards Commission can supplement the regulatory agencies in protecting the public (minority and mainstream) interest, but most nations do not have them yet.

Finally, there is the broad category of *personal involvement.* Here, all four of the case studies furnish examples of individuals inside and outside the government (the "outsiders" including staff members of existing media operations) who appear to have made a considerable difference by continuing to press the case for change.

It should be clear from the case studies that policymaking takes time. Berlin wins the race among the four contestants (with the advantage of having established a city service rather than a national one) in 18 month's time. South Africa's process took just under 5 years. Australia comes in a close third, at a bit over 5 years. The United States finishes last, at roughly 8 years (the influence of the lawyers, perhaps?). Berlin, South Africa, and Australia each created something new, whereas the United States was working with an ongoing problem, and the FCC had to discover what the enforcement of EEO regulations could and could not accomplish before addressing the matter of preferences for ethnic minority owners.

In fact, the FCC case is a fine example of how policymaking may involve all three of the purposes (as spelled out by Portney) that I noted at the beginning of this chapter. Certainly, the FCC was passing rules leading to private activities that should be useful/desirable to society (*distributive*). Those rules also enabled users to develop and share a scarce resource—the frequency spectrum—so the FCC clearly had a *regulatory* purpose. And it had to revisit policymaking (enforcement of the EEO regulations) that had not worked as well as it should have, which is *redistributive.*

Where ethnic minority activity in the electronic media is concerned, the policymaking processes followed by most nations pose additional barriers. Many ethnic minority groups are relatively impoverished, which means that it will be especially difficult for them to become involved in that process. Traveling to the nation's capital and residing there often are out of the question, as is paying for the assistance of legal experts and lobbyists knowledgeable in the ways of governments—regulatory agencies in particular[47]—and of the broadcast industry. Religious organizations, foundations, and charitable organizations occasionally have helped minority groups to represent their causes, as did the United Church of Christ in the WLBT-TV case, but such assistance is neither common nor constant.

Minority groups appear to have been most successful when they have taken advantage of a favorable social climate, mapped out a strategy that identified one's allies among the policymaking forces, and then have worked through those allies to keep the pressure on the policymaker itself, whether the legislature, the regulatory agency or whoever else, until a (reasonably) successful outcome was reached.

There is one further issue to consider: What influence does policymaking have on *participation* of ethnic minorities in the public sphere? All four of the case studies feature policies that certainly could help to bring it about. South Africa's development of a licensing category for community radio was based on the hope, and possibly expectation, that community radio could (and should) serve such a purpose. The FCC's development of preference policies to encourage ethnic minority ownership of stations followed in the same path, and the court decisions were quite eloquent in proclaiming such a benefit. Only Australia's creation of the SBS is less obvious in revealing such a motive, but here too there were expressions of hope, and possibly expectation, that the service would help its audience to participate more easily in the public sphere, and to enrich the lives of mainstream Australians by making them more aware of the cultures and lifestyles of the ethnic communities.

By the final chapter of this book, we should have a better sense of whether ethnic minority electronic media have performed in ways that have encouraged their communities to participate in the public sphere. Two questions arise immediately: How all-encompassing *is* that sphere; and what has *policymaking* done and not done to facilitate and to hinder the role of ethnic minority media in encouraging participation?

I noted in chapter 1 that the concept of the public sphere has attracted much attention from media scholars. Husband (2000: 209) argues that there is a need for ethnic minority electronic media outlets, but that they need to be part of the public sphere at the "most all-encompassing level" if there is to be true dialogue among and between groups in society. If they become "media serving audiences defined exclusively in terms of distinct identities," then they well may become "a Babel of parallel and exclusive public spheres that would have no sympathy with a right to be understood."

I agree with Husband, but I have seen little evidence that service at the most all-encompassing level actually takes place. Part of the problem can be laid at the doorstep of media policymakers, who seem to have spent very little time considering just how all-encompassing they could and should expect ethnic minority services to be. If policymakers wished to ensure that those services both (electronically) reach and (programmatically) serve minority and mainstream audiences, they could include licensing conditions that require broadcasting at sufficient power to reach the largest possible audience, just as they could insist that programs be provided for more than one audience.

Practically, they are unlikely to do anything of the sort, because (a) spectrum space often is a scarce commodity, especially in larger cities, so ethnic services might not be able to achieve a wider reach even if they wished to; (b) if space were available, many of those services could not afford to purchase and maintain the transmitting equipment necessary to achieve such a reach; and (c) the dual programming requirements would demand far more staff members (many of them with specialized qualifications) than are likely to be available or affordable to most ethnic minority groups. Also, the ethnic service operators could raise the legitimate complaint that they were required to do far more than were main-stream licensees, unless the policymakers were to make this a *universal* require-ment. Such a development would seem most unlikely.

Policymakers could moderate their demands by requiring only that an ethnic minority service devote, say, 10% of its airtime or Web site space to material intended for the mainstream audience. Even so, it is doubtful that they would escape the complaint I have just mentioned. And if they did, one vital issue would remain: given the proliferation of electronic media services in most indus-trialized nations and in growing numbers of less-industrialized ones, would minority services stand much chance of attracting mainstream listeners, viewers and Website readers? Does that proliferation itself contribute to the invalidation of the concept of a single mainstream audience?

At that point, policymakers well might be inclined to drop any requirement that ethnic minority services provide programming for the mainstream audience. They could impose a requirement that there be service to the ethnic communi-ties themselves, which presumably have their own public spheres (even if multi-ple spheres do not appear to be what Habermas had in mind). The FCC attempt-ed to do just that with its preference policies, but eventually was overruled by the U.S. Circuit Court, and has not managed to resurrect them. There appears to be a general assumption by policymakers that service to ethnic communities will come as an almost inevitable consequence of licensing ethnic minority media. From what I have observed, it almost always does,[48] but what is provided by those services may or may not encourage participation in public spheres at any level. Furthermore, I very much doubt that its provision can or should be required as a condition of licensing. It would be exceptionally difficult to enforce, and highly invasive if attempted. Encouragement of participation is far more likely to come about as the services and their audiences interact, which should take place from the moment that goals enter the picture.

FINANCING THE SERVICES

The road to creating an ethnic minority media service may be long and full of deviations, but at least there is a point at which it either enters into operation or does not, and that particular battle is over (although relicensing may entail revis-iting parts of the battle). Sustaining the service is quite another matter: The battle is never over. That is true of all media services, but particularly for those operat-ed by ethnic minorities, where a shortage of cash is likely to be more acute. For most of them, it is necessary to sew together a patchwork quilt where the patches themselves are of differing sizes and durability, so that the quilt is under almost perpetual alteration. As we see here, a number of pieces are potentially available, but it takes sustained effort and considerable ingenuity to procure them. I present them in no necessary order of importance; the first three seem to be the most common, as well as most lucrative of the forms.

Government Appropriations

I noted earlier that governments at all levels, most commonly national, have pro-vided financial support for ethnic minority electronic media. Sometimes the sup-port is conditional: for a specific purpose such as purchasing equipment or train-ing; for a limited period of time; only if the service employs a certain number of staff and is on the air for a minimum of X hours per day. Occasionally it is recur-ring, but probably will be subject to scrutiny as the government's annual budget is under discussion by the executive branch and the lawmakers. Even when it is recurring, there is no guarantee that the appropriation will increase to meet infla-tion or demand, and it may be reduced or even eliminated.[49]

The greatest problem faced by the ethnic minority electronic media is that the groups themselves often have very little influence over the size and scope of appropriations. Each group by itself usually is small, and it has not been easy in any nation for an assortment of groups, or even the members of a given group, to unite in order to lobby more effectually on their collective behalves. Indigenous groups sometimes have had more success in persuading the executive branch and lawmakers to support their media, since they can claim to be the "first people of the land," and thus entitled to governmental support—a claim that minority groups who have arrived more recently cannot make. However, the latter *can* appeal on grounds of having been brought to a nation against their will (as in the case of slavery) or of having assisted a nation in time of war (as with Vietnamese, Lao, and Cambodian citizens who assisted the United States during the war in Vietnam), but that rarely seems to have much impact.

Sheer numbers, especially if accompanied by widespread geographic distribu-tion and a degree of political organization, seem to work about as well as any-thing, especially when members of one's group have attained political offices. That appears to have made a difference in Australia where both the SBS and the community broadcasting sector (including the five fully ethnic radio stations) are concerned. Both major political parties have pledged their support for SBS and the community sector in recent national election campaigns, and by and large have delivered on their promises. (The ethnic minority "bloc" is too large for politicians to ignore.)

In no situation I know of does government support account for the entire bud-get of an ethnic minority media service, and with very few exceptions, such as SBS,[50] it will cover one third or less of the total. That leaves the bulk of the sup-port to several other sources.

Advertising

For the vast majority of electronic media services, advertising is regarded as a source of income—and often *the* source of income. As I indicate in Chapter 5, advertising can serve more purposes than that, and sometimes does where ethnic minorities are concerned. However, there is no disputing its financial importance, and many ethnic media services rely quite heavily on it.[51] There are increasing numbers of those services that rely almost completely on it, such as Radio One, BET and Univision in the United States, Sunrise Radio in the United Kingdom, Radio Beur in France, and others.

Other ethnic minority services gained a foothold in broadcasting through the licensing of community and access radio services in the 1970s and 1980s; in some nations, such as France, those services were licensed as noncommercial operations. The hope on the part of governments and regulators was that this would force licensees to forge strong ties with their audiences, although the restriction served another purpose, as well: It kept the new stations from posing any sort of financial threat to the nation's commercial broadcasters. That prohibition eventually was relaxed—slowly in some nations, more rapidly in others. Part of the reason was that many governments provided modest amounts of financial support to the noncommercial services, and did not relish the prospect of increasing that support as the numbers of such stations grew; in fact, some of them hoped to shrink or eliminate it, whether for philosophical or fiscal reasons. As a result, most of the noncommercial services, ethnic minority or not, now carry advertising, although the amounts of airtime devoted to it often are limited by law to considerably less than what commercial services may carry. Australia, for example, limits "noncommercial" radio advertising to 5 minutes per hour.

Ethnic minority noncommercial services in particular may find it difficult to sell even that much advertising time. Some of the smaller ethnic communities will not have their own grocery stores, repair shops, and the like, and probably will not be able to interest mainstream advertisers in buying time. Larger ethnic communities may or may not have much success in doing so. If they are really large, there may be ethnic minority commercial stations serving them already, so that there is little interest on the part of ethnic or mainstream advertisers in turning to the noncommercial sector, where audiences usually are smaller, anyway. It also may be that the regulations governing noncommercial services contain provisions limiting the nature of advertising, such as no political ads, or its duration, such as 30 seconds maximum per ad, or even the sorts of appeals the ads may contain, such as nothing that denigrates competitors. And finally, ethnic communities may place their own limits on what is advertised, as some indigenous communities do (although many do not) where possibly addictive substances and services (alcoholic beverages, gambling) are involved.

Despite those potential problems, many ethnic minority services realize important shares of their income (10% to 20% or even more) from ads, although often this source is the first to feel the effects of a recession. And certainly there are ethnic minority advertisers, as well as a few from the mainstream, who advertise over ethnic services as a way of showing their support for them. Finally, many governments find those services an excellent way to reach minority listeners, viewers and readers with ad-like messages designed to alert those audiences to training programs, health care and other government-run programs. The Black Britain Web site carries a number of such messages, which are paid for by individual government departments. The Black township radio stations in South Africa realize a small but steady income from just such advertising, which also tends to be more reliable than most commercial advertising. A number of the Swedish närradio services, some of them with considerable ethnic minority involvement, have similar arrangements with city governments: Radio Sydvast staff indicated that the service received half or more of its income from the City Council and the Greater Stockholm Council, both of which regarded the station as an excellent way to reach the area's growing ethnic minority population.[52]

Corporate Sponsorship and Foundation Grants

Unlike spot advertising, corporate sponsorship was permitted for noncommercial services from the beginning in many nations. Usually there were (and often still are) regulations governing its acknowledgment by a media service, most of them along the same lines as those already noted for noncommercial ads. When messages recognizing corporate sponsorship began to appear over U.S. noncommercial radio and TV in the 1960s, they were limited to little more than the mention of the sponsor's name, along with a simple visual for TV that consisted of nothing more than that name, and in the same character style for all corporate sponsors.

Times have changed. Now the messages may extol the virtues of the company and its products or services, complete with visual displays of happy car drivers, airline passengers, or whomever else the company serves, along with the company's corporate logo. In other words, they are basically indistinguishable from "normal" advertising. The FCC relaxed the limitations on corporate sponsor messages over public broadcasting in 1984 (Witherspoon & Kovitz, 2000: 80), in part because the Reagan administration had pressured the U.S. Congress to eliminate government support for public broadcasting. Congress finally agreed to reduce that support, and at the same time indicated that it would look favorably on a relaxation of FCC rules governing sponsorship.

Whether the trade-off was favorable to the public broadcasters still is debated, but it certainly is true that the more controversial PBS programs such as *Frontline* and *Now with Bill Moyers* are few in number, and attract relatively modest corporate sponsorship. The various PBS programs featuring ethnic minorities, such as *American Family* (a 2001-2002 series[53] about a Mexican-American family's life experience) and *Tony Brown's Journal* (a long-running but featuring a Black reporter/host) also may attract sponsorship (usually modest, although *American Family* was sponsored quite substantially by Kodak and *Tony Brown's Journal* by the African-American firm W&W Spices), but often do not.[54] Corporate sponsorship may turn out to be a mixed and uncertain blessing, depending on an ethnic service's programming priorities.

Foundation support may come through funding from some of the same businesses that provide corporate sponsorship. The Ford Motor Company has sponsored numerous U.S. public television programs, whereas the Ford Foundation has sponsored studies of the effectiveness of public broadcasting as well as individual programming ventures. The difference is that corporations acting in their own names are quite apt to limit their sponsorship to programs that will win them a measure of public support, whereas foundations tend to finance broader ventures that represent certain socially important causes and issues, such as civil rights, family planning, or mental health where there may be an array of messages in differing forms and delivered through a number of media.

Several foundations have emphasized support for communication initiatives in the so-called Third World. The German Friedrich Ebert Foundation has supported the development of community radio stations in Africa through the financing of production equipment, staff training programs, and conferences where African broadcasters can exchange ideas with one another. Support from ethnic minority foundations or corporations[55] is fairly rare because most of them have little money to spare, but the Anchorage, Alaska based Cook Inlet Region Inc. (CIRI), a regional Native American corporation, helped to fund Koahnic Broadcasting, a Native American/Inuit radio station and training center in Anchorage. Part of that support also went into National Native News (NNN), a daily radio news service distributed by satellite throughout the United States and Canada. However, CIRI cut back on its funding at the end of 2002, and NNN had to be moved to Albuquerque, New Mexico. There were allegations that CIRI exercised some influence over Koahnic's journalistic activities, and indeed a few Koahnic journalists left the station or were fired (Rock on Olympia, 2002), but none of that was linked to the departure of NNN.

Annual License Fees

Fewer and fewer nations assess annual license fees that each TV set-owning household must pay to support the national PSB, although most of the western European nations and Japan continue to do so. In many cases, a portion of that fee supports ethnic (and particularly linguistic) minority broadcasting in one form or another. In the United Kingdom, Welsh, Scots, Gaelic and to a lesser extent Irish Gaelic language services on BBC radio and television, as well as BBC's Asian Service and Radio 1Xtra (a satellite-only radio service for young B Black listeners, featuring music) receive such financing. In Norway, Sweden, and Denmark, the Sami ("Lapp") radio and TV services are part of the PSBs, and license fees cover their operation. In France, the PSBs—Radio France and France2/France3—have regional services in languages such as Breton, Basque, and Provencal, all of them minority languages within their home regions. Spain's national PSBs have robust radio and TV services in Catalan, Galician, and Basque. In Germany, where the fee is paid by households in each *Land* (state), the

WDR covers most of the costs of operating Funkhaus Europa, the multilingual radio service for residents (some of them German citizens) who have come from other European nations, but also from Turkey and the Arab World, as well as Kurds.

Whether the mainstream population would be happy to realize (as few probably do) that a portion of the fee goes to support ethnic minority broadcast services is another question. It is a very small portion of the fee, to be sure, and it well may be that many in the mainstream would regard it as a small price to pay if it seems to assist in making the minority groups proud of their heritage even as it makes them proud to be living in a nation that is broad-minded enough to provide them with such services. I have never seen a survey that would indicate the degree to which that opinion is held by mainstream or minority populations. In any event, that particular use of the fee seems safe for as long as the fee itself exists. Certainly, it is a good example of the sort of service a PSB can provide and that a commercial operation rarely does—a useful attribute in a time when the relevance of the PSBs to society and the appropriateness of the license fee both have come into question.

Institutional Support

A number of institutions, most of them religious or educational, have provided partial or full support to ethnic minority media services. The Catholic Church and some evangelical Christian denominations have been quite active in supporting indigenous minority radio services in Central and South America, some of which they actually helped to create. There are several such stations in Mexico, Guatemala, Brazil, and Ecuador,[56] a few in Africa, and a very few in Asia, mostly in the Philippines. Colleges and universities in Canada, Australia, New Zealand, the United States and elsewhere sometimes have hosted community radio stations that provide considerable amounts of airtime to indigenous and other minority groups.

In a few instances, a college or university has regarded a specific ethnic minority population as its primary student body. Many of the Black colleges and universities in the United States have played that role for a century or more, and a number of them have student radio services, some of which can be received by the local population in general. (Others are wired into dormitories and student centers, and cannot be heard outside of those locations.) A few, such as Howard University's WPFW-FM in Washington, DC, are professional operations with fulltime staff (and volunteers as well). A few of the roughly two dozen U.S. Native American radio stations are connected with colleges, and one of them (Tuba City, Arizona) is based in a high school.

There always is the danger that shrinking educational budgets could lead school administrators to eliminate a station in order to economize. That occurred when the University of the District of Columbia (a largely African-American school) had to cut its budget for 1996-1997 and decided that selling off its radio station, WDCU, might be one way to meet the crisis. The station was very popular with African-American young people, thanks in large part to its jazz format, and the university received many petitions to retain it. However, it was finally purchased by C-SPAN (a public TV service that covers the U.S. Congress and other governmental activities) and converted into a public affairs service with no specific ethnic orientation (Barlow, 1999: 292-293). On the whole, however, institutional support is quite reliable. The one potential drawback is that the religious or educational institution will impose ideological control over program content that rules out the presentation of certain important topics, for example, birth control or higher levels of financial support for ethnic minority studies.

Voluntary Donations by Individuals

In the early days of broadcasting, more than one radio station attempted to interest listeners in donating money to help offset operating costs. Few of them had measurable success, and none managed to survive on donations alone. When public broadcasting stations in the United States became more ambitious in their programming practices starting in the 1960s, a number of them sought to supplement their incomes by soliciting public support. They have enjoyed some success, in part because they do offer a real alternative to commercial broadcasting,[57] but also because those who donate ("pledge") receive something in return—sometimes a program guide, often a membership card entitling them to discounts for various cultural attractions and perhaps a few retail stores.

Some ethnic minority radio stations and a few ethnic television stations, usually noncommercial, have followed that lead, and issue membership cards. Given the often tight financial circumstances of many ethnic community members, the expectation for minimum donations is low—perhaps the equivalent of U.S.$5-10 a year.[58] (In the United States, where there is no annual license fee, it is in the $30-50 range for radio and $60-80 for TV.) Thus, it is not a large source of annual income, but it can be a significant force in terms of showing community support, especially where larger numbers of individuals donate less than the minimum (but often receive a card anyway) and even that represents a real financial sacrifice.

Audience members usually do not enjoy being asked to contribute, so any service relying on that source of income probably will have to come up with an assortment of reasons for why they should donate. Perhaps the most unusual example that I have encountered was an unusual appeal ("Ransom the Fish") made by Melbourne's community TV service (which carried several programs produced by ethnic minority groups). After the station manager had resigned in 2000, it was discovered that the station had numerous unpaid bills, and the budget would not begin to cover them all. The station faced the prospect of declaring bankruptcy, and appealed to corporate donors and to individual audience members for financial help. The campaign seemed to be lagging until one staff member came up with the idea of using the inhabitants of the station's tropical fish tank (live images of which were used to fill "dead" airtime, and thus well-known to viewers) as hostages. An announcer would identify one of the fish, give it a name, and tell viewers that, if X dollars had not been raised within Y days, "Stripey" would be removed from the tank to die. General media attention was considerable, viewers seemed to enjoy the ploy, and the campaign succeeded.[59] Most ethnic services lack fish tanks, but it usually is possible to come up with at least a few imaginative appeals for funding.

Sale of Media Services and Products

Most radio and television stations have a certain amount of sometimes idle capacity on their hands, usually in the form of studio space and equipment or of staff members. The latter also represent a source of expertise, particularly on selling goods and services through the media. Some stations, including a few ethnic minority services, have marketed that capacity, and earn a modest (usually well under 5%) share of their total income by doing so. Advertisers and advertising agencies often do not wish to create their own production studios and employ crew members, so leasing facilities and crews through the stations makes good financial sense. Some stations "lease" their DJs for, for example, private parties, community-sponsored dances, splitting the fees with the DJs.

A number of ethnic minority stations have established themselves as recording studios for local musical groups, and have helped those groups to produce and market tapes and CDs. Australian Aboriginal station 8KIN has arranged with local tourist information sites and the Alice Springs airport to sell CDs and tapes produced by the station. Although it is a minor source of income, it helps to encourage and publicize a growing Aboriginal activity, it cements the bond between community and station, and, because the lyrics of some of the songs call attention to the problems and aspirations of Aborigines, it contributes to participation in the public sphere.

Surtaxes

Several nations have attempted to levy additional taxes on basic services, usually electricity, in order to generate income to support their PSBs. Tunisia and Algeria at one time imposed a modest tax on monthly electrical bills for that purpose, reasoning that at least a portion of the electricity was used to power radio and TV sets. In only one case of which I am aware does a surtax help to support ethnic minority media activity. It is imposed by some of the German *Länder* (states) on households served by cable television, and is called the *Kabelgroschen*. ("Cable Penny" comes fairly close; the surtax is very small.) Many of the larger

German cities and some of the smaller ones have established cable access services, and ethnic minorities often are heavy users, so they benefit directly from the surtax.

Volunteers

Perhaps volunteers should be considered as an "anti-source" of income because a part of their importance to an ethnic minority service is that they do *not* cost money. It is fair to say that they are more important to such a service than they are to most mainstream services, although community stations of all sorts make heavy use of them. Not only do they not cost money; they also are vital to an ethnic service's identification with the community. And for the volunteers themselves, their work with the services often brings them a sense of self-worth and even redemption that is moving to behold: I have had many conversations with Aboriginal, Native American, Maori, Sami, and other media volunteers who have told me that their work with the services turned their lives around and gave them a sense of dignity and purpose.

Given that list of virtues, it may seem churlish to state that there are prices that ethnic media services *do* pay for relying (often heavily) on volunteers. Volunteers soon become aware of their importance to a service, especially if they become popular with listeners, have political influence within the community, possess sources of information and entertainment (especially collections of recorded music), have special skills (accounting, equipment repair), and so on. Many of them bear that sense with pride, grace, and possibly humility, but there probably will be a few who use their prominence to claim and even demand airtime for their friends, more airtime for themselves, or special favors such as being allowed to insert favorable mentions of individuals, groups and businesses that pay the volunteer for such publicity.[60] Volunteers who have been with a service for years or even decades do tend to acquire a sense of ownership of "their" time slots or nonproduction positions, and it can be very difficult to tell them that their skills or approaches no longer meet the service's needs. If they are politically prominent, they are almost certain to resist, and they can count on generating a good deal of negative publicity for the service.

Several of the community and ethnic minority radio stations that I have visited in Sydney, Melbourne, and Adelaide, Australia face a fairly common volunteer-related problem. Most of the stations were created in the late 1970s, when "ethnic minority" generally meant *European* ethnic minority—Greeks, Danes, Germans, French, Portuguese, Italians, and so on. The founders of the stations themselves often were members of those groups. As Australia's ethnic communities have grown to include substantial numbers of Vietnamese, Pacific Islanders, Somalis, Afghanis, and others, and as many of those communities have sought to use radio, and sometimes TV, to express themselves, they have encountered situations where the program schedule either is filled up or has bits of airtime in early morning periods only. There may be survey data indicating that listenership for the Greek, Italian, German, and other programs has decreased, but it is another matter to get the volunteers who identify themselves with those programs to relinquish any of "their" airtime because that would be associated with loss of prestige for the individual and the community.

Even the access radio and TV services mentioned earlier face this problem, since they have airtime to fill, and find volunteers who are willing to commit themselves to a fixed and ongoing time slot as the proverbial "bird in the hand" (worth two in the bush). If such volunteers take the best time slots, that makes it even more difficult for occasional users to reach communities with their messages under conditions favoring maximum impact. One compromise would be to reserve a certain portion of airtime, including "best" slots,[61] for occasional users, with filler material (perhaps repeats of broadcasts) available when users fail to appear. Such an arrangement might even be feasible for a "nonaccess" station, perhaps in the form of one or two scheduled programs per week in which individuals and groups can call the station to complain, celebrate, question or assert, as long as they do so by avoiding libel, slander, and other illegal forms of expression. Certainly, volunteers are important members of the public sphere, but novolunteers can contribute to it in important ways, as well, and deserve a place in that sphere.

Summing Up Financing

Financing takes a host of shapes, in ethnic media as well as in mainstream media. The most important difference is that ethnic minority services are more likely to be on the thin edge than are mainstream services. That can lead to a mentality where it is difficult to not accept money from any and all sources. Nearly all of the ethnic services I visited have faced that prospect at one time or another; most of them have considered the potential drawbacks noted here, and have either rejected a given form or have created safeguards to minimize negative effects. The point here is that they have considered the risks before taking action. The supervisors of two Maori radio stations—Te Upoko o Te Ika in Wellington and Tumeke FM in Whakatane—did not do so when they decided in the early 1990s to switch the station formats from "ethnic community based" to "geographically based" and chose heavy concentrations of pop music (with playlists in the case of Te Upoko). That was supposed to increase mainstream appeal and generate more income, but it severely reduced the Maori character of the stations in both instances. The changes did not last long, as the Maori communities and some of the individuals who had founded the stations regained control of them, but the trauma was considerable and should have been predictable, if the risks had been weighed through a process of consultation with the community. As the old adage has it, "Look before you leap."

SUMMARY

I began this chapter by indicating that there were several *geographic* levels at which media policymaking could take place, but that few of them were all that active where ethnic minority media were concerned. Recalling what I said in Chapter 1 about the continued viability of the nation-state, it should not be surprising that it reigns supreme in media policymaking. Nor should it be surprising that, of all *institutional* forms of policymaking activity, national legislative bodies and regulatory agencies appear to have the lion's share of the action.

Still, the four case studies of policymaking should have shown that there are several other role players in the policymaking process, and that they can have a major impact on the final outcome. When we consider goalsetting in chapter 4, we see that some of the same actors—regulatory agencies, other media, tribal councils (somewhat like cabinets), lobbyists, and the devoted labors of a few individuals—surely are present in the one case study of goalsetting that I provide.

Although there is little that is strictly formulaic about the process of policymaking, the schema I have offered should help in understanding how it works, and even may be of use in assessing how the process might be influenced, or at least where to apply pressure when seeking to exert influence on it. I also have indicated that ethnic minority media activities may face some obstacles that might not loom as large (if they loom at all) for mainstream media groups. That is regrettable and sometimes unfair, but recognizing that certain barriers do exist should provide a starting point for overcoming them.

I have not provided a case study of failures in ethnic minority media policymaking. Doubtless there are some, but I have not discovered them, at least on the scale of the successes I have presented. Certainly, there are successes that have not lasted, such as the dismantling of the FCC's ownership preference policies by the Republican-led Congresses, courts and FCC itself during much of the late 1980s to late 1990s. That should illustrate the limited power (and possible lack of desire?) of a regulatory agency to defend its own policies, especially when their beneficiaries do not have much political power—usually the case with ethnic minorities.

Policymaking may be unpalatable, but it *is* understandable, and ethnic minority groups and their supporters that make the effort to do so *can* influence the process to the point where they are able to claim at least partial victories. The same may be said of financing media services. It is time-consuming and sometimes boring to pour over balance sheets and income flow charts, especially when there is a financial crisis looming and *any* source of income looks good. Weighing alternatives will not necessarily lead to salvation of a service, but it may lead to the conclusion that it is better to limp along for the time being in the hope that something better will turn up rather than to accept support from a source that is almost certain to reshape the service in accordance with its own goals.[62]

NOTES

1. See *Tuning into Diversity* (2002) for extensive summaries of media policymaking with respect to ethnic minorities in Italy, France, and The Netherlands.
2. I treat electronic media policymaking in greater detail in Browne (1999a: 38-62). For an introduction to the overall subject of ways to consider policymaking, see Portney (1986: 1-18).
3. I have taken the liberty of elaborating on the brief treatment Portney provides.
4. This is a little researched subject where ethnic minority media policymaking is concerned, but see Ha-il (1992).
5. For a review of international policymaking and regulatory procedures regarding the mass media, see O Siochru and Girard with Mahan (2002); fo a more philosophical approach to the subject, see Raboy (2002).
6. Both documents were obtained from www.troc.es/ciemen/mercator/UE18-GB and UE23-GB.
7. The Commission also has supported the European Multicultural Media Agency, which holds annual contests in which European teenagers produce video documentaries on various aspects of racism; the winning documentaries are broadcast on mainstream TV services.
8. See www.humanrights.coe.int/Minorities for the annual reports.
9. The Manifesto is available through the Web site of The Multicultural Skyscraper (www.multicultural.net/manifesto).
10. Hargreaves (n.d. but likely 2001: 5) notes that the CSA had commissioned a report on ethnic minority portrayal in broadcasting in 1999, and released a summary of the findings in June 2000 The summary drew numerous criticisms on the grounds that the methodology used was flawed and that the CSA was trying to prepare for the introduction of "ethnic quotas." The then-chair of the CSA, Herve Bourges, stated that the agency was not advocating and would not support such quotas, although it already had released a report indicating that it *would* impose some form of requirement that broadcast services "take more fully into account France's ethnic and cultural diversity" (Hargreaves, 2001: 5). The final report was printed and ready for distribution by autumn 2000 but then was withdrawn in the face of pressure, for "further revisions."
11. The BSC was brought under the Ofcom in December 2003.
12. One particularly notable BSC-commissioned study is "Include Us In" (Sreberny, 1999). It features reactions from ethnic minority audience members regarding their portrayal through British radio and television.
13. Probably because the indigenous groups and their mainstream supporters could argue that, as the original (or only surviving original) inhabitants of the present nation (or parts of it), they deserved primary consideration in the licensing and funding of their own broadcast services.
14. The changes brought about in the United States during the 1970s by petitions to deny renewal of license did provide more opportunities for ethnic minorities to express themselves through mainstream commercial radio and TV, but few of those changes have lasted. Some already had disappeared by the early 1980s, as the Reagan administration deregulated broadcasting.

15. My observations here are based on several visits to the Independent Broadcasting Authority headquarters in London and to several ILR stations in England and Scotland during the period 1976-1986. More recent visits (mid-1990s to 2003) indicate that the effort to include ethnic minority-oriented programming in ILR station broadcasts has dwindled. There never were any formal requirements that either the BBC or the independent broadcasting services include programs for ethnic minorities, and the appearance in the 1990s of limited power local commercial radio stations, a number of them serving primarily ethnic minority audiences, probably further reduced ILR's enthusiasm for providing such programs.

16. STOA/Miramedia is a particularly interesting organization, in that it has been very resourceful in finding ways to bring pressure to bear on the Dutch government, the broadcasters, and even on the ethnic groups themselves, to improve the quantity and quality of ethnic minority portrayal. It also has prepared a quite detailed report on the various agencies in the Netherlands, government and otherwise, that have roles to play in bringing that about. See STOA (2002: 387-428). I also draw upon my visits to the organization in September 1995 and April 2001.

17. The mentoring services were intended to help inexperienced ethnic minority station managers and program directors "learn the ropes" by pairing them up with mainstream managers and directors, who could invite them to see how things worked in mainstream stations, could be in telephone (and later, e-mail) contact with them to provide advice on how to handle immediate problems and similar concerns. That arrangement continues, and the NAB still has a minority affairs unit within its Office of Human Resources.

18. Fairchild (2001: 199) notes that Ontario's Community Radio Ontario Program (CROP), which had made funds available to a number of Native American radio stations for equipment, relocation, and program development, as well as running workshops for station staff, was "discontinued by the right-wing provincial government," but provides no date.

19. For further detail on the *raison d'etre* for this arrangement, see Browne (1999: 227-229, 256-257); Hoffman-Riem (1996: 114-158).

20. See Kepplinger and Hartmann (1989), Herkstroeter (1995), and Lilienthal (1995) for a more detailed account of the councils. Browne (1999a: 249-253) summarizes their activities.

21. I visited several of the associations during the 1990s, and noted that, much like community radio and TV stations, they depended heavily on the willingness of staff to work for little or no financial compensation.

22. There was a fairly large influx of Europeans and Americans, as well as Lebanese, Chinese, and other "non-Whites," during the latter part of the 19th century, thanks to the Australian gold rush and the building of railroads.

23. The Australian Broadcasting Company (ABC) began to provide English-language lessons by radio shortly after World War II. They proved to be unpopular, perhaps because of their somewhat condescending tone, and they were dropped in the early 1950s.

24. There were two exceptions to this, however. In 1964, the Australian Broadcasting Control Board (ABCB) permitted Radio 3KZ in Melbourne to carry up to 10% of its total broadcast time in foreign languages. In 1965, the ABCB imposed the same limit on Radio 2CH in Sydney, which eventually broadcast as many as 17 hours per week in foreign languages, all of them European, but stopped doing so in 1972

(Government of Australia Committee of Review, 1985: 3). As of late 1973, only 19 of the 118 commercial radio stations in Australia broadcast in foreign languages, for a total of 36 hours a week (Special Broadcasting Service, 1984: 233).

25. Australia already had a robust commercial sector, dating from the dawn of radio, and a license fee-supported national service, the ABC, dating from the early 1930s.

26. In a personal interview with the author (Melbourne March, 2001), George Zangalis, widely acknowledged to be one of the prime movers in the foundation of ethnic minority broadcasting in Australia, stated that the conference was organized not by unions, but by the various ethnic community groups. That made it particularly effective in pressing the Labor government to support the creation by the ABC of Melbourne community radio station 3ZZ.

27. Mike Thompson, Head of the Community Broadcasting Association of Australia (CBAA), participated in some of the Labor Party talks concerning the foundation of community broadcasting, and assisted me in understanding some of the political maneuvering that accompanied the process (personal interview, Sydney, March 2001). Also helpful on that subject were Thornley (2002); public broadcasting "pioneer" Jeff Langdon (personal interview, Melbourne, March 2001); and Davies (1998).

28. He also was a founder (1974) of the Public Broadcasting Association of Australia (the CBAA's predecessor), and its first Convenor (Thornley, 2002: 3).

29. 3ZZ was on air for only 26 months, and was the most controversial broadcast service that Australia had ever experienced. One of its chief participants has written a thorough, colorful, and self-admittedly biased account of the station's life and times (Dugdale, 1979). Harding (1979), and Inglis (1983), although somewhat more detached than Dugdale, in the main agree with her judgment that the ABC was uncomfortable with 3ZZ and did little to support it.

30. And still is. There is no national ethnic minority broadcast service anywhere in the world that comes close to offering the range of language services provided by SBS. The only operation resembling it—Germany's Funkhaus Europa—was not established until 1996, provides a relative (to SBS) handful of language services, on radio only.

31. There are differences of opinion concerning the role of the Labor Party in bringing about change, chiefly over the procedure it followed. Davies (1998) generally gives the Party high marks for its initiatives; Griffiths (1976) sees the Party as having been less open and consultative than it made itself out to be in the process of "redrawing the media map."

32. This was achieved with the support, particularly in the form of legal assistance, from the United Church of Christ.

33. Weissman (1981: 576) argues that the policy was not as meaningful as it could have been because the FCC applied a standard—"zone of reasonableness"—that placed on any challenger the burden of proof that minority employment practices at a station were substantially lower then they were for the local minority workforce in general, and for minorities as a collective entity, rather than as specific ethnic groups.

34. Personal conversation with Henry Geller, Aspen Center, Queenstown, MD, May 1996.

35. The question of whether minority ownership does lead to more minority-oriented programming has been hotly debated, and the FCC sought in the mid-1990s to

gather evidence on that point, but the questionnaire it devised for the purpose was regarded as flawed. Craft (2000) has a detailed treatment of the question with respect to U.S. practices; Mason, Bachen, and Craft (2001) provide a specific consideration of its application.

36. Krasnow prepared the NAB petition for the rulemaking.

37. House of Representatives (1995). However, the Republican Party-dominated Congress and those federal courts with Republican appointees in the majority already had begun to dismantle the FCC's preference policies, and some of the preference policies themselves were not without problems when it came to minority implementation of them. Wilson (2001: 95-110) provides a summary of those problems and the dismantling process.

38. Some time later, Radio Pretoria, one of those stations, continued to broadcast after the expiration of its license. Police were sent in to close it down, but its staff and supporters were armed, and it took several weeks to evict them. Two anti-*apartheid* groups in Cape Town applied for licenses, as well, but received no reply, and later began to broadcast illegally. One of them, Bush Radio, was on air for 4 hours in late April 1993, when it was shut down by the authorities for operating without a license.

39. In addition to two personal interviews with Adrian Loew, Program Manager, Bush Radio, Capetown, September 2002, I have drawn on several sources for this account of activity taking place in the early 1990s. In addition to Loew, see Community Radio Manual (1999), Gorfinkel (1992), Government of South Africa (2000: Sec. 2.1), Independent Broadcasting Authority (n.d., but likely mid-1995: 2-3), and Stevens (n.d.). Also likely to be useful, although I have not yet read it, is a recent PhD dissertation on the station by its present manager, Tanja Bosch (2003). It includes a detailed account of the history of Bush Radio in the context of general developments in South Africa.

40. Two personal interviews (September 1995 and April 2001) with Dr. Friedrich Voss, head of SFB4-Radio MultiKulti, have been of great importance to me in writing this case study. A personal interview (July 2002) with Gualtiero Zambonini, Director of Funkhaus Europa in Cologne, Germany, also provided important information on the context of the times where the foundation of multicultural broadcasting was concerned. Vertovec (1996) also provides background on the creation of the service. See also Buettner and Meyer (2001) for contextual information.

41. There are two forms for the term *Ausländer* when it is applied to collections of individuals: *Ausländer* (masculine) and *Ausländerinnen* (feminine). In the interest of space, I have chosen to use the term *Ausländer* to cover both genders.

42. Personal interview with Martin Kilgus, advisor on ethnic minority policy, Suddeutscher Rundfunk (SDR), Stuttgrat, Germany, September 1995.

43. There also was a "left-wing" private radio station in Berlin, Radio 100, that broadcast programs in a number of foreign languages, but it was in existence for only 4 years (1987-1991).

44. The SFB *Intendant* (general manager) at the time, Guenter von Lojewski, was regarded as conservative and not very supportive of expanded service for *Ausländern* (Seefeld, 1994: 18). Braun (1994) noted that such a service was "not exactly a pet project of *Intendant* Lojewski" (translation mine). Schneckener (1994) states that Lojewski did show some interest in using an existing radio frequency for foreign language broadcasts, but did not make a formal proposal to do so, and in fact certain actions taken by SFB, including the "banishing of the SFB

Ausländerprogramme to the unloved medium wave (AM) band," sent the opposite message (translation mine).

45. According to Schneckener (1994), Wendland "realized that, with this idea [for a new multicultural radio service], the former conservative image of SFB could be lifted a bit, and the station could play a leading role in ARD" (the Association of German Public Broadcasters).

46. Although U.S. citizen's groups had lobbied for changes in radio programming policies starting in the mid-1930s, they were few in number and active at the local level only. Such groups became more influential (and far more numerous) following the 1969 U.S. Circuit Court decision noted earlier. See also Guimary (1975) and Montgomery (1989: 51-74, 123-153), the former for details on the growth of citizen involvement through the early 1970s, the latter for two accounts—one African American-related, the other Chicano-related—of ethnic minority citizen group pressure on the networks.

47. A few regulatory agencies, most notably the Canadian Radio-Television and Telecommunications Commission and the Australian Broadcasting Authority, do hold license renewal hearings in the larger cities, so ethnic minorities living in those cities at least have an occasional opportunity to register complaints about their portrayal in the presence of those bodies and without having to incur the expense of a trip to the capital city.

48. See also Craft (2000) and Mason, Bachen, and Craft (2001) on actual effects of ethnic minority ownership.

49. Alia (1999: 113) describes a succession of cuts in Canadian federal government support to the Inuit Broadcasting Corporation (IBC) in the 1990s; the 1996 cut represented a loss of nearly 15% in the IBC's budget.

50. SBS has had to find additional sources of income, especially over the past decade, as legislators have increased the pressure to do so. That has resulted in the creation or expansion of a number of SBS-operated services, such as translation, that may be commercially viable. Judging from my personal interviews and observations in the course of two visits to SBS (February 1996 and March 2001), there is considerable disagreement among SBS staff members as to whether such services have helped or hindered the institution in carrying out its basic mission, particularly inasmuch as staffing for the expanded mission saw little or no increase in most cases.

51. Ofori (1999) covers some of the problems encountered by advertiser-supported ethnic stations in the United States.

52. Personal visit, Stockholm, April 2001.

53. Rebroadcast in the fall of 2003 and with new episodes added in April 2004.

54. The critically acclaimed documentary series on the U.S. Civil Rights Movement, "Eyes on the Prize," was produced by Henry Hampton through the African-American production house Blackside, Inc. Hampton struggled to secure financial support from the Corporation for Public Broadcasting and various foundations, and had to cut back considerably on the scope of the project. After the series had received high critical praise and several awards, he produced a sequel, "Eyes on the Prize II," but funding problems were at least as severe the second time around ("Eyes on Henry Hampton," 1995)

55. Some of the Native American-run gambling casinos contribute to some of the Native American-operated radio stations, although annual giving often amounts to US$1,000 per station or less.

56. See Hein (1988) for a detailed description of Bahai involvement with radio services for Indian groups in Ecuador.
57. The U.S. public broadcasting sector did not develop to an appreciable extent until the late 1960s, when Congress passed the Public Broadcasting Act of 1967. The United States never has had an annual license fee, and that option received very little consideration when the Act was passed, so it may be that U.S. citizens are somewhat more willing to donate to support public broadcasting because they do *not* pay such a fee.
58. That is a considerable sum when measured against average annual incomes in many ethnic minority communities.
59. Personal interviews with station staff, Melbourne Community Television, March 2001.
60. On my visit to GNP the närradio service in Gothenburg, Sweden, in May 2001, the service was trying for the third time to discipline a valued Iranian volunteer who had engaged in such behavior before, apologized for his conduct, and then repeated it. Threats to deprive him of "his" program slot, including one actual suspension, had not kept him from returning to the practice, and the service administrators were on the point of considering his dismissal, even though they knew that it would result in protests from powerful members of the city's Iranian community.
61. One problem here is that "best" can vary from group to group and among types of programs, and that problem is compounded when dealing with a number of ethnic groups, especially if they represent highly disparate cultures and traditions. Still, few would argue with the assertion that, aside from long-distance truck drivers, night-shift workers, insomniacs and early risers, the hours between midnight and 6 a.m. are not likely to be "best" times! Everitt (2003: 112) notes a solution to this problem that was implemented by U.K. access radio station Bradford Community Broadcasting: "by operating a three-monthly programming cycle; it is made clear to all involved that at the end of each quarter the slate is wiped clean and volunteer presenters' and producers' 'franchises' come to an end and may or may not be renewed." He adds that two other access stations have borrowed the idea.
62. That is exactly what happened in the case of Native American radio station KILI-FM (Porcupine, South Dakota) in 1992, when financial disaster loomed and the Lakota tribal government offered to provide financial assistance if the station would drop certain programs and otherwise become more accommodating to the council's wishes. The station manager secured a loan from a nearby bank to tide the station over (and was roundly criticized by the council's supporters for doing so), and the station maintained its independence. See Browne (1996: 198-199) for a more detailed description of the situation.

Audience as Community, Community as Audience

One of the clearest distinctions between ethnic minority and mainstream electronic media is in their perceptions of the audience. Many, and perhaps most, ethnic minority services appear to regard the audience as a community, which they see as essential to work *with* rather than speak *to*. Mainstream electronic media services, and commercial services in particular, tend to regard the audience as something with which to establish contact, but not to the point of declaring even so much as a limited partnership. Community radio and television services fall somewhere in between; at their extremes, they (or certain of the groups which broadcast through them) may be very close to their communities or quite distant from them, but more often occupy the middle ground.

There are many forms of community involvement with ethnic minority electronic media, but as a starting point we may divide them into two broad categories: Those forms initiated by the *community*, which I cover under *audience as community*, and those forms initiated by the *media service* (including anything along those lines that is required by law), which come under *community as audience*. Both forms can be, and often are present in the self-same media service. Also, it is rarely the case that anything more than a modest number of audience members will become involved with an ethnic media service at any one time. Most of them simply do not have sufficient time for that, and many still seem to think of media services as something that is "just there when I need it," or perhaps wonder what they could possibly offer by way of useable skills or resources.

Audience as community includes activities initiated by audience members with little or no specific prompting from the media service, and ranging from *informal* (letter-writing, telephoning, e-mailing, casual conversations with media service staff, and personal visits to the service) to *formal* (community government-sponsored open meetings such as reviews of community-funded activities, community government-appointed boards of supervisors for media services, citizens' groups wishing to monitor media performance). Community as audience comprises media service-originated activities, which likewise range from informal (an "open-door" policy at the service, presence at community events where service staff make themselves available to answer questions about their work, provision of a call-in line for community member comments) to formal (advisory boards appointed by the service or the national or state government, annual [or more frequent] general meetings).

What matters with any form of involvement is whether community members feel that it is meaningful, not only on a personal level ("the service actually listened to me/us!"), but also in terms of impact, especially at the community-wide level ("and it *did* something about the situation"). It also matters that the openness of the service to individuals and to the community be a fundamental and continuing commitment, and not something that varies according to who happens to be in charge or who wishes to be heard. That is not to say that a service always can or should do something to address a complaint or honor a request, but that it should be willing to listen or read, and then to state why it cannot or will not act as requested.

Establishing a sound working relationship with the community/audience often begins even before the service is launched. The initial act in the process is likely to be *goal setting*. Goal setting is a crucial step in establishing relationships between a service and its community: It can indicate just how much, and in which specific ways, the community might expect to play a meaningful role in working with and through the service.

GOAL SETTING

There is a major distinction between ethnic minority media services and their mainstream counterparts when it comes to setting goals that will shape their practices. Mainstream commercial services assume that operating at a profit is a major goal, and that achieving it means reaching more viewers and listeners than do their competitors. Reaching the right sorts of viewers and listeners (demographics) usually matters just as much, and often more. Ethnic minority commercial services must be concerned with audience size and composition as well, but face less direct competition for the audiences they most hope to reach, and as a consequence are at greater liberty to take account of other, more "community-friendly" factors. But most ethnic minority electronic media services are not commercial,[1] and with few exceptions place a high premium on close relationships with their communities.

Ethnic minority media and the communities they serve frequently engage in setting goals, particularly as they prepare to implement their services. Usually, those goals are shaped by what the ethnic groups feel they *do not* receive (or are likely to) through the mainstream media. Sometimes, there is widespread agreement within an ethnic group that a given goal is an absolute necessity, in which case the media service will adopt it with little or no deliberation or consultation. Often, however, there is disagreement over the level of importance of a goal, and perhaps over whether a particular goal even should be pursued. Where there is disagreement, goal setting may resemble policymaking: Several forces are likely to be involved in the process, and the process itself sometimes can become chaotic and prolonged.

Those forces often cannot be identified as clearly as courts or regulatory agencies. They are much more likely to be composed of social and cultural entities such as religious institutions, artisans and artists, teachers, senior citizens, young people, women, and family groups. Their members may have affiliations with several entities, and may find themselves conflicted as they try to determine which affiliation is most important to them in a given situation.

Although it may be of limited assistance in such circumstances, the various forces have ways of examining the situation that can make it somewhat easier to assess a course of action. One way is to consider whether the dilemma is one of *resources* (is there sufficient monetary and/or human capital?) or one of *purposes* (how essential is this goal, why, and what is the feasibility of meeting it, regardless of resources?). Another is to determine whether the dilemma is one of *messages* (what do we want to say, and how should it be presented) or one of *messengers* (who among us will deliver it?). Yet another would be the relative suitability of the available medium for the various goals the community and service have in mind because no single medium is perfect for each and every goal.

The list of goals presented here, and much else in this chapter, stems from my discussions with ethnic minority media staff, as well as books, articles, and reports dealing with ethnic minority media, and what I have learned from scholars and practitioners who have studied and operated ethnic minority media and then have presented their findings and experiences at conferences such as the OURMedia conference held in Barcelona in July 2002 (www.ourmedianet.com). I have organized the list in two categories: Those goals that seem to be universal, or close to it; and those that are not, often because they are controversial issues within ethnic minority communities.

The *universal goals* are as follow:

- Providing/restoring a sense of pride in ethnic minority accomplishments;
- Preserving, restoring, or expanding the use of a minority language (where it differs from mainstream languages).
- Combating negative stereotypes of minorities, especially those provided through mainstream media.

- Providing information on employment, health care, education, financial aid.
- Encouraging and promoting the work of ethnic minority musicians, writers, businesses, and so on.

The *less common goals* are as follows:

- Maintaining informational and cultural links with the ancestral homelands.
- Directly challenging the mainstream by calling attention to proposals or actions by government that are against the best interests of minorities; calling on minorities to oppose government proposals or actions.
- Advocating separate nationhood for the ethnic group.
- Encouraging/cultivating ethnic minority community leaders.
- Showcasing how minorities and the mainstream can and do work together.
- Educating mainstream audiences in the customs and practices of minorities.
- Showing that minorities are capable of operating media services, including commercial services.
- Creating a greater sense of unity among members of a given ethnic group, and possibly among ethnic minorities in general.

It is not that difficult to understand why the five universal goals are such popular choices. The first three address the desire of ethnic minorities to show that their cultures are significant and display many positive characteristics—qualities that often are not featured in mainstream media accounts of ethnic minority life. The remaining two provide direct assistance to the community and to its economic well-being. If there is disagreement, usually it is about who or what will be the focus of attention, and how much attention they receive. Very few ethnic media services have had to ponder whether they should seek to implement such goals.

The list of less common goals contains some possibly unexpected entries. For example, one might think that ethnic minority media would embrace goals that would lead to a better understanding of minority life on the part of mainstream audiences, if only because that might encourage those audiences to be more tolerant and even supportive toward minorities. My experience has been that ethnic minority media staff generally do not mind if mainstream audiences use their services to become better acquainted with minorities. However, staff members often feel that they have ample work to do just pursuing the more usual ethnic community oriented goals, and do not want to spread themselves too thin by attempting to reach the mainstream population as well.[2] In addition, reaching the mainstream effectively can require different forms of approach and more explanation of what is occurring within the ethnic group, which can be very time-consuming.[3] And finally, minority group members may feel that, since they have been deprived of their own media voices for so long, they should be the sole focus of attention.

Two other less common goals—advocating separate nationhood and challenging government actions—may be rare simply because the ethnic services themselves, with the exception of the internet, are licensed by the national government. There may be concerns that the government could use such acts as excuses to revoke the licenses, even if no laws were broken. But the goal of supporting and promoting ethnic minority community leaders, which would seem very much in line with promoting a sense of pride in ethnic minority accomplishments, is almost as rare. Here, the cause seems to lie with the complex world of ethnic minority politics, where the concept of leadership itself varies greatly, depending on specific circumstances and differing interpretations of those circumstances. The ethnic media often do not wish to place themselves in the position of supporting individuals who may turn out to have little support from the ethnic community at large, especially when those media draw so much of their own support from that community.[4]

The goal of maintaining informational and cultural links with the ancestral homelands turns up somewhat more often, particularly when an ethnic minority service feels a major obligation (or major pressure) to serve the older members of the ethnic community. One of the more interesting features of ethnic minority broadcast services is the contrast between those stations (or ethnic services that are responsible for filling specific blocks of airtime on stations) that rely heavily on older staff members and those stations that rely heavily on younger staff. The former tend to draw on material from the homeland—recordings, wire services, direct relays, Web sites—much more heavily than do the latter. But as the stations and services continue on, younger staff often replace older staff, and younger staff often are second or third generation, with less sense of ties to the homelands. Still, I have seen some services virtually disappear because those who established them would not give up control, continued to emphasize ancestral homeland material, and saw their audiences quite literally dieing off.[5]

The goal of showing that ethnic minorities can operate media services is rare; when it arises, it usually is in connection with a commercial service, such as Murri (Aboriginal Australian) radio station 4AAA in Brisbane, or Maori radio station Mai FM in Auckland. In both cases, administrators hoped that the stations would be successful as business enterprises for the usual economic reasons, but also as prominent demonstrations of the business acumen of indigenous entrepreneurs.[6]

One goal that appears infrequently may be the most surprising entry in this list: creating a broader sense of ethnic minority unity. Members of ethnic minority communities usually seem well aware that size makes a difference when trying to alter anti-ethnic minority perceptions and practices, and especially those held by members of the mainstream population. Yet many indigenous peoples still harbor ancient grudges, mistrust, suspicion and even animosity toward rival tribes or bands of tribes,[7] making it difficult to unify for the common good. The

same sometimes is true of nonindigenous ethnic minorities, where family rival-
ries or disrespect for those who come from a particular part of the ancestral
homeland may keep individual minority groups from uniting around a common
cause. In such circumstances, a frequent tendency of ethnic stations or services
not under the control of a given faction is to lie low rather than seek to promote
the setting aside of ancient differences.

Sad to say, attempts to employ ethnic minority electronic media in creating a
sense of unity among still larger aggregations of ethnic minorities, such as all
ethnic minorities living in France, Japan, or wherever else, are exceptionally
rare. I suggested in Chapter 2 that there probably are several reasons for this,
but the fact remains that there are very few services featuring the level of staff
and financial commitment that would illustrate how such a service might operate. Although it is not a worldwide organization, the Aboriginal Peoples'
Television Network (www.aptn.ca) does present a wide variety of Native
American (Canada, Mexico, Central America, United States) and Inuit programs, as well as some from still other ethnic minority sources, which reflect
many quite different cultural and political traditions.

The process of goal setting cannot be reduced to a simple formula, but the
following case study should provide some idea of not just what goes on, why,
and who becomes involves (and why), but also how long the process can take
and the ways in which external (to the ethnic community) forces can play influential roles in the outcome. In many respects, it resembles policymaking.

A CASE STUDY OF GOAL-SETTING[8]

Fairchild (2001: 175-223) offers a clearly organized and richly detailed illustration of intra group conflict and its effect on the establishment of a Native
American radio station in Canada. The case also provides an indication of how
differences can be reconciled, and the role of something akin to a policy making
process in bringing that about. What follows is my condensation of Fairchild's
treatment, with emphasis on policymaking aspects of the situation.

The Six Nations and New Credit Native American Reserves are located near
Brantford, Ontario, and are only a few miles apart. Because of their proximity, it
was certain from early on that only one radio frequency would be authorized for
the two reserves. A core group of individuals from the reserves formed a working
committee in the early 1980s, and then spent a few years holding public meetings
and discussing among themselves how to establish a station, but suspicion, lack of
mutual respect, and bouts of indecision meant that they never could reach
enough agreement to make any substantial progress.

A key figure during that period was Carolyn King, who had married into New
Credit but whose grandmother was Six Nations. Although she did not always
enjoy the support of both groups, it certainly helped that she could understand

the motivations and misgivings of each. The small sums of money that were raised to establish a station never were sufficient to produce tangible results, and the working committee finally disbanded after making a motion to support King and Brian Johnson (Six Nations) in whatever further efforts they might make.

Other media in the area had been covering the situation, which helped to whet the appetites of people in both of the reserves for a station, so Johnson and King found a way to create one that could serve as a prototype: Johnson used some contacts in Toronto to locate equipment sufficient for a 10-watt operation; King got money from a New Credit band member; King and Johnson purchased and installed the equipment; the New Credit (governing) Council made available a small room in the Council house; an engineer friend of Johnson's helped locate an unused frequency; and the unlicensed station came on air. King and Johnson soon took it off the air because it *was* illegal and it *was* attracting attention through local media coverage. It reappeared in a different Six Nations location, then yet another (still Six Nations), where it received formal support (and rent-free accommodation) from the Six Nations Council.

By that time, two community groups were contending for recognition as chief supporters of the station, but ultimately realized that they should reconcile their alternative goals for it if it were to have a reasonable chance of succeeding. Fortunately, those goals already had been the object of considerable discussion throughout the community, and coincided in most key respects: Promotion of the history, values, traditions, languages, laws of the peoples living on the two reserves. That helped to ensure that the station would serve both groups in roughly equal measure.

Several crises followed, but the station weathered them, applied to the Canadian Radio-Television and Telecommunications Commission (CRTC) for a license[9] in December 1990, and had it approved 1 year later. Its program policy followed the shared goals of the two groups, and even though it continues to attract criticism for such things as too much mainstream culture music and too little time devoted to broadcasts in the indigenous languages (it employs Onondaga, Mohawk, and Cayuga, but English predominates), both groups and the two communities as a whole seem to appreciate its efforts to preserve and teach the indigenous cultures.

How did this come about? Through some of the same agents that appeared in the earlier consideration of government policymaking. The persistence of a few individuals was one key to success, and the "bicultural" identity of Carolyn King helped to maintain a degree of intercultural sensitivity and respect. Media attention to the early tests of the station nourished and solidified broad public support. Formal backing for the station by the Six Nations Council marked a significant commitment to its continuation. The threats of the regulatory agency (CRTC) to license a commercial station forced the two rival groups to set aside their differences and agree to apply for a license themselves, and the station's implementation of those goals that the groups held in common assured listeners on both reserves that they enjoyed equal respect.

AUDIENCE AS COMMUNITY

I noted at the beginning of this chapter that goal setting was linked very clearly with the concept of community involvement—a sense of collaboration *between* media service and audience/community. Most ethnic minority media enterprises operate on that assumption. Some of the internet Web sites, for example, a site for a wide variety of discourse for gay Kurds, Buddhist Kurds, and others through message boards,[10] consider their users as full co-participants. Those who do not participate simply are less active than those who do. There is little sense of "to" or of "audience."

Where community members wish to take the initiative and become directly involved with an ethnic media service, there is a fundamental question: Do most ethnic minority media audience members really want to be co-participants? And if they seem reluctant, how should and how can those who operate the services motivate them to do so? Most ethnic minority media service staffs with whom I have spoken have mixed attitudes toward co-participation. They feel that it is good for the audience to become involved with the service, for three reasons: First, people who learn to express themselves through the media will become more self-empowered, more confident, more willing to work for the betterment of the community.[11] In other words, they will be better prepared to enter the public sphere. Second, the community will come to realize that the service really is theirs when they hear and see the words and images of friends and neighbors; participants and non participants alike will come to place even greater value on the media service that provides them with such opportunities. Third, participants will become even better informed critics of media services in general, which should assist in preparing them to question authority.

Where the staff have misgivings, these run along the following lines: First, it is hard work (requiring much staff time) to motivate people to become involved in meaningful ways, especially where they have been part of a society that does not appear to value their opinions and has not welcomed their involvement. Second, once media service staff members have become adept at what they do, as well as committed to doing it, they do not welcome handing over a share of the action to people who are not as adept (at least in working with the media) as are the staff—or as the staff believe themselves to be. Third, people may display great enthusiasm while in the "early involvement" stage, but many soon fall by the wayside as they become bored, frustrated, and so on. As they all need a modicum of training, most of it provided by staff members, is it not wasteful of staff resources if the "desertion rate" is high? And fourth, do community members necessarily want to hear and see all that much from people like themselves?

Whether the community members themselves are aware of those impressions and, if they are, whether they agree with them, is difficult to say. From my own observations, I have concluded that very few community members are so bold as to volunteer their services before they feel reasonably certain that the media service will welcome them, or at least have the grace to decline them politely, and perhaps offer suggestions of services that would be welcome. Most media staff seem to regard the benefits of community participation as clearly outweighing any disadvantages, and many of the ethnic minority services display ample evidence of some degree of community participation, as will become quite evident through the case study immediately below and in our consideration of programming practices in the next chapter. It is less often the case that staff are aware of the need to *project* a welcoming atmosphere for community participation, and to consider specific ways of doing so.

There are many ways in which community members can become meaningfully involved with an ethnic minority media service, and some of them have nothing directly to do with program making. Ordinarily, a service is grateful for community involvement in the form of administrative assistance or fundraising: Telephones must be answered, reports typed and filed, and often there are needed repairs of equipment, furniture, roofs, windows, and the like. To repeat an earlier observation: People are much more likely to see themselves as important to the media service if they are told in a variety of ways that what they do contributes to the overall quality of the enterprise. Media services are in a particularly good position to do so, since they can tell the entire community about who is doing what and why it matters. What is more, volunteers who see themselves as important are quite likely to think of still other ways in which their presence will be valued. Nor are most services overburdened by community members desperate to become involved. The numbers generally are manageable; if anything, service staff might wish that they were greater.

Still, most community members do seem happy enough most of the time to sit back, watch, listen, occasionally criticize, less often commend. What does that say about involvement; more precisely, what does it say about ethnic minority participation in the public sphere? It may show nothing more than what one is likely to encounter in any society and regardless of minority or majority status: By and large, most people do not feel the need to participate all that often in the public sphere—and certainly not as a daily activity. Many seem quite content to let others speak for them. They may not even care to learn what was said on their behalves unless the issue is one that touches their lives very personally and directly. When they do learn what was said, they may regard this as itself a form of participation, albeit a passive form. Ethnic media can assist in keeping the community informed, and on occasion may be able to assist in motivating some of its members to participate. Certainly, those media can serve as channels through which community members already motivated to participate can share their participation with those who do not, and perhaps that sharing will motivate others to join in. If it can accomplish that much, it will have accomplished a great deal.

A CASE STUDY OF AUDIENCE AS COMMUNITY:
ZOOM BLACK MAGIC LIBERATION RADIO

Although the FCC ceased licensing 10-watt radio services in 1978, that did not stop individuals and groups interested in low power radio from trying their hands at unlicensed operations. Most of the activity involved playing specific kinds of popular music, and hardly could be labeled as social protest, but a few services clearly represented challenges to government authority, and one was operated by an African American: M'banna Kantako.[12] His one watt station, at first called WTRA,[13] and later "Zoom Black Magic Liberation Radio," "Black Liberation Radio," "African Liberation Radio," and more recently "Human Rights Radio," came on air from his apartment in a Springfield, Illinois public housing project (600 units) in November 1987. Its signal did not reach all that far beyond the project—roughly eight city blocks. However, its programming sometimes criticized local officials (law enforcement officials in particular), and its lack of a license bothered the FCC, so it was not surprising that the latter, at the instigation of the former, issued a cease and desist order in April 1989—shortly after the station had broadcast a series in which people in the housing project community and the larger community of African Americans in Springfield shared their stories about police brutality (Sakolsky, 1992: 108).[14]

Kantako shut down the station upon receiving the order, but not for long: Within 2 weeks, it was back on air. His own convictions, coupled with the messages and pledges of support he received from his audience, led him to take the risk that the equipment could be confiscated and that he could be fined (he was, in 1990, but never paid the $750 fine) and sent to jail. His own family was actively involved in running the station, and the audience itself functioned as community to help, sometimes in the form of donations of food and of small sums of money, but most of all in supplying their own talents for on-air presentations and various forms of administrative support.

By the early 1990s, the station had acquired something of a national reputation and even a national community, thanks to media coverage through the *Illinois Times* (Springfield), National Public Radio, MTV (the U.S. music video service), *The Los Angeles Times,* and other outlets. Six media scholars, including Noam Chomsky and Herbert Schiller, contributed $100 apiece so that Kantako could buy a more powerful transmitter—one with a capacity of up to 30 watts (Townsend, 1999). A professor at Springfield State University (now University of Illinois at Springfield), Mike Townsend, and an instructor at Sangamon State University, Ron Sakolsky, advised Kantako on ways to maintain and expand the national community by developing snail mail and e-mail lists, having the station listed on various Web site links, and so on.

The existence of those two communities probably served to discourage law enforcement officials and the FCC from shutting down the station during the 1990s, although the FCC did issue a cease and desist order on December 2, 1998, and again on September 30, 1999 (Townsend, 2000). The housing project community itself was dispersed in 1997, when the city tore down the John Hay Homes project, and Kantako lost his operations base (he was the last project tenant to leave). However, his wife had found an apartment near the Springfield business district and in close proximity to the city's east side, where most African Americans lived. The station was back on air from its new location within 90 minutes of signing off from the old one (Townsend, 1999).

By the year 2000, the FCC was considering a resurrection of the discontinued 10- watt license for low power FM services, and at the same time was attempting to close down the many unlicensed services around the nation. On September 29, 2000, the federal marshals came to Kantako's home and seized his equipment. He broadcast the first 5 minutes of the raid live, recorded the entire raid, and made the recording available to whoever might wish to use it, as did a number of stations, illegal and legal alike. With help from his two communities, he acquired the necessary equipment and began broadcasting soon thereafter. On November 30, 2000, the marshals returned, and this time ensured that there would be no live broadcast of their activities: They hired a private contractor to scale the house wall, disconnect, and then remove his two antennas before they entered his house. They did honor his wife's demand that they remove their shoes before entering the living room. Again, Kantako audiotaped the raid and made it available to whoever might want a copy, as many did. And again, thanks to the support of his communities, he was back on air by March 20, 2001 (Townsend, 2000; "Human Rights," n.d. but likely 2001). It remains on air as of 2003.

It should not have been difficult for the station's primary audience—African Americans living in Springfield—to identify with the station, because it not only highlighted problems with which they were very familiar, but also invited them to bear witness to their own experiences by telling their stories on air. In turn, that encouraged some of the audience to volunteer their services as reporters of daily events concerning their community that were not likely to be picked up by the mainstream media. It also caused many in the audience to be more willing to support the station with contributions of food, money, and service. By taking those initiatives, the audience became more of a community with a sense of genuine ownership in the station.

The formation of a second community—national and international supporters—was more difficult to achieve, because it did not rest on the day-to-day experiences of its members, and the members themselves were more difficult to identify. Media publicity on the station helped to bring it to the attention of the broader public, but the support that was provided by many of that public's members arose more spontaneously, although the $100 contributions by Chomsky, Schiller, and other well-known academics certainly helped to publicize it. The development of mailing lists also played an important role in keeping interested parties abreast of the station's activities—especially important at the time of the federal raids in 2000.

Finally, Kantako himself clearly appeared to others as someone who had an important mission, seemed to be fulfilling it, and did not become discouraged by the authorities. He galvanized both communities by his frequent display of those qualities, and his local community could identify with him because he was undergoing some of the same hardships as they were.

COMMUNITY AS AUDIENCE

There has been increased activity over the past decade by ethnic minority commercial media services. One of the chief distinctions that I have noticed when comparing the approaches taken by those services and their noncommercial, generally nonprofit counterparts is that the latter, as I observed earlier in this chapter, place a high premium on developing community participation. The former seem by and large to follow the lead of the mainstream commercial media, where audience size and demographics are the main criteria for measuring success, and communication *with* the audience is more of a one-way street: Commercial services are *to* and *for* audiences, but rarely by them.

Commercial radio services, ethnic and mainstream alike, certainly encourage some forms of audience participation, mainly in the form of soliciting telephone calls, e-mail, and conventional mail, and encouragement of personal and collective visits to the service by audience members, as well as visits by the service to groups of audience members, for example through service-sponsored outdoor concerts. In some instances, participation becomes a major element in program content, especially with radio station talk shows where hosts (sometimes joined by guests) set out provocative topics and then invite listeners to express their reactions and viewpoints. However, the service itself selects the topics, and callers rarely have the opportunity to ask follow-up questions or to express dissatisfaction with host or guest responses, so there is little dialogue in the Habermasian sense.

Because most ethnic minority commercial services are quite recent arrivals on the media scene (most have commenced operation during the past decade or two), it is too early to form a definitive picture of the ways in which they deal with the community as audience. Those with which I am familiar—BET, Univision, Mai-FM (Maori), and 4AAA (Aboriginal Australian radio), Hispanic radio in Minneapolis/St.Paul—appear to follow mainstream commercial practices, and remain very much in control of program content. Audience members ordinarily are not co-participants in the sense of devising and shaping that content, although most radio services do feature listener requests for music and call-ins for talk shows. The same observations apply to ethnic minority commercial television, where opportunities for such participation are far fewer.[15]

As already indicated, ethnic minority noncommercial media services have developed a variety of ways in which to involve members of the communities they serve, and that range of approaches is far wider than what the commercial services provide. Still, there are many reasons why ethnic minority and mainstream services alike must take the lead in deciding what to provide and how to provide it. They range from meeting licensing requirements for broadcasting, where stations generally are the final arbiters of what they carry, and in large measure responsible for their program content, to facing the prospect of a lot of "dead" airtime if they rely heavily on the audience to fill it in. The key to success in treating the community as audience in a manner that encourages its support seems to be the ability of a service to display its openness in ways that will show the community that it attempts to serve them, not so much as a monolith, but as a diverse yet interlinked entity. At the same time, it must show that it is prepared to lead, and sometimes to challenge the community to grow in understanding, tolerance and acceptance of difference and change. The following case study should demonstrate how one service attempts to do just that.

A CASE STUDY OF COMMUNITY AS AUDIENCE: BUSH RADIO[16]

Bush Radio has served the residents of several Cape Town area Black townships (as well as other Cape Town listeners) for more than a decade. Its history of challenging the *apartheid* government, then becoming the first independent Black-operated community radio station in South Africa, provided it with a reserve of good will, but that would not have lasted long if the station had not decided to implement a policy of serving as many groups within the township communities (and sometimes outside them) as it possibly could. How it managed to do so is close to being a textbook case of how an ethnic media service can identify, serve and involve its community.

To embrace as many in the community as possible, Bush Radio holds regular meetings with it. Most noncommercial electronic media services do so through an annual general meeting. Bush does so *monthly*, and at a variety of locations. Furthermore, it records the meetings, edits them to a more suitable length for broadcast (being careful at the same time to ensure that main issues and disagreements are included), and invites audience comment on them. It also informs the audience about specific actions it is (or soon will be) taking in response to some of the issues raised at the meetings, thus showing that discussion can bring change.

In addition to its provision of music (much of it by local artists) to suit the specific tastes of different groups of listeners, younger to older, the station also makes airtime available for groups that some in the broader community of the Black townships might not care to acknowledge: Prison Inmates and Gays/Lesbians. Cape Town has what is easily the most vibrant gay and lesbian population in South Africa, yet no radio station other than Bush Radio provides airtime for discussion of issues affecting that population or for its presentation of music mirroring its feelings and experiences, some of it performed by local artists. The station received some harsh criticism when it began to broadcast "In the Pink," but station manager Zane Ibrahim persevered because he felt that gays and lesbians very much wanted to be regarded as members of the broader community, and radio provided a means for them to introduce themselves to it.

The inmate program was a more complex issue. Since the preponderant share of the prison population in South Africa is Black, the station could assume that listeners in the black townships would appreciate hearing about life in prison, especially when related by individuals who might be known to some of them. The biggest problem was obtaining the agreement of the prison warden to allow prisoners to record their sentiments, which might contain anything from complaints about physical mistreatment to coded messages through which criminals could manage various forms of illicit business dealings. Eventually, the warden agreed to a limited-time experiment in which the prison administration could audition each edited program episode before it was aired, so that any suspicious material could be removed.

Once the broadcasts were underway, the administration soon began to observe that the prisoners who were taking part in the programs developed more positive outlooks and behaviors. "Suspicious material" turned out not to be a problem. The warden became a strong supporter of the broadcasts, and regretted it when Bush Radio had to discontinue them due to the departure of the staff member who supervised them. As of early 2004, the station was seeking to restore the prisoners' voices to the schedule, and a number of community members were urging it to do so.

The gay/lesbian and inmate programs illustrate the lengths to which Bush Radio is willing to go to include some "nonstandard" members of the community. Its ultimate aim in doing so is to bring the community as a whole to be more sensitive to and accepting of differences among its members. Much the same spirit motivates its efforts to include children of various ages in its lineup of program providers. Bush Radio also sees this as an excellent way to bring itself to the attention of two large and important groups of potential listeners and supporters: children and their parents.

Older children, ethnic minority and otherwise, can be very difficult to attract for any station that does not broadcast large amounts of popular music; younger children usually are not in the habit of thinking of radio as offering anything suitable for them. They may be more willing to listen if others like them are presenting programs, but many services are not willing to invite children as guest performers, much less allow them to plan and execute programs week after week. Bush Radio does: Its Saturday morning to early afternoon block of programming is produced entirely by children of various ages. It has won the station an increasing number of young listeners as well as their parents. Parents may be surprised, pleased or startled when hearing some of the topics (drugs, sex, and parental abuse) and viewpoints that emerge in the course of those broadcasts, but they often are amazed at the level of maturity exhibited by their offspring. From the station's viewpoint, this is one more instance of how its programming can contribute to building a stronger community through broadening the range of participation in this particular public sphere.

Finally, Bush Radio carries frequent announcements reminding listeners that this is their station, and that they should contact it by telephone, conventional mail, e-mail or through personal visits if they have complaints or suggestions to share, or even if they simply wish to see what the station looks like. When it goes on location for remote broadcasts, it distributes flyers containing similar announcements. Many stations do the same things. Bush does them more often, through more channels, and with more by way of specific examples that illustrate how it serves, responds to and includes many different sorts of listeners. If the station lacks anything along those lines, it would be sufficient information about the audience that survey research is particularly well suited to provide.

IDENTIFYING AND CONNECTING WITH THE AUDIENCE

Most media services have some idea of who they want to reach. The very act of setting goals should have made that quite clear, especially if those goals were developed with the active participation of community members. However, few noncommercial ethnic services appear to have gone beyond that level to consider how they might identify, assess and serve their target audiences more systematically, in light of such elements as size and composition of audience, program scheduling, forms of presentation, and appropriateness of the medium itself. Stated as questions, the elements might look like this:

- Who does the media service want to reach, and does it reach them? How many?
- Why does it want to reach those particular groups?
- When (times; days) are those groups most accessible where a given medium is concerned?
- What forms of presentation are likely to appeal to/involve them most readily?
- How long are those presentations likely to hold their attention, and does that vary from one medium or presentational form to another?

The first question arises because audiences are fractionated; "general appeal" programs are rarer and rarer. Not all goals will have universal appeal and those that do (or seem to) will appeal to specific audiences in specific respects. An audience survey with items on gender, age group, occupation, level of education, and for ethnic commercial services, perhaps income (by range)—in short, demographics—will be helpful, and not all that expensive to administer. Many ethnic media services have been able to enlist the cooperation of instructors and students at neighboring colleges and vocational schools in carrying out such surveys.

The second question may not be necessary if the media service has already sought to determine which goals are linked most clearly with which audience groups; that is, who does the service most need to reach if a given goal is to be achieved? Often, however, that linkage has not been determined. It is possible to do so through the relatively simple step of listing goals (and explaining them if there are any doubts that they will be understood) and then asking respondents to rank order them in terms of relative importance *to the respondent*. If that is done in conjunction with the demographic survey, it should be possible to learn which groups favor which goals.

The third question takes into account what is already known about audience behavior: There is a great deal of variety in how people spend their time hour by hour and day by day. It is not safe to assume that, because one 60+ male with a high school education follows a given pattern of behavior, all 60+ males with that level of education will do so. However, a survey question can ask respondents to indicate the periods of the day and days of the week when they usually find themselves listening to the radio, watching TV, or surfing the internet. Those responses generally will show which periods of which days mesh with the media usage schedules of the greatest numbers of such males. Such a question also fits nicely within the demographic survey, and should help the media service to schedule its offerings so that they stand the best chance of being readily accessible to their particular target audiences.

The fourth question addresses audience receptivity to various program formats. Again, what is known about audience behavior indicates that people differ not just in terms of when they listen, view or surf, but also when they are more likely to do so for certain kinds of content and in which specific formats. It is possible to develop survey items that assess receptivity. However, it may be better to gather small groups of people (focus groups) to discuss the types of program content they particularly enjoy, and which program formats they find most suitable for conveying that content. This should provide the media service with a richer picture of audience preferences than a survey would be likely to yield.

The fifth question reflects another "given": that people differ in their attention spans. It probably is the most difficult of the five questions to answer, but can be particularly helpful when a service seeks to inform its audience(s) about a specific topic. For example, if a service were to pursue the goal of community member self-improvement, one aspect might be (and often is) limiting family size. When media services have addressed that aspect, as many have, most of them have discovered that lengthy talks about it are ineffective. However, presentation of the aspect through brief ad-like messages (especially in the form of mini-dramas) and brief fictional scenes (especially within soap operas) seems to work very well.[17] The best way to determine attention span is to present several groups of roughly similar individuals with the same basic message in different formats and at differing lengths, but such research is time-consuming, relatively complex to analyze, and quite expensive. If there is a department of sociology, psychology, journalism, or communication studies at a nearby college or university, it might be possible to enlist its aid in such a project.

On the whole, ethnic minority media services have considerable information about their audiences, but most of it is impressionistic and anecdotal. It comes largely from the sources noted earlier in this chapter: conversations between media staff and family members, friends and acquaintances; telephone calls, letters, and e-mails sent by listeners, viewers, and readers; comments made about the services through other media, for example, local ethnic and mainstream newspapers; comments made by attendees at public meetings held by the services. All of those sources can be useful, but they are likely to underrepresent and overrepresent certain groups within the community, and may completely miss others. More importantly, the services are unlikely to learn much about the range and depth of community reaction to what they are attempting to accomplish by way of community involvement.

The usual audience research methods used by electronic media services— random or stratified sample surveys, audience diaries,[18] focus groups—are less common in the case of ethnic minority services.[19] Relatively few of the ethnic services are commercial, and for those that are, only the large national services such as BET, Univision, and Telemundo are likely to be identified in random sample surveys conducted by research firms such as A.C. Nielsen.[20] Those PBS operations with ethnic minority services often conduct occasional, and sometimes more regular surveys on behalf of those services, as well. Local ethnic minority commercial services can be measured through surveys, but the audience sampling techniques used by the research firms conducting such surveys, such as Arbitron (United States), often fail to identify and contact some of the larger groups of audience members for those services, and especially those that lack telephones or stable mailing addresses. Also, local radio and TV stations usually must pay the firm to be included in their surveys and to receive reports of the data they yield; unless an ethnic station is quite serious about selling air time to advertisers, those costs are not likely to seem worthwhile.

Most of the standard sample-based surveys reveal only how many of what sorts of people (age group, gender) listen to, watch or read one or another of the specific offerings (programs, Web pages) of electronic media services. Those data may be helpful in indicating who seems to be attracted to what, and therefore, whether a given program or Web page[21] is reaching the audience the services hope to reach through it. If a survey also includes an appreciation index,[22] which allows audience members to indicate their relative fondness for a given program or page "used" by them, a media service can begin to discover something about the popularity of some of its material, but not all of it: Audience members usually do not apply the index to programs or pages they seldom or never use, and most surveys are not set up to indicate why people do not use them. (It could be ignorance of their existence, misinformation about their nature, difficulty in understanding them, and/or still other reasons.) In short, most of the usual surveys are of limited value to many of the ethnic minority services.

Ethnic minority services may undertake their own surveys, and a few have done so. However, if a particular ethnic group broadcasts over a community radio or TV station for a limited number of hours each week and does so as volunteers, it is unlikely that group members will have the time, money or inclination to develop and administer a survey. Also, the small size of many ethnic communities may render a survey unnecessary. The individuals producing the program(s) probably are acquainted with many of the actual and potential audience members, and could arrange focus group meetings with some of them.

Focus groups are relatively easy to convene, at least for local services. Ethnic minority communities generally seem to enjoy being consulted about a service that is "theirs," at least in principle. If the topics set for discussion are carefully delimited, and if the group conveners develop the questions to which they seek answers but then are prepared to be flexible in how they are asked, there should be an abundance of useful data at the end of each session. The trick is to take careful notes throughout the discussion, tape record the proceedings, and then be prepared to review the notes and tapes as soon as possible, while memories are fresh. Usually it will be necessary to conduct three or four focus group sessions per topic, and with different participants, before deciding whether changes in, for example, program content, scheduling are required. Whether there are changes or not, letting the community know what the service has learned from the groups should encourage people to think of that form of participation as worthwhile.

CONDUCTING RESEARCH

When I have spoken with many ethnic minority media service staff about their detailed knowledge of the audience, they mention various forms of personal contact with community members. When I have asked whether they have employed survey or focus group research to those same ends, I often have received blank stares or troubled expressions, followed by declarations of hope that someday they could afford to conduct the sorts of survey- or focus group-based studies that would help them to answer some of the questions I posed earlier in this chapter. When I have asked why they feel they have to wait, the usual response is that "None of us understands how to conduct them" or "They cost far too much for our budget" or "Our audience might think of such research as too impersonal or intrusive" or "We don't have any models to guide us in conducting such research on an ethnic minority audience."

It is quite true that there are relatively few research-based studies of ethnic minority audiences for ethnic minority electronic media.[23] Furthermore, those that do exist do not always inspire confidence because they do not appear to take into account the special ethnic characteristics of such audiences[24] or because they are executed using questionable data-gathering techniques, such as telephone surveys in communities where many households lack phones. However, it is possible to create ethnic audience-sensitive studies. I have seen inexperienced (in terms of developing such studies) media staff do so, and at very low cost. Usually there has been some outside assistance of the sort I mentioned earlier: Teachers and students from a nearby college or technical institute. But most of the work has been done by the media staff themselves.

The keys to success appear to be the following.

- Have a very clear idea of what is to be discovered and why.
- Keep the survey or focus group session short, especially if it is the first one the service has attempted, but do not terminate discussion *too* abruptly.
- Restrict the survey or focus group to one or two important issues.
- Phrase the questions as concisely as possible and in user-friendly terms.
- Pretest the survey or focus group on a small number of individuals in the community by having them answer the questions, and then asking them where they encountered any difficulties in understanding how each question was worded, whether they felt at all offended or disturbed by any of the questions, or whether they felt at any time that they could see what the media service wanted to discover but would have expressed the question(s) in a different way.
- After the survey or focus group approach has been revised, let the community know in advance that it will be conducted soon, and that the results will be shared as soon as they become available, as well as indicating what the service expects to do with the results. If it is a random or stratified sample survey, and certainly if there are focus groups, explain why many members of the community will not have the opportunity to participate.

A CASE STUDY: CONDUCTING SURVEYS AT TUMEKE-FM[25]

Maori radio station Tumeke-FM, serving the city of Whakatane and its surrounding area, had been on air for roughly two years before it conducted its first audience survey in 1991. It was already quite well known and very popular, in part because it had an "open-door" policy, and regularly encouraged Maori and *pakeha* (New Zealanders of European origin) alike to drop in and visit the station. Dinny Jaram, its manager and a former teacher, had a general idea of what surveys were, and saw them as particularly useful in the station's continuing development now that some of its growing pains were behind it.

There was some skepticism among the staff that it would be possible to design and conduct a survey, but Dinny Jaram was convinced that it could be done if the staff could agree that it was worth doing. Once they did agree, she had them identify what they most wanted to know. Not surprisingly, the two most common questions were "How many listeners do we have?" and "What do they and don't they like about our programs?" Those became the main points of inquiry for the survey. They also served as stimulus to get station staff to contribute their own suggestions as to what form the questions should take, and to contribute their own labor to processing the replies when they came in.

Dinny Jaram also had procured the assistance of an instructor at a nearby technical institute who had had a bit of experience in designing surveys. He worked with station staff in developing questions that would be direct, simple and specific. Most could be stated in a sentence, but one was not quite so simple: "What do and don't you like about the station's programming?" His first impulse was to recommend that the staff think of as many possible negative and positive responses as they could; that list would be refined by combining responses that featured considerable overlap, and then the responses would be listed under the appropriate column headings. Respondents could place check marks beside any response that they agreed with, and the results tallied.

When the staff discussed that approach, they began to realize that it would entail a considerable amount of work, but might not yield as rich a harvest of data as they would wish. They foresaw two problems: There would be no way to determine how strongly a respondent felt about each response that she or he checked, and thus no sound basis for deciding which problems most needed attention; and the fact that the staff had developed the list of possible responses would keep the community itself from participating in an important act of self-expression.

Since Tumeke-FM had earned its popularity at least in part on the basis of its close links with the community, some of the staff wondered whether it might be better to present the question in such a way that respondents could express their reactions in their own terms. The instructor pointed out that the staff would have even more work to do simply because many people probably would say similar things but in different ways, and that the staff would have to determine which responses went with each other (clustering). He could guide them through that process, and assuming that they understood just how much extra effort would be involved, the approach should help to reinforce the idea that station and community truly were partners.

That approach was tested with a focus group of community residents, whose members indicated that it would be helpful if the survey presented few examples of positive and negative reactions to programming, just to get respondents in a mindset to come up with their own reactions. The revised survey was conducted, largely face-to-face but with some use of the telephone, and in general showed strong community support and approval, with relatively few negative reactions and many positive ones for the item "What do/don't you like about the programming?" It was a good morale-booster for the station, and it did seem to strengthen the already solid ties between station and community. In fact, some of the staff with whom I spoke in October 1993 stated that it was proving quite easy to win back the station's "lost" audience after the disastrous change of program format in 1992 (see footnote 25), because so many of its members had such positive memories of what they regarded as their station, and were happy to see it return.

Tumeke-FM's experience with survey research displays most of the keys to success presented earlier, but also underlines the importance of bringing the community into the process of conducting a survey. For better or for worse, survey research is likely to be thought of as something that applies to the mainstream culture but has little relevance for ethnic minority groups. In fact, the past decade has seen more surveys of ethnic minority opinion, but few that elicit opinions about the electronic media, and very few that have anything to do with ethnic minority media, aside from "pure" demographics.[26] Anything that helps an ethnic minority community to realize that surveys can be directly relevant to them should be welcome, and getting community members involved in developing the survey itself (as Tumeke-FM did) should help to overcome the feeling that surveys are for mainstream audiences only.

MEDIA SERVICE AS COMMUNITY

There is yet another respect in which the concept of community is important in assessing the nature and effects of ethnic minority electronic media: the degree to which a media service itself possesses the qualities of a community. As I prepared to write this book, I thought about the many services I had visited and about what it was that made them effective or ineffective as entry points to the public sphere. Several factors seemed to have some bearing on the relative quality of each service, and I summarize them in the final chapter. However, one is worth raising here, because it is a less immediately obvious dimension of community.

Many of the services came about because the larger community wanted them and often made sacrifices in money, time and/or effort to create them. Most of that community did not wish to become involved in the day-to-day operation of a service. Those members who did had varying motives for doing so. Although in certain instances the motives involved financial gain, personal prestige or the hope (perhaps expectation) that their labors would lead to a better position, most of those with whom I have spoken seemed to be involved because they truly believed that they could assist their communities in important ways. They often have sought to recruit like-minded individuals to join them in realizing that goal. For example, Raidio na Gaeltachta (RNG) was created largely by teachers who were concerned that everyday use of the Irish language was dying out, and some of those teachers formed the administrative core of the station (RNG, 1991, 1993, 1994).

No one who has worked for a small business or service with modest resources needs to be told that this requires considerable devotion, teamwork and a fair amount of personal sacrifice. Operating a media service may demand even more of those qualities because of its unrelenting schedule, relative complexity (if something can go wrong, it will, and there are many things that can go wrong), and exposure to public criticism. If those chiefly responsible for holding to the goals set for the service—the administrators, of course, but advisory or supervisory board members and key program producers and performers, as well—can maintain a sense of community within that service, realization of those goals seems much more likely.

The more successful services that I have visited have several features in common, noted here.

Openness

Although a single individual or small group ultimately must be responsible for decisions, it helps greatly if the broader community of service staff (volunteers included) feel that their suggestions and complaints will be listened to and at least occasionally acted on. When they are, acknowledgment of their source will help to strengthen a sense of community. (Rewards of various sorts also can help.) Bush Radio in Cape Town has developed a number of ways to foster that atmosphere, including a suggestion box, bulletin board, regular and all-inclusive staff meetings, and a Web site with a specific category for displaying staff achievements (personal interviews with Bush Radio staff, September 2002).

Multiple Channels of Communication.

Meetings can assist in maintaining a consultative atmosphere, but they are not sufficient in and of themselves. Administrators who get out of their offices to talk informally with other service staff and to produce programs themselves are likely to learn considerably more about how people feel, what they would like to accomplish and how service performance could be improved than will emerge from a meeting. Put another way, formal and informal channels of communication are necessary if individuals are to sense that they are important to the success of the service.

Periodic Reviews of Performance

Performance reviews involve considerable effort and can invoke considerable anxiety. Four things seem to have helped those ethnic services that use them in minimizing both the effort and the anxiety: Everyone is reviewed; the reviews themselves are informal, the results are shared with all staff, and the emphasis is on what individuals are doing well. That helps to reinforce the message that everyone is in this together and that there are many specific examples of ways in which staff members contribute to the service. When negative actions first appear, they are dealt with on a personal basis, unless they have directly affected the performance of others.

As one example of performance review, Maori radio station Te Reo Iriraki ki Otautahi (Christchurch) held weekly staff meetings at which a range of subjects could emerge, but there always was a review of the past week. If something had gone wrong, the staff discussed it, and those who were in part or wholly responsible (including the manager) were expected to apologize to their colleagues and, where appropriate, to state how they would see to it that it did not reoccur.[27] That helped to underscore the need to maintain a sense of mutual responsibility.

Celebrating Community

Individual reviews, commendations and rewards are valuable elements in developing and maintaining community spirit within a service, but recognition of the *collective* effort can be important, as well. Staff picnics and dinners—6EA (an ethnic radio station) in Perth, Western Australia and Awaz FM (access radio for South Asians) in Glasgow, Scotland have featured the latter—are one way of accomplishing this.[28] Service Web site displays in which staff members are identified and described (preferably by themselves) can convey the message that it takes a host of different talents to keep the enterprise going, and that all of those contributions are valued.

In none of the specific examples that I have provided did I have the sense that they were implemented after careful deliberation. Most appeared to have arisen more or less spontaneously. Staff members wanted to establish and maintain good working relationships and either borrowed from previous experience or went with their instincts. If some of the ethnic services that I have visited do not display much sense of community, it may be because staff members often have quite different reasons for wanting to be involved. I already have mentioned the genuine desire to serve the community, as well as financial gain, personal prestige and long-term career plans. But there are other motivations, and some of them are not particularly commendable, such as attacking one's enemies (individuals or other groups).[29]

With large numbers of volunteers at many of the ethnic services, it is not surprising that some of them have little interest in working as part of the service community: They come in just before their time slots, present their programs, and leave soon after. Javed Sattar, who administers Awaz FM, told me in an April 2003 interview that perhaps one third of the staff (volunteers included) seemed to have a sense of the station as a community, and devoted time and effort to maintaining that spirit.[30] I have heard much lower estimates at other services, and there seems to be general agreement that administrators are not likely to win the participation of a fair share of the staff no matter how much emphasis is placed on the concept of station as community. There is general agreement that the effort is worthwhile, but it can be difficult to sustain, especially if it is perceived as coming from the top down.

SUMMARY

The relationship between audience/community and media service is particularly important where ethnic minorities are concerned, so it is not surprising that most of those services devote considerable attention to establishing and maintaining links with their communities, or that community members seek to involve themselves with the services. What those services actually know about their communities may be another matter: Many of the specific forms of linkage between service and community tend to favor those who really want to become involved. There are other channels through which the habitually uninvolved audience can be reached, random sample surveys among them, but few of the ethnic media services have utilized them. And if that audience were reached, to what extent should or might a media service heed what it said? I have the impression that some media staff with whom I have spoken, when they mention "community" or "audience," mean those who have become directly involved with the service, whether on their own, at the invitation of the service, or both. If there is a strong mutual bond between the *involved* audience/community and the media service, can the *uninvolved* audience/community expect to have much influence on the nature and extent of programming that might serve its needs?

There is another unanswered question where media/community relationships are concerned: how does an ethnic media service reach out to a new community/audience—one that it has not sought to reach either because it had not considered a group to be part of its target audience—for example, deciding after a year or two of operation to establish a program block for the elderly—or because the group had become significant in numerical terms only recently, as with Somalis coming to Minnesota in the early 1990s or Albanians to Ireland in the mid-1990s?

Drawing once again on my personal observations of ethnic services, it seems apparent that how a media service gets to know a community/audience is to some extent culturally influenced: Some cultures seem more determined than others to take the initiative, volunteer, and participate when faced with a new prospect for involvement. It may be that, in certain cultures or groups, there has been very little (and in some cases, NO) opportunity for involvement. Others in the group may hold more power and may discourage involvement, or there may be a cultural bias against taking initiative, or past attempts to do so may have been negated by the failure of others to live up to their promises.[31] It may seem to require the skills of a seasoned diplomat when attempting to involve a new group, beginning with the need to exercise patience as members of the group assess the merit and authenticity of an offer to undertake something that may be totally new to them.

There is no magic formula for success, but in those cases where groups have agreed to participate, it usually has been because someone in a position of authority at the service made the group feel welcome, valued, and *not* under pressure to decide quickly whether to join in, lest the offer disappear. It took community radio station 5PBS in Salisbury (a suburb of Adelaide, South Australia) the better part of 2 years to induce young Vietnamese women from a local high school to do so, and close to that for a community radio station in Launceston, Tasmania (7LTN, 1996) to achieve like success with a group of Philippine women who were being abused by their husbands and wanted to share their experiences with others who might profit from what they had to say.[32] In both instances, the station staff also felt that the broader community they already served would benefit from the presence of those new voices. In other words, those new contributions were deemed important to the diversity of the program—the topic of the next chapter.

NOTES

1. Which is not to say that they do not carry advertising or sponsor messages. In fact, many of them do so, but the service itself operates as a nonprofit enterprise, and revenue thus generated is put directly into service operations.

2. However, staff at SKC-TV, the LPTV station on the Salish-Kootenai Indian Reservation in Pablo, Montana told me in August 1994 that they did provide "two-sided" coverage of stories involving tensions between Native Americans and Whites living on the reservation. WOBJ-FM (Hayward, Wisconsin), the Lac Court Oreilles band of Anishinabe, broadcast discussions between Native Americans and Whites over the sensitive issue of the band's treaty rights to spear fish in some of the area lakes, especially when tensions rose to the level of physical violence in 1992. In a visit to the station (July 1994), staff members noted that the discussions were credited with having a calming effect. Keller (1993: 12) corroborates that observation.

3. The staff at the Salish-Kootenai LPTV station also told me (personal visit, 1994) that they rarely bothered to provide explanations of the various events that occurred in the course of a tribal pow-wow when one was broadcast. They reasoned that their primary audience (tribal members) would not need them, and might feel insulted that the station supplied them, whereas their secondary audience (Whites living on or near the reservation) should come to the pow-wows and ask participants what was occurring, assuming that they really wanted to know.

4. There are circumstances where the ethnic media have little choice but to support certain individuals. If an ethnic minority station is under the direct control of a tribal government, as is the case with many of the Native American radio stations in the United States, it will be very difficult for the station to refuse airtime to tribal

leaders and their allies, or to make it available to those who are seen as opposing the leaders.

5. This was particularly evident in the case of some of the Australian community radio stations that carried programs for the Greek community. Some of the programs had been produced by the same individual for the past few decades, and audience response had dropped off markedly. As the program director at Ballarat Community Radio told me in a visit to the station in October 1993, the target audience—older Greeks—literally was dieing out.

6. Personal interviews with Ross Watson, Manager, 4AAA, Brisbane, October 1993 and Taura Eruera, Manager, Mai-FM, Auckland, New Zealand, October 1993.

7. A young Maori announcer at Southland Community Radio in Invercargill, New Zealand told me (October 1993) that his grandmother wondered why he would want to work at a station that provided programs that served Maori in general, and not just his own tribe. She reminded him that "some of those other tribes are our enemies." He replied that this was exactly the sentiment that he hoped to put to rest.

8. Vargas (1995) offers another excellent study where the problems attendant on goal setting receive major attention. Her focus is on indigenous radio in Mexico, and she presents and discusses at some length the problems encountered by the stations in meeting one of their primary goals: relating to, and possibly empowering, their audiences. The problems generally stemmed from lack of respect shown to indigenous staff by their (generally) Hispanic supervisors.

9. A controversial act in itself: One of the two groups favored *not* applying to the CRTC on the grounds that the agency lacked authority over tribal land; the other agreed with that assertion, but thought it too dangerous to remain unlicensed, since the CRTC was threatening to license a commercial station that would be officially authorized to use the frequency that the tribal station (CFNC—changed to CKRZ when the license was issued because another station already had the call letters CFNC) was using (Fairchild, 2001: 193-194). Barnsley (1997) argues on the basis of a specific experience that the CRTC is not favorably disposed toward Native American radio.

10. Georgiou (2002). Available in English and as a more detailed treatment at www.lse.as.uk/EMTEL under "publications."

11. Community in the broadest sense—from neighborhood to national and even international (if the opportunity exists at that level).

12 There already had been at least one African-American unlicensed radio service before Kantako established WTRA. "Black Rose" had set up Zoom Black Magic Radio in Fresno, California in 1985 (Black Rose, n.d.; see also Elizade, 1996; Soley, 1999: 66-67). According to Albert-Honore, Kantako had affiliated with Black Rose's station for several months in the late 1980s, but then broke off the affiliation "due to ideological differences," and renamed WTRA as Black Liberation Radio (Albert-Honore, in Berry & Manning-Miller, 1996: 211). There have been a number of similar services in more recent years, in Decatur, Illinois; Durham; North Carolina; Tampa, Florida; and San Francisco (Bayview/Hunters Point), California ("Mbanna," 2002).

13. The initials TRA stood for the Tenants Rights Association, a group founded by Kantako in the mid-1980s. It already had enjoyed some success in calling attention to use of excessive force by police and in mobilizing the residents of the John Hay Homes housing project to improve their living conditions.

14. Sakolsky indicates that the Springfield chief of police contacted the FCC to complain about the series.
15. Ismond (1995) summarizes the interviews he conducted with the managers of AsiaVision (later, AsiaNet), a TV service for South Asians living in the United Kingdom. His overall impression was that financial viability and profit were the primary concerns, and that programs about, much less by, South Asians and their experiences in the United Kingdom was a very minor concern. The service primarily carried imported entertainment programming, as did the African-Caribbean IDTV ("Identity TV") cable service (Ismond, 1995). This led Ismond to observe (1995: 203) that "It would seem that commercial forces are molding the content of IDTV away from its narrowcasting potential" and that (1995: 202) ethnic minority media personnel were "invariably 'co-opted and contained' by the dominant [media] value system: one in which it is difficult to redefine ethnic minority agendas." A fuller account of Ismond's research appears in Ismond (1994).
16. I have relied primarily on my personal visits to Bush Radio in September, 2002 and particularly to the assistance of its Program Director, Adrian Loew as well as his colleagues in preparing this case study. The Bush Radio Web site (www.bushradio.co.za) also has been most helpful. Gumicio-Dagron (2001: 211-216) provides useful information on the station, as well. A doctoral dissertation (Bosch, 2003) that I have not yet read also should prove helpful.
17. Singhal and Rogers (2003, 2004) offer numerous case studies and other examples of the uses of "entertainment-education" through soap operas and other forms of media entertainment in dealing with AIDS and family planning.
18. Usually indicating specific programs or web pages accessed within the course of 1 or 2 weeks. Diaries are relatively little-used at present, perhaps because people often find them a nuisance to keep.
19. They are somewhat more common in the case of the larger émigré populations such as the Turks in Germany and The Netherlands and North African Arabs in France, but the surveys and focus groups tend to concentrate on viewing habits for satellite television, even where local minority-operated radio and TV services are available. (Such services usually will not be available through satellite transmissions.)
20. They certainly are identified in Nielsen's separate surveys of African-American and Hispanic-American audiences, but those surveys are for television viewing only; there are no recurring national surveys of those specific audiences where radio is concerned, by Nielsen or anyone else.
21. Ethnic minority groups operating Web sites may find it relatively easy to conduct surveys online, although it does require some sophistication to set them up in a way that makes it easy to process responses.
22. European audience surveys quite often feature such an index; U.S. audience surveys almost never do.
23. And far fewer that utilize focus groups. Ethnic minority communities, and smaller communities in particular, may be especially sensitive to who is selected and why. YLE (Finnish Broadcasting Corporation) researcher Erja Ruohuoma (personal interview, Helsinki, September 1994); and Leirsinn Research Centre (Gaelic language usage) researcher Catherine MacNeil (personal interview, Inverness 2003) both mentioned this, although they did not regard it as an insuperable barrier, so long as one attempted to assemble a reasonably representative group.

24. For example, my interview (1994) with Ruohuoma revealed that a group of researchers carrying out a survey of radio listening among Sami ("Lapps") in northern Finland had not been alerted to consider proper forms of address in Sami, or the appropriateness of certain types of questions where older Sami were concerned. Both concerns, she agreed, were important.

25. This case study is based on my personal observations (Whakatane, New Zealand, September 1991) of Tumeke-FM staff at work on the survey, as well as on discussions with the station manager, Dinny Jaram. I returned to the station in October 1993 for discussions with the station staff and with Dinny Jaram, who by that time was no longer the station manager. She had been replaced by a manager who was hired by the tribal council because he had all but promised the council that the station could be profitable if its format emphasized popular music. Instead, the station lost many of its listeners (as well as a fair amount of money), the new manager was asked to resign, and the staff recreated most of the original format and the "open door" approach that had been so attractive to the community in the first place.

26. The leading U.S. survey research organization for television, A.C. Nielsen, has conducted ongoing surveys of Hispanic-American and of African-American viewership for the past several years, but the data collected are limited to numbers of viewers per program, including demographics (gender and age group).

27. Personal visits to Te Reo Iriraki ki Otautahi, November 1993 and April 1996.

28. Personal interviews with Paul Pearman, Manager, 6EA, March 2001 and with Javed Sattar, Director, Awaz FM, April 2003.

29. Access radio and TV services such as the *närradio* stations in Scandinavia, the *Offener Kanale* in Germany, the access radio stations in the United Kingdom, and the access TV channels attached to cable companies in the United States.and Canada, are particularly vulnerable here, since, if one "side" gets a program slot, other sides will want airtime to respond, and an access service is supposed to be even-handed. Kurdish groups and groups from the former Yugoslavia have been mentioned often as "problems" in my conversations with service administrators, because their programs sometimes feature mutually damning accusations. A few services, for example, 3ZZZ (a largely ethnic radio station in Melbourne), have required such groups to share a time slot and to refrain from mutual attacks as conditions of being on air (personal visit, 3ZZZ, March 2001).

30. Some administrators (particularly in Western nations) have told me that certain ethnic groups seem more inclined to accept the "community" concept than are others, with Asian groups often singled out as less inclined: They came in, broadcast their programs, and left immediately after. Those administrators also were careful to indicate that such behavior was not restricted to Asian groups.

31. Golding (1974: 39-51) provides an interesting consideration of why people may be wary when others from outside come to them with offers of the great benefits to be had from participation in a new venture. Often, it is the feeling that the outsiders understand little of the community, but are quite ready to propose solutions that community members may regard as risky or flawed, based on past experience with outsiders promising quick and/or certain solutions.

32 Personal interviews with Denise Guest, Manager, 5 PBS, Salisbury, March 2001, and with Tim Walker, Manager, 7LTN, Launceston, March 1996.

Programming

Everything that we have considered up to this point has a direct bearing on what we hear, see and read by way of ethnic minority electronic media output. The historical development, policymaking, financing, "watchdog" and pressure group activity, goal setting, links with the audience/community, all come together in determining the nature, amounts, and types of material produced, as well as the extent of its distribution to ethnic minority and mainstream audiences. As I already have noted, the internet is something of an exception here, because it remains largely unregulated, albeit with what appears to be increasing pressure to bring it under greater control in many societies. However, financing certainly is of some concern to ethnic minorities attempting to present themselves on the Web, and ethnic minority Web sites come and go at least as rapidly as do their mainstream counterparts.

Although ethnic minority electronic media services differ in many respects, most of them have one thing in common. They seek to both *entertain* and *inform*. (Some may educate,[1] as well, but that is quite rare.) Even the chief exception to the rule—ethnic minority internet Web sites—is not a total exception: Whereas most of the sites concentrate on informing their users, a number of them also offer some entertainment, and ethnic minority Web-streamed radio is not alone in doing so.

Whether audience members necessarily agree with a service's judgment of what constitutes entertainment or information is another matter, particularly where popular music is concerned: Rap (hip-hop), heavy metal, and many other genres often feature messages of protest, challenge, and dissent. However, because audience members make their own judgments about the nature of such content, I have chosen to follow the distinctions generally established by the media services themselves, while pointing out specific instances of ambiguity.

I begin by defining the genres associated with electronic media presentation and considering some of the ways in which the ethnic minority media present material through them (content, scheduling, style).

GENRES: INFORMATION

An electronic media service really cannot avoid informing its listeners, viewers, and readers, even when playing the most inane music, presenting the most stupid jokes, or reporting on events in ways that make little sense. First, not everyone will agree that the music is inane, the jokes stupid, or the reports incomprehensible. Second, those who feel that they *are* inane, stupid, and/or incomprehensible will have informed their own judgments by reinforcing them. What is more, the information-conveying function of popular songs, soap operas, and many more genres of entertainment is evident, especially in family-planning and community development projects around the world. Still, media staff and media audiences seem to agree that the genres presented in this section are those that most readily come to mind when considering the media as providers of information.

Newscasts

As I observed earlier, it came as something of a surprise to me that few of the ethnic minority electronic media services operating at the local level that I have visited in person or through the Web[2] offered anything resembling a service-originated newscast.[3] The picture is different at the national and state/provincial levels, where original newscasts are far more common. Those levels include ethnic minority services that are part of a national PSB operation, such as the Norwegian NRK's Sami Service, the German WDR's Funkhaus Europa, or the BBC's Asian Service; nationally distributed ethnic services such as Mana Maori Media (New Zealand), National Native News (United States), and the SBS (Australia) a number of which are supported in part through government funding, and may operate in cooperation with local ethnic media services (SBS does not); and national commercial ethnic media services such as the U.S. Univision and BET. There are increasing numbers of exclusively online news services, as well, such as the Catalan service Vilaweb (Lopez, 2002: 37-61).

Typically, those news programs present a mix of world, national, and local news, much as do their mainstream counterparts. The chief difference is in the attempt to regularly include items featuring the activities of relevant ethnic groups: primarily one's own group members, but sometimes members of related groups such as other Polynesian peoples in the case of Maori national news broadcasts. If stories about one's group members are receiving prominence in the mainstream media, there are almost certain to be comparable stories on the ethnic service, but with emphasis on material that provides ethnic group context for what has occurred, which mainstream media rarely include. Some of the stories will be reported by service staff; others come from mainstream and ethnic wire, voice and video services, if the group is large enough to have them.

A few of the community radio services do offer self-originated newscasts. Bush Radio, for example, has a 5-minute per day newscast, with roughly half of the items produced by its own staff. But most community stations and access services do not provide anything of the sort, even though many of their managers express the wish to do so. Thus, there is little daily coverage of ethnic experiences and activities that is available to most ethnic minority community radio or TV audiences.

Why are newscasts generally absent from the local ethnic programming lineup? Cost certainly is a factor, as is the scarcity of trained ethnic minority reporters and editors. Even though ethnic minority electronic media services often are willing to accept (and may encourage) something other than "mainstream professional" production standards, newscasts seem to be the one format where those standards *are* applied, and most volunteers do not measure up. Perhaps the media service administrators feel that the news will be judged as less credible if it is not "professionally" produced; perhaps they fear that less than "professionally" produced newscasts will have a negative impact on audience perceptions of the service as a serious venture. (*"Anyone* can produce entertainment, but news should be left to professionals".)

Administrators also told me that there is a perception among volunteers that it is personally risky to report the news because ethnic minority communities often are sensitive about their images, and in particular may resent an "insider" disclosing things about the community and through a public medium that could reflect negatively on it. Some ethnic journalists also have told me that there can be heavy pressure from ethnic community power brokers to "take the right side" on issues. As one example, the director of BBC Radio Orkney described the station's attempts to establish a cadre of volunteer reporters on some of Orkney's dozen or so inhabited islands because the five-person BBC staff could not begin to cover them all on a regular basis. However, it has proven difficult to identify qualified and willing candidates because any reporting that might be perceived as negative could easily be traced to a few individuals, and they in turn would risk ostracization within their own individual island communities.[4]

Commentary/Analysis/Editorials/Satire

These formats, all connected to varying degrees with the expression of opinion, are relative rarities on ethnic minority radio and TV, but quite common on ethnic minority Web sites. The Black Britain Web site (www.blackbritain.co.uk) frequently offers commentaries by members of its staff, many which deal with the portrayal by mainstream media of Blacks living in the United Kingdom. The Web site also solicits reader feedback on the commentaries; individuals sometimes deliver their views on community affairs through access and community radio services, as well.

As for satire, certainly not all of it is informational, but the few examples I have encountered in ethnic media seem to be. Two Maori reporter-editors for Mana Maori Media developed a 2- to 3-minute routine in the form of a "Letter to Momma" ("Reta Ki a Mama"), with each letter commenting on recent news developments involving or affecting Maori. Leading figures, including New Zealand Prime Minister Jim Bolger, received nicknames that highlighted various personal features. Bolger was called "potato" because he had been a potato farmer before going into politics, but also because of the implication that a potato (head) probably was not very bright or thoughtful. The letters appeared during a 2-year period (1991-1993) and seemed popular, but their authors found the effort of coming up with fresh humor quite tiring after a while, and finally dropped the routine.[5]

A Native American Web site, Indianz.com (www.indianz.com, affiliated with the National Congress of American Indians) sometimes includes political satire under its "Humor" category. For example, its April 1,[6] 2002 offering featured a column by "Tom Wannabetterjob" in which the "report" dealt with the (fictive) "arrest and jailing" of Bush administration Secretary of the Interior Gale Norton and her assistant for mishandling the Indian Trust Fund—an allegation that actually had been made in some news media reports.

An African-American woman, damali ayo, created (2003) a satiric Web site in part as a result of being in all-White settings where she faced a range of questions that showed an almost total lack of understanding of her ethnicity. The site (www.rent-a-negro.com) provides a list of services available, for example, bringing a "Negro" to a lawn party, and sets prices for various options such as touching the hair. Renters are offered a Certificate of Association ("An 8x10 certificate stating your affiliation with a Black person") for an additional $100. The service "comes without the commitment of learning about racism, challenging your own white privilege, or being labeled 'radical' and fits a host of social and workplace situations ("My friends would think I was so cool if we *just happened* to run into a Black friend of mine while we were shopping or eating lunch at our favorite restaurant!"). Ayo estimates that roughly one third of the inquiries appear to be serious, but she hopes that her Web site will help to sensitize at least some of its users (Parker, 2003).

Because many ethnic minority electronic media services do not have their own newsrooms, it is not surprising that they do not provide their own commentaries, editorials, or analysis either. (Invited commentaries do appear on some services.) Furthermore, if ethnic minority media staff really are concerned about possible repercussions because of their reportorial activity, the expression of opinion would seem to be an even riskier proposition.

In addition to newscasts, commentaries, and other more or less traditional forms of information in the media, there are several other informational formats that occur with some regularity through ethnic media services. Some service administrators told me that they regard those formats as perhaps even more valuable than are newscasts in terms of informing their target audiences/communities because they are less formal, more discursive, and thus more in tune with the practices of listeners, viewers, and readers. Often, they are more open to direct and immediate community input, whether through telephone or from a live audience, as well.

Discussions/Interviews/"Talk"

These are perhaps the most common informational formats available through ethnic minority media. They are relatively easy to produce, provided that there's a ready supply of willing participants, and they lend themselves to being informal, offering plenty of time for reflection on a topic, and providing opportunity for audience participation. If an ethnic community has not been accustomed to voicing its opinions over the airwaves, the willing participants may be few in number at first. Provided that the media service treats them with respect (usually the case with ethnic minority services, as I have indicated in Browne, 2002: 170-173) and is active in seeking out individuals who appear to be qualified to talk about specific subjects, it usually will enjoy a fair measure of success.

Interviews are particularly frequent on community radio stations, and some programs are entirely interview-based. U.S. community radio station KFAI-FM (Minneapolis) broadcasts the weekly "Indian Uprising," a Native American interview program hosted by Chris Spotted Eagle. The "uprisings" taking place each week are far more internal than external; that is, guests are encouraged to speak first and foremost about what Native Americans can do for themselves, although assistance and opposition coming from mainstream society enter into many presentations, as well. Health (alcoholism and diabetes in particular) is a common topic; so is tribal governance and housing for Native Americans.

Interviewing ethnic minority individuals for newscasts or drawing them out as participants on discussion shows often requires a special sensitivity on the part of the reporter or host. Among indigenous populations, there is quite likely to be the expectation that a question will be succeeded by a long pause, partly in order to show the questioner that her or his query is receiving a proper and respectful degree of deliberation. Pushing for an immediate response may be regarded as disrespectful. Some cultures tolerate and even welcome interventions in the course of a discussion, whereas others may regard them as discourteous. If mainstream culture reporters and hosts are in charge, and if the broadcast is taking place in a mainstream station, ethnic minority interviewees and discussants may be more forgiving of breaches in cultural etiquette. If it is an ethnic minority service, and especially if the hosts and reporters are ethnic minorities, the expectation is far more likely to be that "minority culture rules".[7]

The Panos Institute's West African office sponsored an interesting interview-based project in Ghana and Sierra Leone between 2001 and 2003 (Panos West Africa, 2003). It involved training producers from community and private radio stations in the two nations to gather oral testimony from "locals" and in their own languages. Although there were set topics and issues, for example, conflict resolution and reconciliation (especially potent in war-torn Sierra Leone), the locals were to determine the content of their observations, rather than responding to a set of predetermined interviewer questions. The producers then edited the responses into specific programs on each topic and broadcast them. Although audience satisfaction with the results has not been measured yet, the producers have expressed great satisfaction with the authenticity of the programs, and have remarked that it enabled them to "listen more to the people in the community."[8]

Talk radio and TV programs usually offer opportunities for community participation, and a number of ethnic media services provide such formats. Because most of the audience contributions are made through telephone or e-mail, the participation of economically disadvantaged members of certain ethnic minority groups may be excluded or hindered; but those programs that I have seen or listened to seemed to include the views of a wide range of people (some of them apparently frequent participants, judging from the recognition they received from program hosts). Although much of the subject matter concerns relatively mundane subject matter, those talk programs that feature more serious issues such as health and politics also attract considerable participation, as do those where highly controversial subjects involving mainstream–ethnic minority relations, such as the fishing rights of the Anishinabe (noted in Chapter 4, footnote 3).[9]

Storytelling

Story telling is far more likely to appear on indigenous media services because it is often regarded as a vital part of indigenous community life. Many of the Native American and Inuit stations in the United States and Canada devote airtime to stories, particularly through radio.[10] Children are a prime target audience, both because storytelling often has been used to acquaint them with tribal lore and because there are real fears among many tribal elders that the "storytelling" of mainstream media entertainment is weakening children's identification with the tribe. Although the storytellers themselves generally seem to welcome the opportunity to present their stories through the electronic media, I have heard of a few instances where they did not because the media broke what they felt was the essential bond between the tellers and their live audiences.

Indigenous people often conceive of stories connected with tribal families as the personal property of the families or even of individual family members, who are the only ones entitled to narrate them. When those individuals tell stories (or are interviewed or take part in discussions), they may need to be reminded that what they say can be heard by audiences outside their communities, and who may not be familiar with the concept of personal story ownership. Some of those audience members may appropriate the stories for their own uses, and possibly cause embarrassment or distress for their originators, and possibly for the groups to which they belong.

Documentaries

Because they are expensive and labor-intensive to produce, documentaries do not appear all that often on most types of ethnic minority electronic media (or, for that matter, on mainstream electronic media commercial services). However, the declining cost of shooting and editing high-quality video productions has attracted a growing number of ethnic minority documentary producers, and a typical week's schedule on Canada's Aboriginal Peoples Television Network (www.aptn.com) includes at least a few examples of their work. Many of their documentaries are archival—the preservation of people's recollections of customs and practices that have disappeared or are in the process of doing so—but others deal with vital and often sensitive contemporary issues such as spousal abuse, alcoholism, and AIDS.

Ethnic services that are part of or linked with a PSB—Ireland's TG4, the Welsh S4C, the Scandinavian Sami services, Scots Gaelic radio, and so on—enjoy the advantage of having resources and tradition that help to support documentary production. The level of financial support is higher than it is at most other ethnic services, but it is at least as important that there is a long tradition of documentary production at most PSBs, which brings with it a greater likelihood that the PSB-supported ethnic services will engage in it. Also, the presence of veteran PSB production staff can be helpful as a source of advice and training.

The history of a given ethnic group is a popular subject for documentaries, but so are the experiences of individuals and groups: writers, painters, performers, educators, politicians, and many others. As one example, TV Breizh (commercial TV service in Brittany; www.tv-breizh.com/fr/grille) made a documentary about a Breton actors troupe making its final tour of the province; the producer lived with the troupe and recorded their public and private faces, complete with teamwork, disagreements, moments of fatigue and of elation, and even expressions of doubt that their activity was contributing much to Breton culture.

Advertisements

There is a tendency on the part of many people to think of advertisements as unworthy of inclusion with newscasts, commentaries, discussions, documentaries, and other *true* categories of information. Perhaps that is because of their one-sidedness and/or their frequent use of music, comedy, drama, and other "noninformational" formats. However, family-planning advocates had realized as early as the 1960s that brief messages supporting various methods of birth control could be presented very effectively through dramatic or comedic skits, songs, and other devices usually associated with entertainment—in other words, messages that sounded or looked very much like ads.[11]

Ethnic minority services have followed similar practices. Maori radio stations have presented explanations of New Zealand's two-step voting system through brief and sometimes comic dialogues between a "skeptic" and an "advocate." Black township radio in South Africa carries many dramatized or musical "ads" advocating safe sex, such as one featuring a smooth-voiced man who proclaims over a background of sinuous jazz that "a *real* lover cares for his partner; a *real* lover always wears a condom."[12]

Apart from such socially relevant uses of ad-like formats, there are other reasons why ethnic minority services in particular may regard advertising as beneficial in something other than a purely monetary sense. Several ethnic service administrators have spoken with me about their perception of advertising as a demonstration of the economic viability of the ethnic community itself, in two respects: First, the community gains increased confidence that it has economic importance because ads would not be directed to it if its members did not have significant purchasing and decision-making power; and second, when ethnic minority businesses advertise through the services, they remind the community that some of its members are "making it" in a competitive society and that they are helping to support an important element of community life—the ethnic media themselves.

Community Calendars, "Swap Shops," and the "Bush Telephone"

We do not know precisely when the first broadcast of a community calendar or "swap shop" (announcements of personal goods for sale or barter) took place, but it probably was not long after licensed radio broadcasting made its debut in the early 1920s. Want ads ("classified") and announcements of community activities had been available through the print media for some time, and it must have seemed logical to consider trying them out on the new medium. The format was particularly well-suited to local radio because it provided a natural and direct source of contact with the audience.

Ethnic minority services were quick to introduce community calendars for much the same reason, but also because, like advertisements, they had the symbolic value of portraying the community's vitality. Swap shops have been far less common—perhaps surprising given the more restricted economic means of many ethnic minority communities, which would seem to make personal selling and bartering more attractive. It may be, however, that community members do not wish to reveal (at least through a public medium) the possible economic necessity of engaging in such practices.

The use of radio as a "bush (remote area) telephone" is yet another way in which ethnic minority media can serve as significant sources of contact with their communities. Again, economics is an important factor here, in the form of a frequent lack of affordable telephone service for households in remote, sparsely populated areas. The central Australian Aboriginal radio station 8KIN (Alice Springs, Northern Territory) began to receive requests for such service almost as soon as it came on air in 1985. Because the station had access to a 50 kW short-wave transmitter, which provided signal coverage of a substantial portion of the territory, it could fulfill those requests.

Such requests usually have taken the form of a brief message, sometimes relayed to the station through a third (or fourth or fifth) party, notifying a family member or friend that an individual had been delayed in returning home, but expected to arrive on the following day or two. Sometimes, the message would be an urgent request for medicine or for a spare engine part.[13] Usually, there would be an expression of thanks to whoever passed along the message because it wasn't always the case that the intended recipients would own radio receivers, or if they did, that they would be listening at the time the message was broadcast.[14]

Although this might appear to be a highly individual-centered use of a mass medium, it does not appear to be regarded as such by the community. Instead, it is seen as a caring and participatory act that demonstrates how community members can and should assist one another. Carrying the messages costs the station little time or effort, and that act also serves to demonstrate membership in the community—perhaps in ways that are even more vital to community life than are the calendars and swap shops.

Chat Rooms and Bulletin Boards

The growth of the internet over the past decade has encouraged many ethnic groups to use it for a variety of purposes. Chat rooms and bulletin boards afford opportunities for ethnic minorities to interconnect, whether within the same rural area, city, state, nation, or across a multitude of them. They have been particularly important for diaspora populations, who use it to maintain ties with family, friends, and the homeland, locate "missing" individuals, share feelings on major developments that affect their lives, as did Muslims in the aftermath of 9/11.[15]

Community Meetings

Several of the electronic media services have provided links between ethnic minority governing and consultative structures and ethnic minority communities. That has been particularly useful where a community spreads over a large geographical area, as do many of the indigenous groups in Canada, Australia, Brazil, the United States, and elsewhere. KILI-FM (Porcupine) serves the Lakota Sioux reservation in western South Dakota, and broadcasts the meetings of the tribal council. Because the meetings are attended by many tribal members and feature frequent questions from them (not always clearly audible), the broadcasts can serve to encourage participation by the tribal population in decision-making as they provide real-life examples of how people raise questions and sometimes take issue with the answers they receive.[16]

GENRES: ENTERTAINMENT

There is some disagreement over just what constitutes entertainment. One problem faced by anyone attempting to categorize it is the differing perceptions that viewers and listeners have of whether something is entertaining as opposed to informative or even educational. A great deal of entertainment is presented in ways that blur the lines between the three interpretations, and there is ample evidence to indicate that audiences accept a great deal of fiction as a reasonably accurate representation of fact, at least some of the time.[17]

Soap Operas

"Soaps" have become one of the most popular genres in television, and can be found in the television (and sometimes radio) schedules of nations throughout the world. Their never-ending story lines, replete with subplots, appear to hold great fascination for audiences of highly diverse cultures. There have been a few attempts to create radio soaps for ethnic minority audiences, but the vast majority of soaps are grounded in mainstream cultures, with some token appearances for minorities and very few feature roles. Television soaps have been much the same. However, exportation of the U.S. radio soap opera "model" to Latin America meant that the genre not only took root there, but also led to the development of a Latin American soap opera model that found its way into the United States as Hispanic television stations began to serve a rapidly growing Spanish-speaking audience.

For the first few decades, those services carried soap operas that had been produced in Latin America for audiences there. By the 1990s, it was apparent that more and more Spanish-speaking viewers living in the United States wanted something more than just the fairy tale-like presentations of poor girls from the countryside coming to the big cities and being exploited by wealthy individuals and those who served them. Accordingly, some Spanish-language soap operas began to be produced in Puerto Rico, and their plot lines dealt with the experiences of Spanish-speakers living and working in U.S. society, facing contemporary problems such as AIDS, having homosexual as well as heterosexual relationships.

In 2003, the Los Angeles-based Hispanic-American TV service Telemundo took the unusual step of producing a soap opera (*losteens*) based on the experiences of Hispanic-American students in a U.S. high school. The class was the usual (for high school-related plotlines) mix of dumb-smart, plain-beautiful, shy-forward, outcast-popular students, and all of the principal characters were Hispanic-American. However, some were recent arrivals in the United States, whereas others were second- or third-generation, and that difference was treated as one of the sources of conflict. Parental divorce, drugs, sexual behavior, alcoholism, AIDS, adolescent suicide, and several other controversial subjects also helped to drive the plot.[18] It was broadcast at 8 p.m. (7 p.m. central time), with the idea that teens *and* their parents might watch it, then perhaps discuss it.

There have been relatively few attempts on the part of other ethnic minorities to produce soap operas, but in 2004 the BBC Asian Network intends to produce a radio soap about a South Asian family living in the United Kingdom. It is to be modeled on the BBC's very long-running radio soap opera "The Archers," although it is to be set in Birmingham and not in "The Archers'" rural England. The BBC is investing a million pounds in the production (Day, 2002a, 2002b).

Yet more fascinating because it is the only example of an interactive linguistic minority soap opera I have as yet discovered is "Rogha an Lea," an Irish-language radio series produced by BBC Northern Ireland. It claims to have neither script nor plot—just a group of characters and some settings. Listeners are invited to contribute their ideas and tune in to see whether and how they are used in the production, which came on air in Northern Ireland early in May 2003.[19]

Ireland's Irish-language TV service, Telefis Gaeilge (TG4), has produced numerous soap operas since it came on air in 1996—and quickly introduced its first soap, which remains on the schedule. "Ros na Run" (the name of the small town that serves as the central setting) features a very soap-like set of story lines, with faithful and faithless lovers, concerned parents, gay characters, con artists, financial problems, and so on. One hope of its producers was that those elements would help to reinforce the idea that Irish is a living language, and perfectly well suited to portrayals of contemporary life (www.rosnarun.com).

Sitcoms

The situation comedy may not be a U.S. invention, but its rapid development there—first in radio, and then on television—also brought it into the export market, and dubbed U.S. sitcoms began to appear in many nations around the world. Unlike soap operas, where the conventions of production called for fresh episodes every weekday, sitcoms were and remain weekly productions, making them somewhat more manageable for production companies with limited facilities and budgets.

Much like soap operas, sitcoms have been a relative rarity among ethnic minority program formats. A Maori production company did receive a grant from New Zealand on Air (which collected and distributed proceeds from the annual license fee until the fee was abolished) in 1993-1994 to produce a 10-episode sitcom entitled *Radio Wha Waho*, and dealing with a fictional Maori radio station[20] afflicted by a series of small disasters caused by the staff, such as dropping a piece of fried chicken onto a record turntable, which caused a particularly annoying line in a recording to repeat *ad nauseam*. The series was aired over Television New Zealand, a mainstream channel, and drew fairly positive reactions from the *pakeha* (white) audience, but mixed reviews from Maori, some of whom felt that it made them look stupid. A few worried that it might induce *pakeha* to think that some of the "humorous" lines between Maori characters gave license to Whites to use similar "humor" with their Maori friends, on the grounds that "Well, they did it on *Radio Wha Waho*."[21]

Variety

Variety shows, with their mixtures of dance, song, comedy, and the like, all guided by a host, have become rarities in U.S. mainstream television. They still flourish in many other nations, and sometimes are part of an ethnic service's program lineup. *Sabado Gigante* (*Big Saturday*) originated in Chile in 1962, and remained a Latin American production until 1985, when Univision brought it to Miami, Florida. With its U.S. location, it began to feature more Hispanic-American performers (as well as more references to Hispanic-American experiences) and to go out to U.S. cities for promotional performances.[22] Univision continues to broadcast it to Latin America, but Hispanic-Americans now can identify more closely with the program.

Scotland's two independent television companies (Scottish Television in Glasgow and Grampian Television in Aberdeen) collaborate to produce *Splaoid* (*Having Fun*), a variety show featuring children. Entertainment in the form of song and dance predominates, and "budding popstars" among the show's viewers compete for the Splaoid Trophy by submitting videos of their Gaelic language versions of favorite pop songs. There also is a "challenge" ("Ceist is Cleas") on each episode in which school teams compete at outdoor centers in the Scottish Highlands and Islands.[23]

Drama

Because dramas generally are reckoned to be more difficult to produce than situation comedies or soap operas, it may be surprising that there are numerous examples of them where ethnic minority media are concerned. The BBC Welsh service has featured many dramas, some written for radio and TV, others adapted from the stage (including an animated feature series of several of Shakespeare's plays translated into Welsh). A series of novels by a late 19th century Welsh author, Daniel Owen, was adapted for television and broadcast in 2002. *Treflan* (*The Town With Many Faces*) portrays a Welsh town at several moments in its Victorian history, with religion as a major but not always positive force in the town's development.[24]

Because the BBC long has had a tradition of supporting original and adapted drama, one might expect to see evidence of it on BBC linguistic-minority services, and especially those languages that could be closely identified with the United Kingdom. A similar situation exists for regional television in France and Spain, where drama in Basque, Breton, Catalan, and other regional languages sometimes (in the case of Catalan radio and TV, quite often) appears on the schedule.

.Not all of the productions are made by the stations themselves. In 1990, the Igloolik Isuma Productions company was incorporated as Canada's first Inuit independent video production company. One of its productions—*Atanarjuat* (*The Fast Runner*)—won the Camera d'Or (Golden Camera) award at the 2001 Cannes Film Festival. In 2003, its 13-part television series *Nunavut Our Land* ran on the Canadian Bravo channel. The series is a dramatization of Inuit life in the Canadian Arctic in the 1940s as experienced by five Inuit families, and is based on accounts of that life as related by Inuit elders, so it borders on being a docudrama. The emphasis is on clashes and accommodation between traditional and modern ways ("Nunavut," 2003).

Although radio drama is simpler and less expensive to produce than is TV drama, it is nearly as scarce on ethnic media services; yet it can be very effective as a form of participation in the public sphere. In 1993 a group of Aboriginal high school students in Broome, Western Australia wrote, acted and produced a series of radio dramas for the Broome Aboriginal Media Association (BAMA). The students wanted to reach the Aboriginal community (with Whites as a secondary audience) through a genre that might get their attention through a form of storytelling, which already was much practiced in Aboriginal culture. The message itself was "You really don't know what your kids are thinking, so we want to clue you in." Each episode dealt with a controversial topic: teenage sexual practices, alcoholism in the Aboriginal community, spousal abuse of each other and their children, and so on. The series led to considerable discussion within both the Aboriginal and White communities; a few were somewhat angry that "private" issues were being made public, and by teenagers, at that. Far more were amazed at what they heard, and grateful as well as proud that the "kids" had done it.[25]

Other groups, too, have tried their hands at drama. One of the access radio stations in the United Kingdom, New Style Radio (Caribbean/African) in Birmingham, broadcast (1993) a 10-part (7–10 minutes per episode) radio drama entitled "George's Wake," based on "To My Country a Child," a play by Black British writer Joe White.[26] The drama also was audio-streamed over the station's Web site (www.newstyleradio.co.uk) and archived there. The play itself featured George, a recently deceased Black businessman, as he hears his family and erstwhile friends discussing his (largely negative) "contributions" to their lives. He tries to argue with or apologize to his "mourners," to no avail. The message of the play clearly is "Do right by others while you're alive if you hope to be well respected once you die," but there is considerable humor along with the moral lessons.

Game and Quiz Shows

A few ethnic services have produced quiz shows, generally designed to test contestants' knowledge of such things as Irish history, Maori customs, or whatever else might be particularly appropriate for a given ethnic audience. TG4, the Irish-language service for the Republic of Ireland, has had quiz shows since its inception; questions often test knowledge of the Irish language, as well as of Irish history. One of them, *Cruinneas*, is a quiz show for children, and its contestants "travel the planets [*sic*] in order to answer questions and win prizes" (www.tnag.ie). S4C (Sianel Pedwar Cymry, or Welsh Channel Four) has them, as well.

"Reality" Shows

TG4 also has broadcast one of the very few[27] "reality" series that I have encountered in studying ethnic minority electronic media, but it is a reality show that also has an educational purpose. *Fiche La ag Fas* ran as a four-episode series in May–June 2003. A production team followed a group of students who were learning the Irish language as they traveled around the *Gaeltacht* (Ireland's west coast, where the language is most heavily used). According to the program description, "The course lasts 20 days, and they learn Irish, break rules, and fall in and out of love." They misused the language on more than a few occasions, so viewers had opportunities to learn from group member mistakes (www.tnag.ie). But the group also experienced interpersonal joys and disappointments, in true reality show fashion. The other reality show, on Welsh TV, is covered in the section on language.

In 2003, the Hispanic-American TV network Telemundo produced a reality series *La Cenicienta* (*Cinderella*), that featured some interesting touches, such as the central figure (Minerva Ruvalcaba) appearing on the opening night with "her family, two best friends, a priest and an astrologer, all to help her choose Prince Charming." But what made the series most unusual was that it challenged Latino sensibilities in featuring a woman who was twice divorced and had a 2 1/2-year-old daughter. The producer of the show said that he wanted "to change the way men see single mothers." A Hispanic-American psychologist indicated that, although she thought that American-born Latinos attached less shame to such status, "It's still very difficult for a society with a strong traditionalist component to accept single motherhood" (Navarro, 2003).

Music

By far the most common and seemingly most popular form of entertainment available through ethnic minority electronic media is music—most of it "popular," but often with at least some "traditional" music, as well. One of the more popular music formats is country and western, which is featured over most Aboriginal Australian radio stations, appears on many Scottish stations, has fairly wide distribution through Native American stations, and more limited availability through Maori radio. The performers often are Aboriginals, Scots, Native Americans, although there are likely to be contributions from U.S. "mainstream" artists.

Ethnic minority media services have assisted in the growth of ethnic minority music industries in a major way, both as disseminators of their recordings and as discoverers of talent. Because a majority of ethnic minority media services is local, it is easy for bands and individual musicians to perform in a service's studios (where they exist) or to drop off recordings for broadcast. Some services go out of their way to induce local performers to share their talents with listeners and viewers, although few have committed themselves to scheduled time slots where local performers will be featured. Those services with adequate technical facilities often will invite performers to come in, be recorded, and then decide whether they are satisfied with the result. Increasingly, however, service staff are discovering that many performers already own or can borrow first-class recording equipment, and will come in with highly professional recordings already made.

Individual singers and vocal groups sometimes craft songs that speak to the problems and aspirations of their ethnic communities. They sometimes do so through "coded" or bivalent messages in their lyrics, as with Tejana[28] singer Shelly Lares and "Here We Stand" (her song about a relationship between a Mexican-American woman and a non-Mexican-American man). As Gonzalez and Flores (1994: 41) state, "If we read the song as constructing a metaphor for the competing forces of traditionalism and acculturation, we can see that . . . the situation is left purposely ambiguous. Both worlds are accommodated." The fact that the song is in English (rare for Lares) adds to its potential bivalence.

For some groups, song and dance are more natural expressions of what they want to say about themselves, their histories, the problems they face, and the triumphs they experience than is the spoken word. A representative of UNAIDS for East and Southern Africa saw a vivid demonstration of that at a seminar

> and the organizers said one of their frustrations was that people just did not participate, And then one of their facilitators went to a meeting of women . . . and asked them if they would like to participate. . . . And the women said, "Of course we would like to participate!" And he said, "Well, how? How would you like to do this?" "We would like to participate by dancing and

singing." . . . And so the next day, they came back already with songs and . . .
those songs had all the lessons, all the ideas of what they thought people
needed to know, in their own language. . . . They wanted to sing their participation. They wanted to dance their participation. This is not "traditional"
for them. This is just the way they communicate. (Makinwa, 2003)

Sports

Sports events are popular with audiences throughout the world, mainstream and
ethnic minority alike. They are one of the most common reasons for ethnic
households to subscribe to cable or satellite TV, especially when the service provides channels from the major ethnic homelands. Some ethnic groups, indigenous
in particular, have their own teams or individual athletes, and are anxious to hear
and see them covered by the electronic media. Although the mainstream media
routinely provide coverage of the "mainstream" major leagues, conferences, and
other gatherings, they almost never do so for contests involving ethnic minority
teams, although they certainly feature ethnic minority athletes who belong to
mainstream teams. Also, there are national sports competitions for some ethnic
groups, such as the Maori games.[29] Although such events may be mentioned by
the mainstream media, they do rarely receive extended coverage. Thus, the ethnic services have the opportunity to provide their communities with some very
popular programming that will not be available anywhere else.

The range of such coverage can be considerable. A *närradio* service in the
largely Sami town of Keitokeino, Norway occasionally has sent its reporters out
to provide live coverage of the local football (soccer in the United States) team in
an important out-of-town match. Raidio na Gaeltachta covered Irish football
matches as well as the annual Irish Games starting in the 1970s. The South
African Black Township station Radio ALX (for Alexandra, the township) enjoys
the advantage of not having to leave the station in order to cover home football
games, because the newsroom windows directly overlook the field. Very few of
the ethnic commercial electronic media services furnish such coverage, although
Univision has done so regularly for Latin American football matches and for
major international competitions such as the World Cup.[30] As some U.S. teams
and players also are involved in those events, the coverage may be particularly
appealing to Univision's U.S. Spanish-speaking audience, but that is not the
prime target, and there are few concessions to those viewers.

GENRES: EDUCATIONAL

It can be (and often is) argued that any material provided through the mass
media has the potential capacity to educate. I have restricted my coverage of that
genre to media material where the primary purpose is to educate. Most of that

education is not linked with educational institutions, and ethnic service administrators often have expressed regret that they have not managed to link up with schools—primary schools in particular. Part of the reason may be that teachers in many nations are not educated to think of the mass media as potentially useful partners. In fact, the media may be treated as the enemy of education. Very few colleges of education or other teacher-training institutions seem to provide courses on such subjects as Teaching With the Media. Also, I have heard teachers (ethnic minority and mainstream) express the fear that, if the schools begin to rely more heavily on the media to provide part of a student's formal education, the need for classroom teachers may decrease. Where that fear is present, the media are not likely to be welcomed with open arms.

Languages

Indigenous electronic media often are seen as vital instruments in the salvation or resurrection of dying or dead languages, and indeed they can have a major impact along those lines. Along with primary and secondary schools (and, less often, tertiary institutions) offering instruction through and in the languages, several hours of daily broadcasts and the availability of Web sites in them does bring about a growth in interest, on the part of younger students as well as adults (Clarity, 1994). That has occurred in Ireland and in Wales, and appears to be doing so in Scotland (Cormack, 1995). The range of programming available is considerable: news, commentary, documentaries, talk shows, game and quiz shows, music (sometimes in variety shows), occasional soap operas, sitcoms and dramas, and sports. It helps that the BBC and RTI (Irish Radio and Television) support the major Irish, Scots Gaelic[31] and Welsh radio and television services, but commercial radio services in those languages are beginning to appear, and cable TV occasionally provides programs in them, as well.

   The growth of such services has not been problem free. There are members of the Irish, Welsh and Scots listening and viewing public who feel that it is a waste of financial and human resources to develop extensive broadcast services in what they regard as largely useless languages, especially if that money and effort could be invested in creating a larger number and variety of mainstream language programs that would reflect life in Wales, Scotland, and Ireland. That appears to be a minority opinion, but it can be highly vocal.

   The issue of using the electronic media to *educate* listeners and viewers in such languages appears to be less controversial, perhaps because there has been a long-standing practice in many nations of employing the electronic media in language education. Radio and TV broadcasts, audio- and videocassette productions, and more recently the internet (often used in a supporting role on media Web sites, rather than on its own) all have played such roles. Whether the resources available to users of those languages will be sufficient to accomplish the task well is another matter. Teaching an individual to speak something other than her or his mainstream language is not all that easy in the classroom. Doing so through the electronic media is much more difficult unless the media and the schools coordinate their efforts, if only because the media usually cannot devote comparable amounts of time to language instruction, will not be willing to prepare and distribute the necessary supporting material (instructional texts and workbooks in particular), and have no way to keep prospective students, not to mention their family and friends, from tuning to other broadcasts—usually abundant and often more enjoyable.

Some of the attempts to reinforce language instruction are quite ingenious. Aside from TG4's *Fiche La ag Fas*, noted earlier, that series also has an interesting collaboration with Ireland's Transition Year Curriculum Support Group. Program episodes of *Ros na Run* are used as classroom aids to improving student comprehension and speaking of Irish. *Ros na Run* producers and the Support Group first developed a workbook based on the program, but soon replaced it with an online version that permitted more interactivity between teachers and students (www.rosnarun.com/education). Welsh TV (www.s4c.co.uk) offers "Yr Wythnos," a weekly 30-minute news program for Welsh learners. It presents the leading news stories of the week, but with some definition and discussion of the terminology.

There is one more dimension of languages and the ethnic minority media that should be noted: the use of several languages within a given service. When an ethnic service aims to reach several linguistic populations in their own tongues, it immediately faces the problems of *choice* and *supply*. Choice in this case means "Who gets the most/best broadcast or screen time." Some of the linguistic groups probably will be largely than others, but size is not the only thing that matters: Certain groups are likely to advance claims of greater prestige, longer time in residence, and greater prosperity. Any/all of those claims may be relevant. Supply is a very different issue: Members of some groups may be readier to become involved with the media service than are others, and some groups may have no more than one or two individuals who have the necessary talent and/or interest to become involved.

There is not a great deal that service administrators can do to keep everyone reasonably satisfied, but Radio ALX, in the Johannesburg, South Africa township of Alexandra, manages quite well by rotating airtimes occasionally, as well as conferring with program producers about the need for some degree of give and take when reconfiguring the schedule. As the station provides programs in all eleven of South Africa's official languages, the task of balancing competing interests is considerable, which may be why the station has found it difficult to retain station managers, and often has had to prevail upon one of the station's founders, Slovo,[32] to take up the reins of management once again. The station is committed to retaining the "all official languages" policy, even though there are brief periods, as Slovo noted in an October 2002 personal interview, when the solitary program presenter returns to her or his tribal area for a visit, and programming in that language ceases for the time being.[33]

Genres: A Summary

Although the various programming examples show that there is no genre that some ethnic minority service somewhere has not presented at one time or another, it would be incorrect to assume that most of the services present a wide variety of genres. The national PSB-supported services often do, and a few others— Bush Radio and Radio Centre-Ville (Montreal) prominent among them—come close to matching them. The Hispanic-American commercial TV networks, Univision and Telemundo, also provide considerable variety, including sitcoms and "reality" programs. Original news programs are lacking on many local ethnic minority services, but are present on most of the national services, public and commercial alike. For the most part, the ethnic minority services emphasize a few entertainment genres (popular music in particular), with most informational genres aside from interviews and discussions a distant second and educational genres generally absent from the lineup.

Certainly, it is possible to convey information and education through entertainment, and it can be done very effectively; nor does it always have to be done consciously. But one might have expected the ethnic services to place greater emphasis on informing and educating their communities, given the rationales that often accompanied their creation (Chapter 4). The rationales themselves still appear to be alive and well, but several realities have compromised their execution.

Financial support is a major problem for most stations, and clearly has an effect on the time and effort a service can devote to the more ambitious and innovative productions. The *media climate* is another problem, in the sense that most ethnic minority groups have had heavy exposure to mainstream electronic media, most of which devote far more attention to entertainment than to information or education, and thus provide few nonentertainment models. Also, ethnic minority media services have little opportunity to learn from one another's experiences. *Employment prospects* for ethnic minority producers, directors, writers, actors, journalists, and the like, have been quite restricted, and that tends to limit innovative approaches to programming. *Disrespect for media* on the part of educators often appears to have hindered the development of educational programming. Finally, *staff turnover* is high in most ethnic minority media services, and discourages programmatic innovation.

Despite the obstacles, ethnic media services generally retain a strong sense of serving their communities. Three of their most commonly cited goals in programming for those communities are retaining and strengthening minority languages (indigenous languages in particular) within mainstream societies; reaching younger community members; and promoting greater mutual understanding. Each of those goals presents its own problems, but there are solutions, too, as is seen in the following accounts.

PRESERVING, SAFEGUARDING, AND EXTENDING THE MOTHER TONGUE

The electronic media often must confront the issue of how to bring indigenous/ethnic languages into the modern era. Irish, Welsh, Scots Gaelic, Basque, Breton, Maori, and many more are ancient languages, and until their relatively recent revival they generally were inadequate for the coverage of science, technology, medicine, and other major features of present-day life in industrialized societies. They simply did not provide enough of the necessary terminology. Major efforts on the part of language boards, teachers, political figures (the Irish, Welsh and Scottish parliaments all use indigenous languages, as well as English), and the media have resulted in the development of far richer vocabularies, to the point where there are relatively few concepts or phenomena that cannot be readily and fluently explained through many of those languages.[34]

All of that should be quite satisfying to speakers of what many regard as their "mother tongue," and to many of them, it is. The problem arises when one examines how the expansion has taken place. Irish has been held to a "purist" approach, in which every effort has been made to develop Irish terms that stem from older terminology, for example, joining *clar* (board) and *toinne* (wave) to create a term for surfboard. Users of the other languages have created such terms, as with TeUpoko Iriraki ki Otautahi (Christchurch) invented Maori term for computer: *roro* for electric and *hiko* for brain. Sometimes it has been possible to rediscover a long-dormant term that is easy to use and can replace a term that owes a great deal to the mainstream language, as with the ancient Basque term *gela* (room), which was used by French Basque radio station Xiberoko Botza to replace the "modern" Basque terms *kanbera* and *sola*, derived from the French words *chambre* and *salle*.[35]

But more often (and sometimes far more often), there is an adaptive approach, where new terms are created by adding indigenous language prefixes or suffixes to mainstream terms. That may be easier for many (sometimes most) listeners and viewers to understand, and less effort to create. However, there is the danger that, with the passage of time, the indigenous language will become less and less indigenous and more and more mainstream. All languages change over time, and some more rapidly than others, but English and French are major languages, and in nations where they also are the mainstream languages, speakers of indigenous/ethnic languages may wonder how they can possibly keep those languages from being swamped by indigenized mainstream terminology, especially if schools and/or the media use it.[36]

There is another form of "purity" that also enters into any consideration of ethnic minority broadcasts in the mother tongue: "Correctness" of pronunciation. The broadcast media have been regarded in many nations as standard-setters for language usage almost from the moment they were introduced. Because they present such a wide range of programming, there is ample opportunity to allow for a comparably wide range of pronunciations and vocalic mannerisms. That is particularly true where entertainment is concerned, since rural and urban settings, occupations, income and other elements can be manipulated for dramatic or comedic effect. There always are critics (many of them educators) who are quick to point out the negative effect that attractive characters with nonstandard speech patterns may have on the population in general, and especially on young people. That can be a particularly sensitive issue for an ethnic media service when the mother tongue is quite close to the dominant "national" language, because the possibility of linguistic assimilation seems more likely, but in fact any ethnic minority mother tongue can face a similar situation.

Many of the ethnic services using nonmainstream languages (the larger services in particular) have developed close working relationships with language boards in hopes of maintaining a balance between the preservation of high standards of ethnic language usage and the sense of linguistic relevance in contemporary society. Catalan Radio and Television (CTV) has a linguistic advisor who also is president of the Grup Catala de Sociolinguistica. He realizes the need for a degree of flexibility, for example, the use of an old, Cockney-like dialect in a comedy, and he argues for greater use of Catalan dialects other than those of Barcelona (which tend to predominate on Catalan radio and TV) in order to preserve as well as recognize the oral richness of the language, but with some degree of standardization (Vallverdu, 1995).[37]

Ethnic and linguistic minority electronic media services using the minority languages sometimes face pressures from two opposing forces: those who advocate using *only* the minority language, and those who advocate using *only* the mainstream language. One of the great debates within the ranks of Maori broadcasters and their chief funding agency, Te Mangai Paho (TMP), has been the issue of whether stations should be required to broadcast exclusively in Maori if they expect to receive support from TMP. Those arguing for such a policy contend that it is necessary to make the language as much a part of everyday life as possible if it is to survive, much less prosper, in a nation where English is so deeply entrenched. Those opposing hold that there are far too many Maori, young and old alike, who are not fluent in the language and almost certainly will not make the effort to learn it well enough to be able to follow broadcasts, so why risk alienating them (and members of the mainstream culture) from Maori culture altogether by depriving them of access to Maori radio and TV, which probably would fade away without TMP support?

Those two arguments represent extreme positions, with relatively few supporters for either one (but probably more of them on the "Maori language-only" side). Ethnic media service administrators usually try to achieve some degree of balance, but more often that balance is tilted in the direction of using English far more than Maori. An increase in the amount of Maori language broadcasting might very well encourage more people to *akona te reo* (Maori for "speak the language"). Welsh language radio and television are credited with helping to increase the use of Welsh, but that may be in part because the stations provide a fair amount of programming for Welsh learners. Such programming is expensive because it requires expert advice and a certain amount of experimentation to create programs that are both interesting and effective in attracting and sustaining language learners, but it may be worth the investment for broadcasts in *any* ethnic minority language.

One can argue, as some have, that developing wider use of a minority language makes good economic sense, in that it encourages the growth of the minority culture "industry" (books, videos, music, etcetera in the language) It may even play a role in increasing tourism, where visiting the nation or region becomes more "exotic" when there is a "native" language—especially when the "natives" can speak the mainstream language, as well.[38] However, the argument is far more likely to be made on cultural grounds: 'This is *our* language, it's part and parcel of who we are, and if we don't support it, an essential part of ourselves is lost'. If the economic and cultural arguments are combined, it is difficult to reject the case for broadcasts and Web sites in minority languages, but it also is essential to realize that sustaining them will take a lot of time, money, and effort, and prudent to recognize that there are some compelling reasons for maintaining ethnic media content in the mainstream language, as well.

Finally, there have been situations in which broadcasting in "foreign" languages has been risky. National governments themselves may be wary of ethnic media services that use "foreign" (nonmainstream) languages, and may discourage or even prohibit such use. Totalitarian regimes tend to be particularly suspicious, although the People's Republic of China and the Soviet Union/Russia have encouraged the development of radio services in ethnic minority languages, generally within ethnic regions themselves and not in the major urban areas in other parts of the nation to which minorities often migrate.[39] Wartime may cause nations to view ethnic media with particular suspicion: The U.S. FCC developed a policy statement in 1942 on "Foreign Language Radio Wartime Control" in which it urged station managers to insist receiving English translations of any foreign-language material before broadcast, and then to check the broadcasts themselves to be certain that there were no changes in their content (Grame, 1980: 18-19; Horten, 2002, esp. ch. 3).

Even in peacetime, however, nations may be uneasy at the thought that electronic media services within their borders are providing material in languages that most of the population will not understand, thus making it possible for those who *do* understand to speak and to hear criticism of national authority. The United Kingdom had begun to experience ethnic minority-operated "pirate" radio services by the 1970s, and some of their program content was in Greek, Hindi, and other nonmainstream languages. When the Conservative Party gained power in 1979, there were debates about the future of "pirate" radio in general, some Party members favoring the licensing of the stations as low-power community services because they were a good illustration of the Party's support for entrepreneurial activities, others questioning the wisdom of rewarding illegal activity by licensing it, still others expressing reservations about what the stations might broadcast. Those reservations were particularly strong regarding the "foreign-language" stations; the Conservative Party Secretary at the time, Norman Tebbetts, was quite concerned that some of them would broadcast in languages that he and his colleagues could not understand, and that they well might be criticizing the government.[40] In fact, the government already had set the licensing process in motion in 1986, but suddenly reversed itself and called it off. (It finally was implemented in 1990.)

In general, nations now seem less concerned about the possibility that "foreign"-language services could pose a threat to public welfare or civic spirit, perhaps because the existence of more and more of those services has not led to serious problems. In fact, there have been several positive developments. Teachers of foreign languages see such services as valuable additions to the learning environment. Fans of "world music" have a greater range of choice when ethnic media services are available. Even candidates for political office are more likely to realize the benefits that come with speaking at least a bit of one or more nonmainstream languages if there are media that capable of reaching portions of the electorate that might be impressed to hear the politicians "talking their talk."

REACHING YOUNGER AUDIENCES

Most ethnic minority electronic media services are keenly interested in reaching children, younger and older alike. According to NRK Sami Service Head Nils Johan Heatta (personal interview, Karasjoh, Norway, May 1993), the Sami television service made that audience its top priority when it began to produce programs in the early 1990s. That is quite logical because those groups are the future of ethnic minority cultures, languages and the media themselves. However, those same groups are prime targets for mainstream media as well, and many of the mainstream services have far more money for program production and for research on the viewing and listening practices and motivations of younger audience members than do most ethnic services. As a result, reaching those audiences is a major challenge for most ethnic media, and one that worries most of the ethnic service administrators with whom I have spoken.

Those operations best equipped to meet the challenge are, once again, the PSB-affiliated ethnic minority services already mentioned: TG4, S4C, Raidio nan Gaidheal, and others. They generally have portions of their schedules that are devoted to broadcasts of children's programs, and make some effort to reach teenagers, as well. S4C has a block of children's programming entitled Planed Plant ("Children's Planet") Monday through Friday from 12 noon or slightly later to late afternoon; it includes Welsh-language lessons for various levels of learners, some entertainment, and a news program in Welsh for young viewers from 4:50 to 5 p.m. TG4 provides two weekday blocks, one running from 8:30 to 11:30 and the other from 2 to 5:30. The TG4 lineup contains a predominance of cartoons (some from the United States, for example, *SpongeBob Squarepants*, and generally subtitled in Irish), although it also includes *Cruinneas*, the children's quiz show mentioned previously. Unlike S4C, TG4 does not include newscasts for young people, or language lessons for them.

Ethnic media services in most other nations do not provide as much by way of children's programming. As of mid-2003, Maori Television offered two programs made specifically for children, *Tikitiki* (portrayals of Maori customs and history) and *Puukana* (variety/light entertainment), but it had contracted for several more children's series in preparation for its debut as a separate and exclusive channel. The central Australian Aboriginal television service, Imparja (Alice Springs), produces a 30-minute children's program, *Yamba's Playtime* (www.imparja. com.au/Yabba/yabba), available every weekday afternoon with a repeat broadcast in mid-evening. Yamba, a honey ant, is played by a costumed adult, who works with a group of children in the studio ("The Playtimers") on projects such as making a scrapbook of "portraits" of friends and family, making "Buddy" biscuits (with boy and girl biscuit cutters), and reading and discussing books. Fridays are reserved for "walkabouts," where Yamba and Rene (the program's co-host) visit places such as a children's care center and bring back videos to share the experiences with The Playtimers. Aboriginal experiences, customs and events are frequent but not exclusive subjects.

Television Northern Canada (TVNC) has broadcast a "superhero" series for children, entitled *Super Shamou*. Its Inuit star deals with problems likely to be encountered by children, such as substance abuse. Another TVNC children's series, *The Takuginai Family*, emphasizes respect for Inuit language and traditions. Both series are produced by the Inuit Broadcasting Corporation, but a third series, also carried by TVNC, is produced by the Kativik School Board. The series, *Allai*, is more specifically educational, and features an Inuit family portrayed through puppets. Inuit language and culture, as well as the geography of the immediate region (Nunavik) are its main focus (Alia, 1999: 106).

The attempt made by some ethnic minority television services to offer several hours of children's programs each weekday may carry a price. Even if services such as TG4 and S4C receive considerably more financial support than do most ethnic minority electronic media, it is far from enough to limit their offerings to their own productions or commissioned works. They usually turn to syndicated material to fill out their schedules, much of it from the United States. Although that material is subtitled in the relevant language, the story line and visual depictions do nothing to reinforce the minority culture, and in some cases may even carry messages antithetical to it—messages that may appear in the mainstream programs that children also watch.[41]

Reaching teenagers poses its own problems, although one is related to the issue I have just raised: reinforcement of culturally negative messages. For teenaged viewers and listeners, that is most likely to occur in the form of popular music. As mentioned in the discussion on music, one of the primary ways in which many ethnic minority radio stations have had a major impact on their communities is through their role in promoting ethnic minority soloists and groups. Still, most ethnic radio services have to turn to other sources to fill out their schedules, and ordinarily those will be mainstream soloists and groups: Their recordings are easily obtainable, and it is probable that they already are popular with ethnic minority teens. The problem is greater for television, given the higher costs of production, particularly for music videos that might begin to match the elaborate, attractive, and very expensive videos made by mainstream groups.

Many of the larger ethnic services have made attempts to attract teenaged viewers with non-musical material, often by combining that material with music segments. There also may be the opportunity for participation in parts of a show. For example, Maori Television has a weekly series for young adults, *Mai Time*, with some unusual features: A program segment ("Mai Live") in which music videos sent in by soloists and groups are played; and the opportunity for young adults to become (one time only) presenters of various segments of the shows.[42] There also are a few soap operas that center around adolescents, such as the already-noted "losteens" on Telemundo.

S4C took the unusual (and expensive) approach of commissioning an animated Welsh-language feature, "The Otherworld," for teenaged viewers in which three teens would travel back several centuries and find themselves as members of an earlier Welsh society, where they would encounter problems with parallels to those they experienced in 21st-century life. The depiction of that society was based on the Welsh historical epic, Y Mabinogi (www.s4c.co.uk/mabinogi). Through it, adolescent viewers might realize that their Welsh history was both exciting and relevant to their own lives.

One of the more commonly used approaches to reaching ethnic minority children and adolescents is to involve them directly in program production. Many fulltime ethnic minority radio stations devote the mid- to late afternoon weekday hours to music (with some talk) programs hosted by high school students. Quite often, the students lack fluency in the ethnic minority language, but then, so do most of their listeners. The hosts usually are encouraged to speak a few of the more common words and phrases, and to expand their vocabularies so that they might inspire their classmates to do likewise; some stations (particularly those operated by and for indigenous groups) may have coaches who instruct the announcers in correct language usage and proper customs.[43]

No ethnic minority service that I am aware of goes quite so far as does Bush Radio in Cape Town to involve children and adolescents in the station's programming. Bush has a Saturday block of programs that is produced *entirely* by them: Bushtots (ages 6–9) from 10 to 11 a.m., Bushkidz (ages 10–12) from 11 a.m. to noon; Bushteens (ages 13–18) from 12 to 2 p.m. In this project (CREW, for Children's Radio Education Workshop), each group works as a team, and there are enough participants[44] that it has been necessary to develop two alternating teams for each time period, with each team preparing its show (with the guidance of station staff) on the Saturday before its studio broadcast. A few of the

Bushteens have proven sufficiently adept that they have their own shows outside of the Saturday schedule. The station also hosts a yearly Radio Kidocracy Conference lasting days. It is aimed at discovering what sorts of programs and subjects young people would like to hear; teaching them radio production techniques, including presentation of radio drama, storytelling, interviewing, news reporting, and so on; and helping them to draw up a Children's Radio Manifesto in which they set forth what they want to accomplish through radio (www.bushradio.co.za/spec_proj).

Some of the access radio and TV services have made special efforts to recruit teenagers as program producers. The Offener Kanale (Open Channel) service in Berlin cooperates with the Berlin State Institute for Schools and Media to offer "Kids On Media" (KOM, at www.kids-on-media.de), which trains groups of schoolchildren (most of them in the 10- to 15-year-old segment, and a number of them members of Berlin's diverse ethnic minority population) to make videos. The training is conducted with the participation and supervision of classroom teachers, and the subject matter usually is what the schoolchildren themselves have proposed, for example, showing how a school class in one Berlin district persuaded the residents of a large apartment complex to allow class members to "beautify" the unadorned building's exterior. Radio Centre Ville (www.radiocentreville.ca) in Montreal has an active program of cooperation with Montreal schools that runs along much the same lines as does the KOM project.

BUILDING ELECTRONIC BRIDGES: PROGRAMMING PRACTICES AND THE PUBLIC SPHERE

From what is presented in this chapter, it should be apparent that the ethnic minority electronic media are capable of providing a wide range of expressions through a wide variety of formats. Some of those expressions and formats are intended to promote dialogue, to build bridges, whereas others are not (which does not mean that they *will not*). But dialogue and bridges with what sorts of communities?

Bridges Within an Ethnic Minority Community: Local, National, and Worldwide

Hartley and McKee (2000: 3) refer to the "indigenous public sphere" as "the highly mediated public 'space' for developing notions of Indigeneity, and putting them to work in organizing and governing the unpredictable immediacy of everyday events." As they discuss the concept, it seems evident that what they have in mind is a "space" where indigenous peoples can come together to learn from each other's experiences, but also a space where nonindigenous peoples (and their media in particular) can come to learn how indigenous peoples perceive themselves. They note that "Thus far, the Indigenous public sphere has hardly been under the control of indigenous people" (3).

As should be clear by now, there is an emerging indigenous/ethnic minority public sphere that *is* under the control of indigenous/ethnic minority groups, working through the electronic media. However, it would be quite correct to observe that the indigenous/ethnic minority media have not yet managed all that often to share information among themselves. Most ethnic minority media activity takes place at the local level, with little exchange of material *among* services.

Ethnic minority electronic media services generally are dedicated to the idea that they should serve their communities as broadly as possible, and try to satisfy a wide range of interests. That is far easier to accomplish if a service has access to many hours and days of airtime or can afford to develop and maintain a multifaceted Web site. With an hour or less per day (typical of what each ethnic group may have on many "rainbow" community stations), the program may include no more than a brief account of community news, an extended interview or discussion with a guest from the community, and perhaps a bit of music, usually but not always by an ethnic group artist.

Even a service with more time/space at its disposal probably will fail to include at least a few interest groups within communities. Sometimes the omission may be a matter of policy: no "hate" groups, no religious programming, no use of the mainstream culture language. Sometimes it may be determined by the wishes of those in charge, who may prefer to avoid openly declaring as service policy the exclusion of views contrary to those of the dominant "power elite" in the community, the nonavailability of airtime for young people, females, rap, hip-hop and rock artists, and so forth. Sometimes it is the result of a lack of equipment and/or facilities, such as recording gear for musical groups, as well as studio space.[45] And sometimes it is a lack of desire on the part of a group to present itself through the media, or even ignorance of the possibility that it could do so. Occasionally, a group may doubt that the broader community would be interested in learning more about it.

The services themselves certainly can do more to address some of those omissions than others. As discussed in greater detail in the final chapter, many ethnic minority services are very weak on self-promotion, to the point where some of them seem almost invisible within communities where they have been present for years. That lack of self-promotion costs a service not only audience members, but also the opportunity to mirror the community as inclusively as possible: Many community interest groups are short on time as it is, and are unlikely to invest it in working with a service that few in the community seem to heed, or even recognize.

The correction of certain omissions may be more difficult, especially when it means challenging the "power elite". I already have noted the example of KILI-FM, which rejected a significant financial offer from the tribal government because to do so would have meant cutting off what station staff felt were important community voices (Browne, 1996: 278, footnote 2). Nor are the elite always members of the local government; sometimes they are the individuals who have taken the responsibility for providing the station's only Greek/Albania/ Peruvian/Lao block of programming, but who also have refused to consider including the voices of women, young people, local musicians, and so on, in what they consider to be "their" program.

Service administrators can attempt to address those exclusions, even at the risk of alienating a longtime, often valued and frequently well-connected (within the community) program presenter. During a personal interview (Sydney, March 2001), Inoke Futa Huakau, the manager of Radio 2000 (a multiethnic service in Sydney, Australia), spoke of his gradual realization that many of the station's presenters were male and often in their 50s or 60s. When the station reorganized its program schedule in 2001, he told all program presenters that, if they wished to retain their program slots, they would have to begin working with a younger person of the opposite sex as a "junior partner." A few took to the idea with some enthusiasm, others with some reluctance, and still others offered reasons not to do so, such as "In my culture, an older man and a young woman should not work together in the same room." (Huakau suggested that a chaperone be invited to attend rehearsals and the actual broadcast.) At the time of our meeting, he was cautiously optimistic that the policy would take root.

A few ethnic/linguistic minority groups have used audio- and videocassettes to distribute their programs to one another. Ethnic women's cooperatives in Canada, Bolivia, and several other nations have produced programs and even series about themselves, featuring accomplishments such as campaigning successfully for a local hospital or better housing and challenges such as spousal abuse and alcoholism (Gallagher & Quindoza-Santiago, 1994; Gumicio-Dagron, 2001; Riano, 1994; Rodriguez, 2001). Many of those programs and series are distributed on tape to other groups of the same ethnicity, which may place them with local stations or access cable services. Tape duplication can be quite inexpensive, although mail services may be slow (militating against distributing highly topical programs).

As leasing time on communication satellites has become more affordable, a number of ethnic groups have begun to use them to distribute programs that would remind local ethnic communities that they are part of a larger picture— that there are Native Americans, Maori, speakers of Irish and other languages in other parts of the nation and even the world. The members of that larger ethnic community might have something to learn from one another, or might help to create a greater sense of solidarity within that ethnic group, which could translate into greater political influence locally and nationally.[46]

Most of the ethnic services with mechanisms for sharing programs and reports among themselves do so on a limited basis. AIROS carries "Native America Calling" for 60 minutes daily, 5 days a week and "National Native News" for 10 minutes daily, 6 days a week; those programs are carried by most Native American stations, but also by some of community radio services. There are other special broadcasts from time to time, but the vast majority of the usual Native American local radio station's schedule is made up of local material, along with recorded music (much of it mainstream, but with increasing numbers of Native American artists). The stations and their audiences may or may not want more material about other Native Americans, but if they do, the expense of gaining access to AIROS stands in the way of a few of them.[47]

Australia's National Indigenous Radio Service (NIRS) furnishes BRACS and other Aboriginal radio stations as well as some mainstream stations with satellite relays of material from several of the larger Australian Aboriginal radio stations. Since February 2001, NIRS also has provided stations with a 4.5-minute hourly newscast in which there is always at least one indigenous story. So far, it has nothing resembling "Native America Calling," although it would like to produce such a program. (However, where Aboriginal communities in rural Australia are concerned, telephones are scarce, so audience participation might be limited.) As with the AIROS-distributed programs, the NIRS material is in English.[48]

The situation is considerably better for Maori radio, where Ruia Mai (www.ruiamai.co.nz) provides the 21 Maori iwi (local tribal) radio stations with roughly 40 hours per week of Maori language material: a 5-minute hourly news and sports bulletin, with emphasis on Maori affairs; a weekday morning 30-minute current affairs program; a weekday morning 1-hour interview-based current affairs program; a weekday evening 30-minute current affairs program; a 30-minute Sunday evening arts and entertainment program; and a weeknight 90-minute bilingual "music countdown," with call-ins from around the country. Also, there is a Maori news Web site, Te Karere Ipurangi (http://maorinews. com/karere) that provides current Maori news items but also commentary and longer articles, as well as links to other Maori information sites, including research on genealogy.

Bridges Among/Between Ethnic Minority Communities

Communication satellites, audio- and videocassettes also play a role in reaching out to other ethnic groups. The Aboriginal People's Television Network grew from the Inuit Broadcasting Corporation, but when it expanded its television schedule and became available on cable TV throughout Canada, the expansion included individual programs and series produced or commissioned by indigenous TV services in other nations and regions, including the United States, Australia, and (less often) Latin America. Still other groups may not identify themselves as ethnic minorities, but render valuable service in distributing material about ethnic group activity. As one example, the Women's International News Gathering Service (WINGS, with headquarters in Vancouver, Canada; Web site www.wings.org) collects reports from women's groups around the world, and the experiences of ethnic minority women often are featured in the weekly audio-tape- and satellite-distributed "magazine" programs that it produces.

A number of Web sites provide forums featuring the exchange of information and cultural expression between ethnic and indigenous minority groups, as well as mainstream groups that support ethnic minority groups. The Worlds Indigenous Peoples Network (http://groups.yahoo.com/group/worlds-indige-nous-people) was founded in 1999 for just such a purpose, and presents several dozen messages each month. Contributions come mainly from Australia, New Zealand, North and Central America, but cover the activities of groups in other parts of the world, as well. Group contributions range from "alerts" about nega-tive developments affecting ethnic minority indigenous and non-indigenous pop-ulations, such as conditions at an Australian government-run "detention" camp for largely Afghan refugees, to celebrations of minority group accomplishments, such as the inauguration of the first fully indigenous university in Canada. Individual contributions might include an Aboriginal Australian family searching for a lost member, or a Navajo poet ("rustywire") sharing a poem about searching for the spirit of the dawn.[49] Users must put up with the fairly frequent interrup-tion of Yahoo-placed ads, but that certainly helps to lower the cost of the service.

Operating such as service is not easy, primarily because groups or their repre-sentatives (some of them quite likely self-appointed) are not always that active in furnishing reports about themselves. A service such as Australia's SBS faces a particularly large challenge in attempting to provide news reports to ethnic minorities in 68 languages on radio and more than 60 on TV. Ideally, those reports would contain items about the activities of specific ethnic minority com-munities around the nation, as well as items about important developments in the ancestral homelands of ethnic group members and about Australian develop-ments (government actions in particular) that are of particular importance to eth-nic minorities. It also would be ideal if the SBS English language news programs could provide all of those dimensions, and present them in such a way that they would be attractive to English-speaking ethnic minorities and to the Australian mainstream population.

Putting all of that into practice is difficult, to say the least. The SBS newsroom has neither the money nor the number of staff that would be necessary to manage such a huge task. It must delegate a certain amount of authority to the journalists within the individual ethnic services. However, those journalists also face pres-sures from within their own communities, and especially from elected or self-styled community leaders. The pressures may take the form of suggesting (or occasionally, demanding) positive coverage of some individuals, groups, and developments, but also may run in the opposite direction—no coverage or nega-tive coverage of other individuals, groups, and developments. But there also are instances where the journalists discover that various individuals and groups with-in the community would rather not have their activities covered, or at least not through such a public medium, because they do not wish to risk drawing criti-cism from other community members, where factionalism at times can be quite prominent. Such an atmosphere discourages investigative reporting, and SBS newscasts do not feature all that much of it.[50]

Bridges With the Mainstream Population

Because most ethnic and linguistic minority services were founded because their communities were not receiving much if any attention (or were receiving too much negative attention) from mainstream media, it is hardly surprising that there are relatively few examples of deliberate attempts at outreach to the mainstream audience. Those that do exist often are bi- or multilingual services with a predominant mainstream language, such as Radio MultiKulti (Berlin), Funkhaus Europa (Cologne), Radio Bilingue (Fresno, California), Radio AGORA (Klagenfurt, Austria), or MultiMedia Radio (Florence, Italy). The broadcast schedule usually is divided into segments where listeners wishing to hear programs in one or another of the minority languages will have scheduled times and days, but where speakers of the mainstream language also will have a block (most often daily) of airtime where ethnic minority program presenters fluent in that language will provide material of particular relevance to their ethnic communities and/or concerning their culture. There is a dual objective here: To reach ethnic minority listeners (predominantly younger people, often second- or third-generation) who have little or no command of their group's language, but also to reach mainstream culture listeners who might be interested in learning more about ethnic minority groups within the country.[51]

Services that do not consider themselves to be bi- or multilingual nonetheless may offer such programs as one (usually small) part of their schedule. Ruia Mai, as I noted previously, produces and distributes a 90-minute nightly music program in Maori and English, and it draws requests from Maori and Pakeha ("White") audiences alike. Bush Radio encourages its program presenters to use Xhosa, Afrikaans, Zulu, and other languages as well as English, and some of them do so frequently. Again, such services often have the dual objective that I have just indicated.

THE AUDIENCE

Few surveys or focus group studies have been conducted regarding audience member listening habits and program preferences for ethnic minority media services. Studies of ethnic audiences for satellite-delivered services from ethnic homelands—Turks in Germany and The Netherlands, North African Arabs in France—sometimes indicate audience reactions to ethnic services originating in the "new homeland," but that usually is an incidental feature of such a study. Also, Welsh and Scots Gaelic audiences have been the object of considerable study, thanks to the efforts of Welsh television service S4C, the BBC, and the Leirsinn Research Centre in Scotland.[51]

The evidence that I have seen indicates that programs featuring material of direct assistance to the community (health care advice, tips on savings and investment, dealing with welfare agencies, etc.) are very popular.[53] So are programs where individuals talk about life in the community 50 or more years ago, although teenagers sometimes express the wish that there be fewer of them.[54] Although music usually is popular, as well, tastes differ widely among various groups within the community, with some "traditionalists" expressing their dislike for hip-hop even more forcefully than do their mainstream counterparts, particularly when the ethnic minority language is used for that purpose. Newscasts are attractive if they contain sufficient material about ethnic individual and group activity; newscasts that appear to repeat the same material covered in mainstream newscasts are not particularly welcome. Comedic and dramatic formats generally are popular so long as they are reasonably professional, do not appear to ridicule the ethnic groups they portray, and do not contribute to reinforcing negative stereotypes held by the mainstream culture.

Although ethnic minority audiences seem willing to tolerate less than "fully professional mainstream" standards as an ethnic service is in its growing period, there is some evidence of expectation that those standards will improve over time. However, there also is a desire that productions recognize and exhibit specific ethnic minority cultural characteristics, and that mainstream language productions with subtitled or dubbed translations substitute figures of speech, proverbs and other "markers" of ethnic minority language practices. Productions that are regarded as close copies of mainstream "models" are not particularly welcome.

It also appears to be very difficult to attract children and teenagers to ethnic minority media services if there is little or no material of specific relevance to them and, in most cases, produced by or at least involving their presence. However, it is important to avoid overgeneralization because listening and viewing preferences often differ considerably according to age, gender and first-/second-/third-generation membership.[55] Parents, teachers and children especially appreciate the instruction value of broadcast productions, especially in their role as reinforcers of language instruction, and welcome programs made expressly for language-learners.

Scant as survey evidence may be on the above points, there is even less of it with respect to programs that appear to be designed for the purpose of assisting ethnic minorities in entering the public sphere or mini-sphere. (Similarly, the few programs that are intended to attract and "educate" the mainstream audience have received very little attention in research studies, aside from occasional indications of size, composition and [rarely] program preferences of that audience.) I have yet to see a survey that assesses ethnic audience, much less mainstream, reaction to the broadcast of a tribal council meeting, call-in programs that deal with significant (to the ethnic community) issues, or forums where a "live" audience and/or callers may Interact directly with hosts and guests, and possibly (especially through the internet) with one another.[56]

SUMMARY

There are very few program genres and formats that ethnic minority media services have *not* utilized, but some appear with greater frequency than others. That sometimes may be due to differing tastes and preferences on the part of the audience, but it also may be a result of what the service budget will cover, as well as the nature of a community's talent pool. A service may be able to nurture talent, as OK Berlin, Bush Radio and others have been able to do in developing programs produced by children and teenagers, or as many services have done in working with teenaged musicians. That takes time and patience, and even then there may be so few who offer their talents that the service is unable to develop an ongoing program, but instead must content itself with occasional appearances by those performers. One can argue that ethnic minority media services should be especially open to including occasional broadcasts, but that appears to be less often the practice now than it once was.

Ascertaining the size or composition of the audience, not to mention what the audience thinks of what it receives, has received far less systematic attention than it should, with the PSB-supported services such as BBC's Raidio nan Gaidhael (Scots Gaelic) and YLE's Sami service for Finland, as well as Welsh, Scots Gaelic and Hispanic-American television services, as major exceptions. Granted, there are problems of cost and execution, but the Tumeke-FM case study should indicate that systematic studies are not impossible for smaller ethnic minority media services, let alone larger ones. Studies of audience reaction to programming that is intended to bring community members into the public sphere may be more difficult to develop and execute. However, if service administrators consider that particular goal to be important (and many state that they do), then the effort should be worthwhile, and media staff members will have a more precise idea of just how well they are and are not meeting it.

NOTES

1. I use this term in the sense of *formal* education. Certainly, there is a great deal of informal education that can take place, through nearly every type of programming. However, most ethnic minority services themselves restrict their use of the term to in-school or after-school *reinforcement* programs, as well as language lessons.
2. Even the BBC's new (2002) satellite-distributed radio service (1Xtra) for "fans of black music" does not have a newscast, although the service's Web site (www.bbc.co.uk/digital/radio/1xtra) does have a "One life Message Board," which has carried messages on such topics as the war in Iraq, being gay/bisexual/lesbian, education, health, and so on. Few of the messages that I had read as of late 2003 had much if anything to do with being Black or any other ethnic minority.
3. Ethnic minority newspapers with Web sites are a different matter, although even here the prevailing tendency seems to be to add little or nothing to the printed version.

4. Personal interview, John Ferguson, director, BBC Radio Orkney, Kirkwall, April 2003.
5. Personal interviews with program creators Waihoroi Shortland and Rereata Makiha, Mana Maori Media, Papatoetoe, New Zealand, September 1991 and October 1993.
6. April Fool's Day in the United States, and a common occasion or mock news stories.
7. Several media organizations have prepared guidelines for reporters covering ethnic community events and people (see Bostock, 1990; Eggerking & Plater, 1992; Langton, 1993; Stockwell & Scott, 2000).
8. A roughly similar study was conducted by Wambui (2003). It dealt with the Development Through Radio project in Sierra Leone, and focused on radio programs featuring women's observations about the wartime periods and their struggles to exist.
9. Although not about ethnic minorities, a case study on the BBC Radio Ulster (Northern Ireland) "Talkback" program provides a thoughtful consideration of what might and might not be accomplished by way of developing a better sense of mutual understanding through the use of "talk" radio (see Coleman, 2002).
10. I have seen some very good examples of storytelling through television, including a colorful animated series of Aboriginal Australian folk tales made in the early 1990s, and distributed primarily through reasonably priced videocassettes.
11. Singhal and Rogers (1999, 2003, Hornik (1988), and the Web site www.comminit.com contain numerous example of ad-like announcements.
12. I heard the former over several Maori stations while in New Zealand in 1996, and the latter while visiting Bush Radio in Cape Town in September 2002.
13. There were precedents for this sort of service in Australia. Both the "Flying Doctor" and "School of the Air" services date back several decades. However, both services could count on their intended audiences owning not just a radio receiver, but a transceiver (combined transmitter-receiver) as well, so that two-way communication was possible. As I learned in my first visit to 8KIN (September 1987) most of its listeners lacked access to a transceiver.
14. Many indigenous radio stations in rural areas have provided similar services. Vargas (1995) cites several examples of what a number of Mexico's Indigenous Radio Network (INI) stations broadcast as "radio post offices" or "radio phone booths."
15. Ogan (1993) provides an insightful analysis of such usage during the 1991 Gulf War.
16. I had the opportunity to hear some of those questions and challenges when driving in western South Dakota in March 1995, as I listened to KILI-FM's broadcast of a tribal council meeting. Some of the attendees were upset over the council's projection of costs for a new road, and pressed members for details on how the figures were calculated.
17. This study does not deal with people's interpretations of what they receive through the electronic media, and my treatment of entertainment genres here is restricted to what ethnic minorities present through those electronic media outlets where they can speak for themselves. There have been very few studies thus far that have examined audience interpretations of such presentations.
18. The Telemundo Web site (www.telemundo.com) provides a detailed description of the series and its characters.

19. "Rogha an Lea—sobal-dhrama idirghniomhach…" on www.bbc.northernireland/blas/radio-dhrama.

20. However, the station was modeled after one at which the writer of the series had worked briefly. Because the fictional station seemed to be run by idiots and incompetents, the manager of the actual station was not at all pleased with the portrait (personal interview with Cyril Chapman, Manager, Tautoko-FM, Mangamuka Bridge, New Zealand, October 1993).

21. A White columnist in an Invercargill, New Zealand paper even said of one self-deprecating "joke" on the program that "I think I'm allowed to tell that one, because it was featured on … Radio Wha Waho" (Fallow, 1993: 2).

22. As it did in Ybor City (Tampa), Florida in December 2000 (Persaud, 2000).

23. The Web site www.ccg.org.uk/press indicates how the series functions and how to become involved.

24. The S4C Web site, www.s4c.co.uk, provides further details. The elaborate staging and costuming alone would be prohibitively expensive for most ethnic minority services

25. Personal interview, Clair Chang, Program Coordinator, BAMA, Broome, October 1993.

26. White also adapted his play for radio, and produced and directed the series.

27. In 2003, Maori Television entered into a production contract for a reality series, *Te Iwi Kohatu*, that would assemble a small group of volunteers and place them in a remote area where they would have to create a *pa* (fortified enclosure) and live together in semi-traditional Maori fashion. Much like the U.S. Public Television reality series *Frontier*, but unlike *Survivor* on U.S. commercial TV, the group would *not* vote participants off the team. It may come on air in 2004.

28. A Texan-Mexican-American woman.

29. The Maori Language Commission also oversaw the creation of a Maori-language dictionary of sports terminology in the mid-1990s; the chief motivation was to assist Maori sports writers and announcers. Although some of the Maori terms bore a close resemblance to their English equivalents, many did not (personal visits to the Maori Language Commission in October 1991 and September 1993).

30. But Univision's local affiliates do not do so for local contests involving Hispanic-American teams, although they may for local professional athletes who are Hispanic-American.

31. The Scots Gaelic television service does not receive *direct* monetary or other forms of support from the BBC, but the latter is obligated under the terms of its Royal Charter to broadcast 90 hours per year of Gaelic TV productions. It does support Gaelic radio (Raidió nan Gaidheal, or Radio of the [Western] Islands). Two Scotland-based Independent Television companies—Scottish Television (Glasgow) and Grampian Television (Aberdeen)—are obligated under the terms of their licenses to produce weekly programs in Gaelic (30 minutes weekly for STV, which also must rebroadcast 30 minutes weekly from Grampian; 53 minutes weekly for Grampian, which also must broadcast STV's 30 minutes). STV and Grampian make no secret of their desire to be released from the obligation. To quote from the Chairman's Foreword to the Gaelic Broadcasting Task Force Report (2000), "it has now been put to us with brutal clarity by the commercial broadcasters that Gaelic broadcasting is an encumbrance which they have to support because of ITC [Independent Television Commission] enforcement but which they now regard

with no interest or enthusiasm." Information retrieved from www.scotland.gov.uk/
library3/heritage/gbtf-01.asp, October 15, 2003.

32. The "working name" of David Mathlany, who greatly admired South African
Communist Party official Joe Slovo.

33. The most difficult language to staff, Slovo said, is Venda, due to a shortage of
Venda speakers in the Alexandra area.

34. Thomas (2001: 113) observes that "if you underestimate the capacity of your *language* to develop when society is changing, you prepare it for the realm of nostalgia,
which is often the comfortable face of despair."

35. Those examples were related to me by staff members at Raidio na Gaeltachta in
September 1990, Te Reo Iriraki ki Otautahi in November 1993, and Xiberoko
Botza in September 1989.

36. I have treated the subject of minority languages and the electronic media in greater
depth elsewhere (Browne, 1996: 165-190). See also Cormack (1998), where the
author discusses the problems faced by linguistic minorities in attempting to enter
the public sphere.

37. Whether Catalan should be considered as a minority language within Catalonia is
another matter because a majority of those living in the area speak it fluently, but it
does bear a fairly close resemblance to Spanish (which Basque certainly does not),
and Catalan households can receive plenty of radio and TV programming in
Spanish, so it faces some of the same problems encountered by other languages living side by side with a roughly similar but far more powerful linguistic "neighbor."

38. Grin (1989, 1997). Grin and Vaillancourt (1999) expand on the "economic benefit"
argument, and provide an interesting assessment (pp. 27-50) of Welsh-language TV
channel S4C in terms of its success in encouraging the use of Welsh, although they
see room for improvement in its appeal for teenage audiences.

39. In 1998, just a few years after the dissolution of the Soviet Union, a private multi-
ethnic radio station was founded in Moscow. Although Krasny Most ("Red Bridge")
broadcasts almost entirely in Russian (it occasionally carries poetry readings in
Armenian, Georgian, etc.), its program content is directed to the Azeris, Armenians,
Georgians, and other peoples from the old Soviet Republics, aside from the Russian
Republic (Solovyova, n.d., but likely 1999).

40. Quite possible, because most ethnic minority groups in the United Kingdom were
not that well disposed toward the Conservatives.

41. However, the imported children's programming carried by TG4 and S4C appears
to have been carefully selected to eliminate the more violent cartoons and to
emphasize such widely accepted values as being kind to others through such cartoons as *Super Ted(-dy Bear* and *Clifford the Big Red Dog*. Guyot, writing about the creation of the Breton commercial TV service TV Breizh, expresses his concern that
the Breton-language portions of the schedule will consist of subtitled or dubbed
"Japanese cartoons, American series, advertisements" that would make Breton an
instrument for translating such shows—clearly not a noble purpose, in his view
(Guyot, 2001: 13).

42. The program's Web site (www.maitime.nzoom.com) informs contestants that they
need the approval of their families and their schools in order to participate. If
accepted, they work with one of the show's directors to prepare for the experience.

43. Many station managers who have used the late afternoon hours for such programming have told me that at first there often was criticism from older and more fluent ethnic group members that the station was setting a disrespectful example by putting such "beginners" on the air. Their usual reply was to point out that young people were the future of the language and culture, and that one had to start at their level, then work to raise it; in other words, "Give us time."

44. According to station staff (personal interviews, September 2002), Bush Radio tries to attain a balanced geographical and ethnic representation of participants from within its coverage area.

45. I have visited a number of stations where the only studio present could hold a table and chair, but very little else, and where the announcer had to possess the skills of a contortionist to enter and leave!

46. A few services, such as Ireland's Raidio na Gaeltachta, have used satellite relays to bring their programs to Irish speakers in other nations, but the purpose usually is cultural maintenance, although the services could make use of that audience as evidence of their relevance, locally, nationally and internationally.

47. The connection expense is not all that large in absolute terms, but a number of the Native American stations operate on the thin edge of solvency.

48. One project ("Moorditj: Australian Indigenous Cultural Expressions," 1998), commissioned and distributed by the Western Australian government's Department of Aboriginal Affairs rather than NIRS, used CD-ROM technology to display the artistic work of 110 Aboriginal and Torres Strait Islanders (Hartley & McKee, 2000: 167).

49. Examples were drawn from the group's Web site entries for June 2003.

50. During personal visits to SBS in February 1996 and in March 2001, I spoke with a number of journalists, editors and heads of language services. I also have relied on accounts of SBS journalistic activity provided by Davies (1998); and Jakubowicz (1994).

51. Friedrich Voss (manager, Radio MultiKulti) and Gualtierro Zambonini (Manager, Funkhaus Europa) were particularly helpful in explaining the operation of this dual approach where their services were concerned (personal interviews with Voss, September, 1995 and April, 2001; and with Zambonini, July, 2002). An interesting feature at both services is that the German-speaking program hosts, reporters and other interviewers are encouraged to use their ethnic languages on air when it seems necessary to help a German-speaking ethnic minority guest, interviewee or caller express her or himself more clearly or comfortably.

52. There is a summary of audience research conducted by the center between 1993 and 2001, accessible through www.scottish.parliament.uk/S1/official_report/cttee/educ-01/edp01-18.pdf.

53. A more complete list of earlier surveys appears in Browne (1996: 264-265). Some of the research from the 1990s includes DeMay (1991: 417-430); Karam and Zuckernick (1992); Nihoniho and Young (1993); Ruohuoma (1995); Sueddeutscher Rundfunk (1993); Veldkamp Markonderzoek (1995). In addition, I have examined reports by the BBC on audiences for Welsh-language programming, by the Leirsinn Research Centre (www.leirsinn.smo.uhi.ac.uk) on audiences for programming in Scots Gaelic, and by Australia's Special Broadcasting Service (see Ang et al., 2002). There also are several qualitative studies, most of them with limited numbers of respondents, in Ross (2001).

54. I recall speaking in 1994 with three teenagers in Galway, Ireland about their
     favorite radio stations and programs. All three claimed to be reasonably fluent in
     Irish, but spent very little time listening to Raidio na Gaeltachta. When I asked
     why, they all said that there were too many people talking for too long about "the
     old days," and too much time taken up with detailed descriptions of wakes (funeral
     receptions), including lengthy life histories of the departed.

55. On generational differences, see Hargreaves & Mahdjoub, 1997: 459-477; Ogan &
     Milikowski, 1998: 13-21; Hargreaves, 2001; Ogan, 2001; Milikowski, 2001. The
     studies generally emphasize audience reactions to satellite-delivered services from
     the ancestral homelands and say little if anything about reactions to "new home-
     land" ethnic minority media.

56. Price and Cappella (2003) dealt with online discussion of public issues—here, U.S.
     political campaign issues during the period April-December 2000. They found that
     more than 70% of the discussion group (663 out of 915 respondents) had attended
     at least one of the eight online sessions, whereas roughly 40% (350) had attended
     half or more of the sessions, with older respondents most likely to attend frequent-
     ly, with political knowledge as another significant predictor of attendance.
     Furthermore, actual participation, as measured by online "talking," was distributed
     very evenly. Their findings would seem to indicate that this form of participation in
     the public sphere holds considerable promise, although the small number of ethnic
     minority discussion group members makes it difficult to generalize regarding its
     appropriateness for that population. Price did tell me in a brief personal conversa-
     tion (Minneapolis, September 2003) that in general the data for ethnic minorities
     matched up closely with the data for the overall group.

Conclusions and Projections

Given the plethora of ethnic minority electronic media services, their differing natures, and the wide variety of goals they set for themselves, it would be futile to attempt grand-scale comparisons or to develop a list of structural factors that might contribute to "ideal" services. However, and in line with the questions posed in Chapter 1, it is worthwhile to try to determine whether certain factors seem particularly significant in the influence they have on the success of those services.

THE IMPORTANCE OF STRUCTURAL FACTORS

The broadest and most obvious common denominator among those factors, in terms of its significance, is *financial support*. As we have seen, that support can come from a number of different sources, and most ethnic minority services must rely on more than one of them in order to exist in the first place, much less to survive and to meet their programming goals. The PBS-supported services appear to be the most stable in that regard; in fact, many of them have experienced considerable growth over the past decade or two, while none of them, so far as I can determine, has ceased to exist.[1]

That may be the result of a real sense of commitment on the part of at least some PBS senior administrators to serving minorities, but it also may be reinforced by a growing recognition on their part that the traditional public service broadcasters need to identify and justify fresh reasons for their continued financial support through household license fee revenues and/or annual government appropriations. The growing numbers of ethnic minorities in most industrialized nations, coupled with the likelihood that most commercial broadcasters will not be interested in serving them, at least on a national level, make them a logical high priority audience.

What is less obvious, but well worth noting, is that almost all of the *non*-PBS ethnic minority-operated media services that existed at least 20 years ago have managed to survive. As indicated in previous chapters, most of them have had to struggle at one time or another, as some of them do constantly, in order to make financial ends meet, and a few have gone off the air for short periods of time. That is a remarkable record, but the *communities* served by the operations often have made the difference, simply because they cared enough to assist in finding ways to continue. Sometimes, it is money, but often it has been goods (food, fabrics, furniture) and their own (largely volunteer) labor. Far more often than not, the media services (local in particular) have worked hard to develop and maintain close identification with their communities, so one might observe that they are rewarded for their efforts in a very literal way. Also, failure to maintain that identification, as we have seen in the case of TuMeke FM in Whakatane, New Zealand, can result in a rapid loss of community support and audience size.

How the ethnic minority internet services will fare financially is difficult to say, because most of them have not been in existence for all that long. There is a high mortality rate among internet services of all sorts, as anyone who has used a 2- or 3-year (or even month-) old internet address list soon discovers. Ethnic services often face even more difficult financial prospects than do most other internet services, if only because (a) many ethnic minority groups have low internet usage rates; (b) there are no direct equivalents to public PSBs when it comes to internet services (although almost all national PSBs have their own internet services); and (c) if advertisers have been slow to advertise through mainstream internet services, they have been even slower to do so through those operated by and for ethnic minorities. (Government departments and agencies have been readier to use ethnic minority Web sites, as we have seen.)

When we consider those factors that appear to be most influential in determining *each* of the specific outcomes—the creation of ethnic minority services, their continuity, and achievement of their principal goals—several of them come into play, some more than once.

Based on my observations, the most important factor influencing the *creation* of a service is not structural; rather, it is the willingness of individuals, often working as small groups, to commit themselves to its achievement. In nearly every instance where I have visited a service, staff members have expressed doubts that they would have had a service if not for the efforts of a handful of individuals who simply would not give up in the face of financial, regulatory, and technical obstacles. Usually, those individuals felt that the ethnic community (or a fair proportion of it, at any rate) supported their efforts, but that, if they did not persist, no one else was ready to step in and take over.

The individuals themselves come from many walks of life, but three categories seem most prominent: ethnic minorities with pre-existing media experience; teachers (including clerics: priests, missionaries, rabbis, imams, etc.); and community activists.[2] It is not particularly surprising that any of the three would wish to support the creation of ethnic minority media services, nor surprising to discover that they often bring certain biases with them.

What matters is whether they recognize those biases and how they manage them. The "media experienced" may want the service to operate on at least some of the same lines as do established media services, which is fine as long as the community does not come to feel that participation is limited to those who can exhibit something close to mainstream professional standards or that the service itself strikes them as a pale copy of the mainstream stations. Teachers and clerics are apt to regard the service as a way of teaching the community about the disappearing elements of its heritage (language and customs in particular) or providing it with religious instruction; again, that can be valuable, but also can lead to an inability to see some merit in contemporary cultural or religious expression through rock or rap music, or the mixing of mainstream terminology with the ethnic minority language. Community activists may see the service as a way of helping the community to rid itself of various evils (disease, child/spousal abuse, etc.), which certainly is helpful, but less so (and probably less effectively) if the activists pursue a top-down approach that minimizes community participation.

Policymaking by governments has been an important factor in the creation of a number of ethnic media services (if not as many as one might suppose), through development of exclusive licensing categories or preferential licensing consideration for would-be ethnic service operators, provision of start-up funding, and in a few instances, initiation of services such as SBS. Such policymaking has been heavily influenced by the *social climate*, which accounts for the fact that there have been periods marked by the creation of considerable numbers of ethnic media services, as well as periods with little of such activity. Most governments have been slow to assist ethnic minority groups in establishing local radio and TV services, and very few have done so at the *state/province/area (subregion)* or national levels. However, governments in Australia have provided exclusive licensing categories, start-up funding, and annual financial support for local ethnic minority services, *and* have created the world's largest ethnic minority national broadcasting service—SBS. Canada also has done comparatively well by its ethnic minorities, the indigenous populations in particular, as has New Zealand (Maori and Pacific Islanders). No other government has come close.

When I presented the Australian policymaking process as a case study (Chapter 3), I noted that several elements came together to lead to the creation of the SBOS. The climate of the times certainly helped, as it did in the case of SFB4–Radio MultiKulti in Berlin, and any attempt to develop a *strategic approach* to policymaking on behalf of ethnic minority media would do well to weigh the odds for success in that light. Periods of fiscal austerity coupled with lack of sympathy on the part of the ruling party or coalition may not be the most opportune moment for implementing the strategy. But there is real merit in identifying friends in high places (especially those who are ethnic minorities), cultivating the mainstream media to raise public awareness and support, and devoting what may seem like never-ending efforts to keep the pressure on and to apply it where there is reason to believe that it will do the most good. All of that assisted in the SBS campaign. And if the law of the land (and perhaps the policies of supranational bodies, for example, the European Community, in which the nation holds membership) contains anti-discrimination provisions, or pro-minority provisions, that can help the cause, as it did in the creation of a viable Maori broadcasting system in New Zealand (Browne, 1996: 131-163).

Although *community support* frequently plays a role in the initiation of ethnic services, it is more apt to take the form of cheerleading—encouraging those who form the nucleus of the effort to keep up the good work. *Local and tribal governments* sometimes will promise to make space available to the service, and usually those promises are kept. If a local *religious institution* is involved with the project, it may be able to secure cooperation in the form of funding, gifts of equipment, and training, from national and international religious bodies with which it is affiliated.

There does not appear to be one dominant factor in the continuity of ethnic minority services. Certainly, *community support*, as noted earlier, is very important, especially for the many local and neighborhood services. Government *policymaking* in the form of continuing authorization of financial support through annual appropriations to such services, local and national, is important where it exists, but somewhat unreliable because of changing financial and political climates. The greater readiness of the PSBs to support ethnic radio, and sometimes TV, has been particularly helpful at the national level, and because financial support most often comes from annual license fees, it is quite secure, even if increases in the fees often fail to keep pace with rates of inflation. *Institutional support* has been vital in many cases: support by PSBs, as already noted; support for local services by *religious* organizations, particularly for indigenous services in developing nations; support by *educational* institutions in a few instances.

There is one form of support that is more difficult to quantify, but may be of the greatest importance to survival: *human capital.* Most ethnic minority media services would shrink or disappear if they did not have the participation of *volunteers* and the presence of *low-paid staff.* Although there clearly are disadvantages to relying heavily on volunteers and on "permanent" staff members willing to work long hours for minuscule wages, both are essential to the viability of most local ethnic minority broadcasting.

In a related vein, the persistence of a service over time, particularly in the pursuit of its goals, seems highly dependent on *organizational stability.* There are several reasons for stability, or lack of it, in an ethnic media service's output, but most of them can be found at the top: The continuing presence, vitality and adaptability of the service administration, as well as the most highly valued volunteers. I have mentioned the burnout factor more than once in previous chapters, but we should consider why some services manage to avoid burnout (by and large, since no service I have ever visited was entirely burnout-free) and others are plagued by it.

The single most common reason, according to present and former service administrators and staff with whom I have spoken, is overwork. That often is connected with heavy dependence on volunteers (Chapter 4), who can be the joy and the bane of an administrator's existence: Joy when they maintain their commitment, remain fresh and vital, and rarely miss or are late for their program slots or other responsibilities; bane when they become irresponsible, casual, or tired. Usually, the administrators must fill in when volunteers fail to show up; if such problems arise frequently enough, they can and have prompted administrators to leave. A second major cause of resignation seems to be the "tug-of-war" syndrome: being pulled back and forth between displeased and sometimes powerful groups of community members. Administrators tend to feel underappreciated after a few years (or less) of such treatment. The third probably is monetary support: The usually meager salaries available to many ethnic service administrators may wear over time, especially as family responsibilities begin or increase, or as offers of better pay and shorter working hours come from other media services.

Those media services that have been able to maintain their administrative teams over time also seem to maintain strong ties with the community, in large part because they feature several forms of consultation and contact between community and service.[3] Both parties appear to take the attitude that sustaining the service is a mutual responsibility, which improves the likelihood that a distressed manager will turn more readily to the community for help, rather than simply leaving. Managers and other top administrative personnel who have had previous experience in administration and/or ready access to sources of expert advice also seem to be better able to weather the various storms that are likely to arise. That is a good endorsement for administrative training programs and for the mentoring services noted in Chapter 4, as well as for the experience that can be acquired through short-term experiences under restricted service licenses (described in Chapter 2).

To better evaluate the role of factors in the *achievement of principal goals*, it would be of great help to know what the goals were as well as what they are so that there can be an informed assessment of what has changed over time and what has remained more or less constant, and more importantly, why it has changed or not.[4] Information on original goals often is not available; most ethnic minority media services are no better than their mainstream counterparts in keeping records of their birth and growth. Still, I have encountered very few examples of what has been described as "digging up the plant every week to see whether it's taking root," and that would seem to indicate a certain degree of stability.

However, just as there certainly are cases of commercial radio stations changing their formats once or twice a year, there also are ethnic minority commercial and noncommercial radio stations that have changed formats, some of them more than once. That usually is due to declining ratings or to sale of the station rather than to indications of dissatisfaction on the part of the target audience, but in either case, the motivation to change is primarily economic, however much it may be justified in the name of "providing our listeners with even better programs." Rarely is there evidence of consultation with the community in order to determine how to improve the level of service.

Certain goals may be easier to sustain than are others, often because there is greater consensus among media service staff and within the community regarding their importance. *Reviving the language* is one such goal, even though there probably will be some who feel that too little or too much airtime is devoted to it, or that the language used is not sufficiently pristine or is far *too* pristine.[5] *Highlighting the accomplishments of community members* is another; again, there will be those who claim that the "wrong" people/groups get too much attention (and/or the "right" ones too little), and that is something that can bring about changes in management if those who feel that they are being neglected and their enemies glorified are sufficiently powerful.[6]

Fostering ethnic minority musical talent often is a popular and lasting goal, although some individuals may be disturbed over the use of the ethnic language to express love or hate in particularly strong terms. *Focusing attention on ethnic minority children* is at least as popular and as long-lived, but not necessarily once they reach their teens and become more disposed to question authority. *Dealing with health and monetary concerns* also is a common and stable goal, especially because, sad to state, those concerns seem to be widespread and never-ending.

Goals may shift because those individuals mainly responsible for carrying them out lose interest in doing so or simply decide to move on to something else or to take a well-earned rest. They may be forced out because there is a general lack of community support for what they are doing, how they do it, who does it, or all three. There may be other individuals and groups within the community who come to regard the station as a useful instrument in their acquisition of greater influence, and who are able to take control and promote their own goals, which may or may not coincide with earlier goals. When one of those goals is using the service to *generate revenue for the community*, it may be that programs implementing the existing goals will not disappear from the schedule, but will be placed in less popular time slots (or, for internet services, be given less prominent display) and perhaps given less airtime.

It is not always easy to determine why goals shift because the parties involved will have their own explanations for the change. Local members of the South African Rural Women's Movement were largely responsible for creating Moutse[7] Community Radio Station (MCRS) in 1997, and sought to ensure that it would serve the entire regional community, but with special attention to the experiences, achievements and problems of women. The South African broadcast regulator, ICASA, offered it a license as a "community of interest" service for women, but the women held out for a "geographical community" license in order to emphasize their commitment to a broadly inclusive service. But the first 2 years were difficult: ICASA was slow in granting a license, the local bank baulked at setting up an account for the station, and ". . . Internal tensions grew as they few remaining women lost their grip on the project." According to project consultant Tracey Naughton, "the reality of MCRS today is quite different from the one envisaged by the women who started it and by the donors who funded it. . . . A project that had a well-defined starting point has experienced a gradual slippage from a clear development orientation . . . to a male-dominated culture of enter-tainment-focused, ego-boosting broadcasting" (Gumicio Dagron, 2001: 251). In such a situation, it is difficult to tell who bears responsibility for what occurred.

One potentially important source of influence on continuity appears to play a very modest role in that regard. *Government regulation* could impose requirements that hold broadcast stations (and, if regulation were to reach that far, internet services) to the promises they have made as a condition of receiving and retaining their licenses. In fact, during the 1960s and 1970s the U.S. FCC required radio and TV stations to file annual reports in which they identified problem areas within their communities and how their programs had dealt and would deal with those problems. However, stations rarely were questioned about their practices, and fines or license revocations were almost nonexistent.[8] The general practice of government regulators seems to be to avoid the imposition of specific require-ments, but instead to wait for community members to complain about program-ming practices before looking into a station's activities. That should work well enough *if* community members know how and where to lodge their complaints, and have some confidence that they will be taken seriously.

FACTORS, ETHNIC MINORITY SERVICES, AND PARTICIPATION IN THE PUBLIC SPHERE

I have chosen to discuss the influences of factors on ethnic minority electronic media and the ways in which they may serve to assist participation in the public sphere as a separate but related part of my consideration of the overall subject because I feel that such participation is the single most significant function that those media can perform. Also, it appears to be the least understood of their vari-ous functions. After I review several dimensions of the public sphere and ways in which ethnic minority media services have addressed this particular function, I provide a set of illustrative examples.

The Nature of the Public Sphere Revisited

I observed in Chapter 1 that Habermas does not take note of the existence of eth-nic minority electronic media, and thus does not consider their possible role in promoting ethnic minority participation in the public sphere. Nothing in his dis-course on the sphere would indicate that he would deny their utility as entry points, although he might wonder, given their tremendous variety and relative lack of coordination (e.g., few national networks), whether they would be particularly effective in that regard. Also, as he does not seem to conceive of the sphere in anything other than broad terms (national and all-inclusive), I suspect that he would be uneasy with the notion of mini-spheres which serve very specific, narrowly drawn communities. Yet, that clearly is where the vast majority of ethnic minority electronic media services operate.

To be sure, there are increasing signs of cooperation among ethnic minority media services, as well as the creation of ethnic minority national services, that might promote ethnic minority participation at the national level. For example, there are nationally disseminated news services: indigenous satellite-delivered radio (and in some cases, TV) news broadcasts in Australia, New Zealand, Canada, the United States, Scandinavia, Ireland, Wales, and Scotland; similar services for nonindigenous ethnic minorities in Great Britain for Asians, France for North African Arabs, the United States for African and Hispanic-Americans, Australia for the ethnic minority groups in general, Germany for a smaller number of such groups.

In some instances, however, national newscasts make little provision for material originating at a subregional or local level. Also, some of the national services feature brief newscasts (5 minutes or less), and even they may include relatively modest numbers of items dealing with the experiences and concerns of minority populations. Still, many of the services have been in existence for relatively short periods of time. Presuming that ethnic minority journalists become more numerous, that their levels of experience increase, and that ethnic minority audiences become more demanding, those services could become more significant in helping ethnic minority individuals and groups to participate more readily in the national public sphere.

There are other sorts of ethnic minority programming that are distributed nationally, ranging from the heavily entertainment-oriented fare offered by Hispanic- and African-American national TV services to discussion programs such as "Native America Calling" over AIROS and audience participation pop music shows such as "SIPS–Stay in Play" over Maori radio network Ruia Mai. Also, the notable increase in ethnic minority popular music groups has led to the creation of many national production and distribution services for their work.

The growth of ethnic minority national services has not been matched by the growth of research studies that might provide us with some idea of how effective those services are in reaching ethnic minority and mainstream audiences.[9] A.C. Nielsen now conducts national surveys of African- and Hispanic-American TV viewers on an established schedule, but they provide demographic information only. There have been numerous studies of ethnic household listening and viewing behaviors (and occasionally, motivations) in The Netherlands, Germany, France, Great Britain, and other European nations. They generally show high user figures for nationally available satellite or cable-delivered ethnic services, most of them imported from other nations, but usually do not indicate whether the audience members regard their content as having any direct bearing on their own experiences as ethnic minorities in another society.[10]

Because most ethnic minority media activity occurs locally, it should be easier to encourage participation at that level, and certainly there is much more of it, particularly through radio. Also, it appears in a greater variety of forms, both political and cultural. Although many of the ethnic stations do not originate newscasts, the vast majority of them have discussion and call-in shows where political issues arise, and a few have programs that deal exclusively with such issues. A few indigenous stations also provide live coverage of tribal government meetings, including questions and comments from the floor. A number of ethnic minority political figures have made efforts to attract the attention of ethnic stations, and a few have managed to secure their own weekly or monthly program slots, although the latter (at least in my experience) usually do not include provision for direct audience participation. Many ethnic stations are very active at election time, and hold open forums with the candidates, election-oriented call-in shows, candidate interviews before "live" audiences, calls for people to vote and explanations of how and where to do so, and other programs where community members can raise questions and express their views.

Cultural forms of possible participation are even more numerous and varied. Participation through music is perhaps the most common, and many stations provide encouragement to local groups of musicians. That is most apparent through broadcasts of their work (and, for the ethnic internet, through publicity for their live performances and their recordings), but some of the better-equipped stations also serve as recording studios. Because ethnic minority musicians quite often express concerns and triumphs (their own as well as those of others) through music, there is opportunity for entry to the public sphere. Discussion and interview programs, as well as call-ins, encourage participation on subjects ranging from health and money management to intergenerational understanding and the observation of traditional customs and practices. Sitcoms and drama may play roles in raising important issues and perhaps bringing people to become active in addressing those issues, even if they very seldom involve direct participation by audience members.

Programs made for (and in some cases, by) children and teenagers, although perhaps dealing with politics, more often are cultural: learning about an ethnic group's history and practices, raising concerns about parental and spousal abuse, confronting thorny issues such as teenage sexual behaviors, and so on. And of course there is considerable language instruction, although its effect on participation in the public sphere is more indirect, perhaps increasing ethnic pride to the point of inspiring personal involvement.

In the preceding chapters, I have placed greatest emphasis on how ethnic minority media services and communities work together to achieve participation, some of which may constitute entry into one or another public sphere. As we have seen, some types of services (local, noncommercial, several forms of contact with their communities) seem better suited to providing such entry points than do others (national, commercial, little contact with their communities aside from quantitative surveys), especially in the form of permitting and even encouraging community members to speak for themselves. However, there are no guarantees that members will participate, and if they do, whether that will bring them into a public sphere where information and ideas are exchanged. By the same token, we know that ethnic minority media services possess the capacity of to promote ethnic minority participation in the public sphere. It certainly is not inevitable that they will do so, and some in fact provide little or nothing that would encourage it.

The issue of what it is that drives media service as well as community behavior in ways that are not conducive to participation is complex.[11] Although it is easy to identify certain elements, such as empty promises (we say we want you to/you say you want to, but one or the other of us really does not) or narrow perspectives (you can participate/I will participate only if you do it my way), that begs the question of why such elements exist in the first place.

For example, an atmosphere of strict *professionalism* at an ethnic media service often seems to discourage widespread community participation. Does that atmosphere exist because those in charge of the service feel that it would confirm negative mainstream stereotypes about minorities who "can't run a media service that sounds/looks/reads like the real thing," or might it be that those in charge are professionals themselves, and cannot conceive of any other way to function or see this as a stepping-stone to careers in mainstream media? Do community members refuse a service's offer to participate (and perhaps provide training) because they just do not have the time, lack self-confidence, do not wish to expose their views to the full scrutiny of the community, or do not think that what they say will lead to any sort of change? Rigidity on the part of either party might be present for legal or quasi-legal reasons (avoidance of libel or slander charges), but it also may be that defining in narrow terms what one will or will not do makes it easier to justify why the offer of participation was not accepted.

Uses of the Electronic Public Sphere by Ethnic Minorities

A number of the brief case examples that follow involve media services operating at the community level, thus promoting participation in the mini-public sphere. Certainly it is much easier under most circumstances for a locally based media service to encourage the active involvement of community members. However, the Kabylie case example illustrates that one can develop community participation on an international level through use of the internet, while the Chiapas case example and the Chapter 4 case study on Zoom Black Magic Liberation Radio indicates that it is possible to generate support from a broader community by careful use of modest resources.

The amount of participation likely to be generated by the services varies a great deal. Some of the messages clearly were intended for narrowly defined communities, whereas others had broader targets. However, in each instance it appears to have been the intent of the individuals or groups to generate discussion—in other words, to enter and/or assist others to enter the public sphere.

Often there would have been a certain degree of risk involved—certainly for the originators, but perhaps on occasion for the listeners who entered into the discussion/dialogue.

Mayan Women. Starting in 1997, a group of Mayan women in Solala, Guatemala learned to make video and to use the internet in order to preserve their cultural heritage, induce greater participation by Mayan women in community affairs, and teach other Mayan women how to make videos and use the internet. The group now operates as the Centro de Mujeres Comunicadoras Mayas (Mayan Women Communicators Center), and works with the Council for Mayan Communication in Solala, which has established a telecenter for bilingual (Kakchikel and Spanish) teachers and for first- through sixth-grade students. Some of the children have created a musical theater production based on Mayan legends concerning the Spirit of Lake Atitlan, and have used it to draw attention to current environmental problems.[12]

Aboriginal Teenagers. A group of Aboriginal teenagers in Broome, Western Australia approached the local Aboriginal radio station in 1995 with a proposal to make a series of radio plays about the sorts of problem that Aboriginal teenagers face: Teenage sex, abusive parents (particularly alcoholic fathers), White prejudice. The children produced the entire series. The plays stirred up considerable discussion in the Broome community. However, the praise they received far outweighed the criticism.[13]

Cree Women. A Cree Native American women's group in Northern Quebec produced (mid 1990s) a set of video documentaries about unemployment and its effects on home life in their community. Because this was not the sort of issue that had been discussed in public (shame, fear of retaliation), that was a very bold move, and brought the community to discuss it and then take steps to decrease the levels of violence, drinking, and gambling that had been going on. The effort probably would have been confined to the community, but news of it spread, and other communities used it as a model.[14]

Serbo-German Rock Band. A rock band composed of Serbian and German musicians introduced a number of songs with lyrics that celebrated the virtues of joining two different cultural perspectives and coming up with a third culture that included the most attractive (to them) elements of the first two, as well as a few of their own devising. But they also mentioned the criticism they received from members of their own respective cultures—principally but not solely younger members—for having "abandoned" their own cultural heritage. They also answered this criticism in song, noting that they all felt that they had three cultures to draw upon, and were all the richer for it. Originally produced in 1995 for an episode of the ZDF (Second German Television) series *Nachbarn* (*Neighbors*), their work was distributed on video, and likely used by many of Germany's cable access services (Zweites Deutsches Fernsehen, 1995).[15]

German-Australian Teens. A group of German-Australian teenagers in Melbourne produced a monthly program in German and English (mostly the latter), aimed at their peer group. The program formed part of a "German Hour" on a Melbourne community radio station (3ZZZ), and was the first youth-oriented segment to find a place on the "German Hour." When it came on air in 1999, some of the older German-Australian listeners objected strongly, because "the kids" played "distasteful" music—particularly music that contained "four-letter words" (often six or more letters, in German, and principally *scheiss*, or "shit"). "The kids" defended their choice, explaining to the audience that they had developed the program to appeal primarily to their peers, among whom songs with "rude" lyrics often were popular. They also hoped that older listeners could use what they presented to gain insight on the sorts of things that interested their sons and daughters, nieces and nephews, and younger friends ("3ZZZ Youth Program," 1998).

Peruvian Women. A number of Peruvian indigenous women have participated in a health and family planning series ("Bienvenida Salud!" or "Welcome to Health") broadcast by *La Voz de la Selva* ("The Voice of the Jungle," a community radio station in the Loreto district of Amazonian Peru) by writing letters to the program producers in which they express in general and specific terms what the program has led them to change in their practices, but also how it has increased their sense of empowerment. The letters themselves are read on the program to encourage others to follow their examples (McKinley & Jensen, 2003).

Tanzanian Fishermen. The video production project *Maneno Mengi* ("Small words," in Swahili) assisted fishermen in southeastern Tanzania to illustrate the problems they were encountering with marine resource management, revenue sharing, personal income management and developing collective bargaining power. The videos made by the group included interviews with government ministers, the district executive director in charge of the fish market, and their own discussions of the problems. With the videos acting as catalyst and as visual evidence, they were able to get the Tanzanian Navy to intervene in halting dynamite fishing, to strengthen their own association, to gain access to a share of the tax levied on them by the fish market, to create a savings and loan program, and to encourage other communities to build fish markets (Gumicio-Dagron, 2001).

Iranian Women's Program. Leila, produces a weekly radio program over a Stockholm community radio station (Radio Sydvast) about Iranian women living in Sweden. She often discusses the plight of women in abusive relationships, and she has received numerous threats over the time (approximately 7 years as of

2003) she has produced the program. She continues to do so because she has received mail, telephone calls, and personal visits from women who state that they have been helped and sometimes empowered by what she has said, and have taken various actions based on it, for example terminating abusive relationships or gaining respect from males for their views on politics and other "male" subjects.[16]

Kabylie on the Internet. The Kabylie[17] living in France have had a number of small-scale media services for several years, including a number of programs on Beur-FM (the Paris-based network for North African Arabs living in France). In 1998, the Association Kabyle-France-Internationale (AKFI) initiated an internet service—www.Kabyle.com—for Kabylie and the larger North African Berber population. The aim of its founders was to strengthen Berber cultural identity, and they were careful to distance the site's own editorial content from anything that would become involved in "Berber politics" because, according to the site's editor "Politics isn't our cup of tea. . . . Berberness is a very sensitive subject which divides Kabylies" (Gabin, 2001, translation mine). The site provides news, interviews, practical information, a press review (several Algerian papers, but also some French papers as well as *El Mundo, The Guardian* and Associated Press), forums and chat rooms, and an interactive Amazigh (Kabylie language) dictionary as well as a distance education course in the language. The forums, all of which have moderators who try to keep exchanges from becoming too tendentious or parochial, have proven especially popular; many of them have attracted Berber participants from France, North Africa and beyond, with some non-Berber participants as well (Sagot, 2002).[18]

Chiapas and the Internet. The Mexican state of Chiapas became a prominent name in media reports in the mid-1990s, largely thanks to the use that the members of the EZLN (Ejercito Zapatista de la Liberacion Nacional) and their supporters inside and outside Mexico made of videos and the internet: They provided Mexicans and the outside world with running accounts of clashes with Mexican government authorities, injustices experienced by the indigenous peoples of Chiapas, the statements of EZLN leader Commandante Marcos, and other information relevant to publicizing their cause. Although at first the group did not operate a Web site, the reporting done by themselves and their supporters was concise, often verifiably accurate, timely and available in Spanish and English. Because this particular use of the internet was quite novel, those accounts began to appear in newspapers and over radio stations throughout North America, but also in Europe.

By 1998, some of the inhabitants of Chiapas had begun to make and distribute videos of abuses by the Mexican Army, but also to portray lifestyles, practices and beliefs of the Maya living in Chiapas, and to cover a mass assembly (Convocacion National) held in San Cristobal to discuss future steps. The videos were copied and distributed within Mexico and abroad, and several communities have set up ongoing workshops to train others in making videos. The movement now has its own Web site (www.chiapasmediaproject.org.). In effect, the EZLN and its supporters have created a public sphere where such a thing would have seemed nearly impossible at the beginning of the 1990s (Gumicio-Dagron, 2001; Froehling, 1999; Knutson, 1998; Russell, 2001).

A Summing Up of Ethnic Media and Participation in the Public Sphere

Regrettably, there are very few detailed studies of the program production process followed in ethnic minority media services, and those few are concentrated on a particular category of program activity (Alia, 1999; Madden, 1989, 1992). We need many more such studies before we can more precisely determine the range and nature of program practices that facilitate ethnic minority participation in the public sphere. What I have offered here may serve as an indication of what is available and what people do with it, and hopefully will help to guide those who conduct more detailed studies, but it must be regarded as indicative rather than definitive. With that cautionary note in mind, I offer the following observations:

- Any assessment of participation in the public sphere through the electronic media, whether it involves ethnic minorities, mainstream populations or both, must be made with the realization that it can take place in a wide variety of formats, including some that usually are associated with entertainment.[19] Also, the electronic media seem able to *stimulate* participation by providing material through formats that do not involve direct participation by the audience, as in the Aboriginal teenager radio dramas mentioned above. The cultural dimension of participation in the broader public sphere brings a potential added benefit: The presence of ethnic minority voices and views in cultural presentations, when they contain political messages, probably will be more acceptable to the mainstream public than overtly political material would be.
- Although men continue to outnumber women in most ethnic minority media services, the numbers of women in the more important administrative and production positions appears to be increasing. This is particularly the case for community radio stations and in the newsrooms of indigenous stations. Furthermore, most ethnic minority stations provide programs particularly for women, and some of them provide considerable amounts of airtime for that purpose. Ethnic minority Web sites remain heavily male-dominated, although a few are operated by (and usually for) women.[20] I regard the presence of women in decision-making positions within ethnic media services as important, not only because that presence more accurately reflects the composition of

society, but also because those female ethnic minority decision makers whom I have met in the course of my research seem particularly supportive of getting community members to participate in the public sphere.[21]

- Children and teenagers are becoming increasingly important as program producers and participants at many ethnic services, although far less so on the internet than through radio and TV. It is too soon in most cases to determine whether those who become involved carry their participation and/or support for ethnic media services into adulthood, or whether they will be strong supporters of programming that helps to bring audience members into the public sphere, but early indications are promising.

- When searching out reasons for participation and nonparticipation, it is necessary to realize that this is a two-way street: Media services and community members must work together, openly and willingly, if meaningful participation is to be achieved.

- Mini-spheres *do* exist, and ethnic minority media have played roles in creating and strengthening them, at least where ethnic communities themselves are concerned. What we do not know is whether they exist in a state of balance with the broader public sphere. That is, do they promote participation within their communities *only*, or do they also encourage community members to participate in the broader sphere? It well may be that the participation they do promote will come about indirectly. I think it more probable that they will stimulate curiosity, provoke small group discussion, perhaps even offer models of how one might conduct oneself in the sphere, than that they will offer actual opportunities for direct participation.

- Media service administrators in charge of access or community services that promote ethnic minority participation have observed that the more recently arrived ethnic communities, many of them from nations lacking a tradition of media diversity, openness and credibility, often appear reluctant to participate, even when they are offered free training. Those communities often are the fastest-growing ethnic minority groups in most industrialized nations, and the differences between their country-of-origin cultures and the new host country culture seem more likely to lead to misunderstandings, legal problems, etcetera. Clearly the electronic media—and not just access and community services—can play an important role in acting as a bridge between cultures, but their administrators will need to consider just how to achieve that still-elusive goal.

The apparent shrinkage in airtime available to incidental users over community, access and ethnic radio and TV services noted above has special relevance for the more recently arrived émigré populations. Most of those individuals have come from nations lacking in traditions of citizen participation and freedom of expression through the media. They are likely to need more time and more persuasion if they are to take their places in the broadcast schedules of such services. They probably will not wish to undertake commitments that involve broadcasting or Web site maintenance on a continuing daily, weekly or even monthly basis until they feel much more confident that this is a worthwhile undertaking. But will there be incidental airtime available to them so that they may gain that sense of confidence gradually? And will that airtime be available at hours that are convenient to them and to their prospective audiences? If not, they are not likely to be interested, no matter how much *potential* good they might do for their communities.

• More than a decade has passed since the introduction of the internet. Many ethnic minority groups now make use of it, for a variety of reasons and in a variety of formats. In some cases, there appears to be a real sense of community on the Web site, with several types of forums, chat rooms and other interactive options, as well as a carefully selected and lengthy set of links. In far more of those that I have visited, there are few interactive options or links available. A medium that possesses tremendous potential power in terms of facilitating participation in the public (mini) sphere has yet to demonstrate that power where most ethnic groups are concerned, whether because of lack of access to the necessary equipment or the impression that the medium is yet another instrument to promote the domination of the English language and the Western thought process. It shows greater promise in helping to bring together ethnic minorities with similar concerns, indigenous and diasporic populations in particular, through such Web sites as the Indigenous Information Network (iin@iin.co.ke), the Inuit Circumpolar Conference (www.inuitcircumpolar.com), the Quechua Network (www.quechuanetwork.org), Turkish Media (www.turkish-media.com), Iranet (www.iranet.com); and the Native Nations Network (www.nativenationsnet.net). The creation of community telecenters as a way of making the internet more familiar and accessible to ethnic minority users also shows some promise, but is far from being a cure-all.[22]

Wireless internet is growing in popularity, although there still are relatively few locales in which it can operate effectively, thanks to the need for a host of transceiver (transmission and reception) installations in cities of any size, let alone entire nations. Also, it is quite expensive. Still, it seems likely that its use will spread, and some ethnic minority groups already are using it. The Makah

Indians, a small coastal tribe in northwest Washington, have developed a wireless network and are using it for a variety of purposes: interconnecting to discuss tribal issues; selling their crafts through the internet; and learning their tribal language, which relatively few of them now speak. There were 150 Makah with wireless keyboards and access codes to the Makah Web site (www.makah.com)[23] by June 2003. The Economic Development Corporation of the Affiliated Tribes of Northwest Indians, which sponsors the Makah project, hopes to build on the project by using it as an example to other tribes of what can be accomplished (Gohring, 2003).

- Although it is quite evident that most ethnic minority media services have been influenced (and often *heavily* influenced) by their mainstream counterparts in their presentation of material, many of them have reflected their community's own cultural practices in such specific ways as use of pauses, slower rates of speaking, absence of frequent interruptions during interviews, regard for emotional implications of what is presented, respect (sometimes too much) for those in positions of authority (Browne, 2002).

- No ethnic media service can sustain itself on community participation alone. Even the so-called access services rely quite heavily on "regulars" to fill the airtime or screen space, because they and other ethnic services know that, with occasional exceptions, those groups and individuals will do so reliably, efficiently, perhaps professionally. Still, it is possible that, in return for that security, the services may find themselves losing touch with some parts of the community, which could come to regard them as more and more inaccessible (less and less community-oriented).

I close my consideration of the public sphere with a pair of broad questions: First, can there be a single broadly public sphere in an industrialized world where media outlets are multiplying so rapidly, with the possible exception of those moments, for example, 9/11 when a single event may galvanize "the public" in the broadest possible sense? My brief answer is that, in most of the larger industrialized nations, such a sphere is becoming more difficult to sustain, largely because of the increasing number of licensed electronic media services (broadcast, cable, satellite) and the growth (uneven, to be sure) in internet services. Second, where there is a broad public sphere, and where there are mini-spheres, what is the role of the electronic media in carrying out one of Habermas' chief goals for the sphere: The facilitation of *dialogue*? Here the answer cannot be brief, because we need to subdivide our consideration of mediated dialogue: With *whom* is the dialogue being held within and among mainstream and ethnic populations? For what purpose(s)? Cultural? Political? Economic? How do mainstream- and minority-produced programs and internet services help to facilitate it?

To answer those questions, we need far more in-depth research on the dialogue-promoting experiences of electronic media in many nations, and not only of ethnic minority media. The present study does not provide that research, but I can offer some impressions. First, the electronic media traditionally have not been all that interested in promoting dialogue. Throughout most of their histories, they have regarded themselves as "senders" and their audiences as "receivers." The internet has not followed that model, although some of its more commercial users promote only very limited dialogue with their customers. Community and access radio and TV services have been somewhat more open to involving individuals and groups in program production, but have tended in recent years to favor those who are willing to commit themselves to ongoing, regularly scheduled programs, leaving less time free for more incidental users. Nor have most of the programs on those services promoted dialogue with and among the audience, aside from call-in and listener request offerings, and even they often have treated dialogue as entertainment or self-promotion (for their hosts).

Second, when dialogue is promoted, it appears to be largely with and among a fairly narrow segment of the audience: "repeaters" who are regular listeners, viewers or readers, and who are ready to offer information, views and opinions on a variety of subjects from political to cultural to economic, and a great deal more. Whether they are ready to acknowledge the contributions of others is less certain: The practices of most program producers, coupled with technological limitations, makes it difficult for audience members to speak with each other as well as to engage in true dialogue (often requiring more than one question or statement per participant) with program hosts and their guests.[24]

Again, the internet can circumvent some of those limitations, although it requires a certain amount of skill and spare time to participate in "real-time" exchanges, especially when using visual devices such as avatars,[25] which are slow to download unless one has sophisticated software and high-speed connections. If community members themselves can become involved in the development of internet services and structures appropriate to their needs, capabilities and manners of expression, there should be better prospects for success in developing various forms of participation through the internet.[26]

Where mainstream and ethnic minority services seem better able to promote dialogue is in their provision of *stimulation*: opening up topics for discussion among listeners, viewers, and readers by making available sets of facts and views pertaining to those topics, and doing so in ways that will bring audiences to talk about them. Provocative hosts and guests can help, but may do more harm than good if they belittle each other, disrespect callers and Web site visitors, or seem interested mainly in promoting themselves. If their provocation sometimes takes the form of action-stimulating questions and remarks directed to the audience ("Has this come up in your home, workplace, etc.?" "Have you and your family/neighbors/co-workers wondered what to do about this situation?" "It's easy to obtain more information/organize a discussion group/initiate a petition.

Here are some phone numbers/addresses/ Web sites..."), that may be helpful in promoting dialogue. Holding community forums on air (as Bush Radio does) and broadcasting "live" meetings of local or tribal governments and associations (as KILI-FM does) also can help through their provision of specific examples of civic dialogue where "ordinary people" take part.

It would be wise to bear in mind that dialogue in the public sphere or mini-sphere may not always be readily apparent. It may go unrecognized by observers unfamiliar with the practices of a specific culture. Words and phrases in all languages can have very different meanings depending on the context within which they are expressed. Nonverbal (oral and visual) expressions vary a great deal among cultures, and even within a given culture. Emotional words, phrases, and expressions may be the least uniform of all elements of communication, yet dialogue often features them. Put another way, one person's harangue may be another's invitation to an exchange of views.

Also, it may take considerable time for dialogue to develop, especially if a community has been ripped apart by conflict. Think of Sarajevo and its Bosnian, Croatian, and Serbian populations, or the many tribes in Sierra Leone and Liberia, or Los Angeles following the numerous disturbances that have erupted because of interethnic tensions or perceived injustices. One of the goals of the Panos West Africa project noted in Chapter 5 is to generate discussion within towns in Sierra Leone that might help to re-establish a sense of community, but no one presumes that dialogue will blossom immediately following the first broadcast. At best, the creation of programs that provide a sense of what dialogue can sound like perhaps will bring individuals to consider initiating it.

One further consideration: Thanks to the existence of mini-spheres, it is quite likely that ethnic minority and mainstream audience members increasingly will find themselves in the position of working harder to develop a sense of dialogue by listening to, viewing and reading the electronic media. Although mini-spheres and the broader public sphere provide opportunity for the presentation of a wide variety of viewpoints, the presentations themselves often do not take the form of dialogues. In fact, it is not unusual for them to come across as one-way statements: Accept them or not, they are not open to discussion. Both Dahlgren (1995) and Murdock (1999)[27] see the need for the promotion of dialogue through the media, but for me it remains open to question whether individuals and groups are willing to make the effort to combine the strands of separate presentations made through different media outlets and fashion them into dialogues.

THE "DARK SIDE" OF ETHNIC MINORITY ELECTRONIC MEDIA

My intent throughout this volume has been to portray and analyze the ways in which ethnic minorities have used the electronic media. Although I have been critical at times, my fundamental assumption has been that such activity is a positive thing for society. I also indicate that some of the services have had to over-come opposition to their existence, usually from groups within mainstream soci-ety, but occasionally from within the minority communities themselves. That opposition tends to see what could be labeled the dark side (*pace* Darth Vader) of ethnic minority media: the *problems* they may create or exacerbate in mainstream and ethnic minority societies. Although I disagree with such assessments, it is important to take note of them because they are not likely to disappear; also, they have some bearing on what I present in my subsequent treatment of ethnic minority electronic media and the public sphere.

One of the most common opposition arguments is that ethnic minority media services are divisive—that they tear at the fabric of society. The argument often is expressed in terms of the arguer's personal experience: "I have lots of black/Asian/Native American friends at school, in the workplace, in my church/syna-gogue, and they're just like us [members of the majority culture]; if they have their own media that only gets in the way of keeping us together as a society.'[28] A roughly similar argument sometimes is used to indicate that such media services, but especially the noncommercial services, are a waste of money, particularly if government funding is involved.

A third argument arises from some individuals who claim to have ethnic minority interests at heart: helping minorities to maintain their own languages and customs disadvantages them in the "real world," where they shall have to compete for jobs with people who are fluent in the mainstream language and understand the mainstream culture, and thus will have an advantage in the employment process.

The first argument can be regarded as cultural narrow-mindedness or even paranoia. Still, it might help the cause of those who believe in ethnic minority media as strengthening society if the minority services themselves were to reach out to mainstream cultures a bit more often. That could be accomplished provid-ing material couched in the spirit of "This is us, and we think that, if you listen/watch/read this material attentively, you'll get to know us better." Such material has been in relatively short supply (and sometimes totally absent) in the output of most ethnic minority services that I have visited or am otherwise aware of. It need not take up large amounts of time or space; even 1- or 2-minute inserts of the "Did you know?" variety can be useful in countering some of the negative stereotypes held by mainstream audiences. Such material also can help to counter the second ("waste of money") argument, and might even include indica-tions of just how little (if any) financial support governments actually provide.

The third argument can be a bit more difficult to confront, although there *are* circumstances in which ethnic minority individuals can be disadvantaged by their lack of command of the mainstream language(s) and/or their unfamiliarity with mainstream culture. Ethnic services that provide material in both ethnic minority languages and the mainstream language(s) can argue that they serve speakers of either or both sets of languages, and act as an additional resource to mainstream individuals who seek to learn ethnic minority languages and to increase their understanding of minority cultures. In doing so, the services can justly claim that they provide enrichment for both ethnic and mainstream cultures. Also, rarely is it the case that audiences for ethnic minority services of any sort cannot hear, see or read material transmitted by mainstream media, and the latter usually far exceed in quantity of output what the former can provide.

There are two further negative views on ethnic minority media services that surface from time to time. We already have encountered one of them: the "danger" that services broadcasting in foreign languages may disseminate "negative" messages, wittingly or unwittingly, and that the mainstream public (including the government) will not realize that the fibers of society are being weakened. The sort of negativity most often noted is anti- (mainstream) authority: defiance of police and resistance to laws. I have seen no documented cases of incitement to large-scale resistance, much less outright rebellion or revolution, on the part of licensed ethnic minority stations.[29] A Turkish TV station did broadcast a message urging Turks abroad (who presumably received the station via satellite, directly, or through cable) to join the Turkish army and help contain the Kurdish "threat" within Turkey. A warning from the German government that it would block the satellite signal if the message continued to appear (it was interpreted as a glorification of war, which the German constitution outlaws) brought its rapid withdrawal.[30]

Most of the negativity that has come to my attention involves intra-ethnic affairs. Serbs and Croats, usually appearing in German cable channel access radio programs or during programs they have produced on community radio stations in Australia sometimes engaged in verbal attacks on one another during the breakup of Yugoslavia in the 1990s. Such attacks generally were short-lived, as station managers intervened and threatened to strip the groups of their airtime. A Greek-Australian broadcaster criticized a Greek-Australian evangelical organization in allegedly offensive and demeaning terms in an August 1996 program that she hosted on Adelaide ethnic station 5EBI; the station was instructed by the Australian Broadcasting Authority to report on the program's specific content and, if warranted, to take steps to ensure that there would be no recurrence.[31] Although the Serb and Croat attacks could be seen as injurious to society, it is harder to make that case for the 5EBI incident, and the incidents like it that I have heard of during my visits to ethnic stations.[32] There also have been isolated cases of individuals, usually from the mainstream population, using their programs on access radio to attack ethnic minorities.[33] In almost every case, self-regulation has prevented recurrences of the offense. Measured against the overall foreign-language broadcast output from ethnic minority stations, such incidents are very rare indeed.

The second of the present-but-infrequent negative views involves a "bread and circuses" argument, this time made chiefly by ethnic minority group members and their supporters and along the following lines: "Ethnic electronic media activity has no major effect on ethnic minority status in mainstream society. It's made available to us as a sort of safety valve through which we can bemoan our situations, criticize mainstream authority figures for what they haven't done to help us, to play our own music and tell our own stories, and feel that we've really accomplished something when we haven't changed anything significantly."

From the evidence I have gathered through listening, viewing, and reading ethnic media, there has been comparatively little airtime or Web site space devoted to people bemoaning their situations or criticizing mainstream authority; it has been far outweighed by celebrations of achievement on the part of ethnic minorities. The relative absence of the former has surprised me, because there are some vivid demonstrations of ways in which videos, for example, have been used to show those in authority just how bad a situation is and how many promises have not been kept. Some of that activity has brought results, as in the case of the videos made in the Tanzanian *Maneno Mengi* project referred to above, or in the videos made by the Kayapo tribal members showing the negative impact of "outsiders" seeking to exploit mineral and agricultural resources in the Kayapos' Amazonian homeland (Turner, 1991).

Because ethnic minority broadcast stations are licensed by mainstream governments, there will be some general limits set on what those stations and all other stations can carry, but in most industrialized nations (developing nations sometimes are another matter), those limits do not include tough, honest, accurate criticism of those in authority. Therefore, regulatory restrictions are not likely to be an impediment to airing criticism of those in authority. And there are some ethnic services—Bush Radio, the Native American Web site www.indianz.com, Aboriginal People's Television Network, among others—that operate in quite varied sorts of circumstances, yet manage to present a fair amount of critical material. It is quite possible that many ethnic minority services display such material in less obvious forms, such as rock or rap, but it also may be that some of those services regard cultural activity as their chief purpose, with less attention to ethnic minority political activity.

ETHNIC MINORITY MEDIA, MAINSTREAM MEDIA, AND SERVING THE PUBLIC

There is the possibility that mainstream media could regard the presence of ethnic minority media as a justification for reducing or eliminating whatever types and amounts of ethnic portrayals they have been providing. That justification might be supported by reasoning along the lines of "Ethnic minority media will know best how to reach their communities, so why should we provide something that's second-best, or even culturally inappropriate?" Because there are very few ethnic minority services available on a *national* level, such an argument simply is not tenable there (which has not prevented people from expressing it). Furthermore, if a national service is supported by household license fees or annual government appropriations, as are many of the public service broadcasters, the fact that ethnic minorities are among the fee and tax payers also invalidates the argument, even if the PSB itself provides some specifically ethnic services. Nor is it that difficult to enlist the help of ethnic minority groups in determining what *is* culturally appropriate, even if there may be disagreement on that point among community members.

At the *local* level, where ethnic minority services are more common, there are many towns and cities where no such services exist, even though minority groups live there. Some of those groups are likely to be too small to mount a production schedule that would make them audible or visible to the general population with any frequency, and some groups may lack funding that would support such efforts. The largest metropolitan areas, where the greatest variety of ethnic minority groups is likely to be found, probably will have several radio stations and a few TV stations that will provide some airtime for those groups, but certainly not for all of them. Thus there remains a need for local mainstream services to help fill in the gaps.

Along with the need for mainstream services to reach out to ethnic minority audiences, there is the equally important need for those services to present *mainstream* audiences with portrayals of ethnic minorities. For one thing, mainstream audiences are far more likely to listen to, view and read mainstream electronic media services than they are to seek out the ethnic minority media. There are several possible explanations for that, ranging from the likelihood that the ethnic services will have more limited transmitter power and will occupy the less desirable positions on the broadcast bands to the fact that some of them will sound and look "different" (perhaps less immediately attractive, possibly incomprehensible at times) when compared with mainstream services.

Mainstream services could be required by law to devote portions of their airtime to portrayals of ethnic minorities, although I am unaware of any nation where such a requirement is imposed. Those services sometimes have their own codes of practice and sets of guidelines in which program producers and performers are enjoined to display sensitivity in their portrayals of ethnic minorities.[34] Such codes and guidelines may be influential in shaping the perceptions and behaviors of media professionals, but much depends on the willingness of top-level administrators to underscore their importance[35] and to act decisively when they have been breached.[36] If they are made know to the ethnic minority communities themselves—and often they are not—they can provide members of those communities with an instrument for demanding more frequent and more accurate portrayals.

There also may be a lack of knowledge on the part of the mainstream audiences that the ethnic services exist. Most of them have come into being during the past 20 years—a period when many industrialized nations have experienced the rapid growth of electronic media outlets. The mainstream services that existed prior to the expansion already commanded the loyalty of mainstream audiences. The newly emergent services often have spent a great deal of money and effort in trying to erode some of that loyalty, publicizing what they have to offer and where viewers can find them on their sets and their computers.

Many of the ethnic media service administrators with whom I have spoken are aware that they are not well known to mainstream audiences, and for some of them, that is perfectly all right, since they often regard that audience as secondary (even a very distant second) to the achievement of their goals. When I covered goal setting in Chapter 4, I made that same observation, and noted that, with all of the ethnic community-directed goals that could be present, it should not surprise anyone that serving the mainstream audience usually would have a low priority. Still, stinting on publicity may cost an ethnic service more than just a mainstream audience.

Some ethnic service administrators seem to regard the publicizing of programs and the service itself as a luxury, and a low priority luxury, at that. However, my conversations with members of the ethnic community (including some media service production staff) indicate that ethnic community knowledge of the existence and nature of those services, as well as where to find them, sometimes is quite low. Thus, the absence of publicity may cost ethnic services in terms of reaching more of what should be their core audience members as well as some of the mainstream audience. Although absence of publicity is not the fault of mainstream media, publicity itself is an activity where those media could assist their ethnic counterparts by providing advice and perhaps even training, although competitive enterprises usually are not known for their charity toward other media services of *any* kind.

Because mainstream and ethnic minority audiences alike generally spend far more time using mainstream media than they do ethnic minority media, mainstream media services have an obligation to provide mainstream and ethnic audiences alike with balanced, accurate images of ethnic communities and individuals, whether through newscasts and other informational formats, through entertainment, or through both. I use the term *obligation* deliberately: In most nations, the airwaves belong to the public, and not to the mainstream public alone. That applies even to specialized ("niche market") media services. Whether media regulatory agencies are willing to codify and then enforce such an obligation is another matter, particularly in this deregulatory era. A final observation: Given the growing presence of ethnic minority communities in nearly all of the industrialized nations, not only is it in the self-interest of mainstream media to recognize that presence (many community members are potential mainstream audience members, and their children almost certainly will be); it also is a matter of helping to foster healthy societies in which mutual respect is the norm and mutual mistrust the rare exception.

THEORIES AND CONCEPTS

I noted several theories and concepts in Chapter 1 when I discussed various authors whose work had influenced my research. Although my own database is broad, I do not feel that it is sufficiently deep for me to claim the right to propose a new theory about ethnic minorities and their uses of electronic media. However, I am quite willing to reconsider those theories and concepts in light of my findings.

Where *cultural* or *media imperialism* is concerned, the sorts of media services I have studied almost always are intended to provide an alternative to the mainstream media, and usually they do. However, the extent to which they do so is not always easy to determine, because many of the services sound and look a good deal like their mainstream counterparts when one first encounters them. Often it is necessary to listen, look and read carefully before one begins to notice a number of subtle and not-so-subtle differences, such as length of pauses, respect shown to interviewees and other guests, rate of speaking, mixing of mainstream and minority languages, use of minority slang, "accents," types of internet links provided, and of course themes emphasized in both factual and fictional material. It has been rare in my experience to find ethnic media services that did *not* exhibit at least a few mainstream media characteristics, just as it has been rare to find any such services that lacked ethnic minority characteristics. Minorities *have* found their own voices through their own media, and many (although not all) of them no longer need depend entirely on the mainstream media for their portrayals.

Still, the mainstream media continue to command a far larger share of ethnic minority audience attention, if not loyalty, than the ethnic services can manage. That is likely to be true long into the future. Also, the mainstream media will continue to attract ethnic minority producers, writers, actors, journalists, and so on, who gained some of their media experience through working for ethnic services. Some of those individuals may be able to alter various mistaken and negative perceptions of ethnic minorities held by their mainstream colleagues, and sometimes that may result in positive and lasting changes for mainstream media portrayal of minorities. But sometimes they will not be able to alter anything, and some of them may not try. Cultural/media imperialism *does* exist, and ethnic minority media can do only so much to influence it for the better, but they do make it possible for ethnic and mainstream audiences to realize that ethnic minorities are more than what mainstream media choose to present. The *hegemony* of the mainstream electronic media and audience *dependency* on them no longer is unchallenged.

The concept of the *public sphere* as set forth by Habermas is too narrow to be readily applicable to ethnic minority media: It is concerned mainly with political and economic dialogue at the national level, and fails to take into account the wide variety of ways in which dialogue may be initiated and stimulated (through music, drama, poetry, etc.). However, the reinterpretation by Dahlgren (1995),

Curran (1995), Stevenson (2002), Keane (1996), and Fraser (1992), among others, of the public sphere as consisting of various mini-spheres, alternative spheres and/or subaltern spheres seems to fit nicely with what most of the ethnic services provide for their communities; also, Dahlgren recognizes the validity of music and other "nondialogic" forms of expression for the exchange of thought, as do Hartley and McKee (2000). The internet in particular is well-suited to promoting dialogue (and possibly participation), and many ethnic minority Web sites offer chat rooms, forums and other features for that purpose.[37]

Downing and Husband (2002: 11) wisely observe that, in order to promote true dialogue, and not a "uni-directional right to freedom of speech, of publication, of broadcasting, [where] (t)he essential interactive dynamic of *communication* is corrupted to a myopic concern with personal expression," there should be a "Right to Be Understood." Although understanding may be difficult to achieve, a mutual recognition of the right to see and to be seen, to speak as well as to listen, itself would constitute a major step forward, and here I have no doubt that Habermas would agree.

There is the possibility that, as mini-spheres multiply, they may dissipate the force of arguments, whereas the concept of a unified and singular public sphere carries with it the likelihood that arguments presented through it would be more likely to reach a larger public, to involve more of it in dialogue, and to implement those actions that it advocated. That would be a powerful selling point for the "unified sphere" concept, but the rapidly changing and growing mediascape makes me doubt that the concept remains practicable, even if it once was. Like Humpty Dumpty, it cannot be reassembled, and the individual spheres are acquiring lives of their own, for good and for ill.

I noted in Chapter 1 that I had not found any theories dealing with institutional structures and the effects of those structures on programmatic outcomes, although the structural perspectives offered by Krasnow, Longley, and Terry (1982) and by Hirsch (1977) have been useful to me in their emphasis on *interactions* between agencies. So has a model for developing codes of media conduct proposed by Husband and Alam (2002), because their approach emphasizes the need to carefully assess what one hopes to achieve at each stage of the development process—something that I have attempted to follow in presenting my own structural approach.

Organizational interactions turned out to have considerable explanatory power with respect to the creation of policies and services affecting ethnic minority media, as I have indicated in my policymaking case studies (Chapter 4). They also appear to explain to some degree why some ethnic media services have been more successful in maintaining their commitment to major goals than have others. And finally, examining ethnic media in light of structural elements and their interrelationships highlights the elements themselves and, for me at least, makes it easier to pinpoint strengths and weaknesses within the media services and the principal agencies that influence them.

FUTURE DEVELOPMENTS

I do not doubt that the ethnic minority electronic media will continue to grow, particularly in view of the rapid increases in ethnic minority populations throughout the industrialized world. At the same time, I feel obliged to sound some cautionary notes regarding certain issues that must be faced if those media are to continue to play a role in serving their communities, much less promoting participation in the public sphere. Those issues are *improving financial prospects; the systematic development of advocates; the need for research;* and media proliferation and *the need for publicity.*

Improving Financial Prospects

I begin with this issue in part because it seems to be the greatest worry for ethnic media administrators, but also because it is fundamental to promoting growth and stability. That is true of all electronic media services, but especially for ethnic services, because so many of them operate on the thin edge of solvency. Improving the situation likely will continue to require dependence on an assortment of financial sources, which is not all bad: If one source suddenly vanishes or shrinks, there are others that at least will sustain the service.

It would help greatly if *governments* could realize, as some already do, that ethnic minority media services are a social good, both for minority populations and for the mainstream. That should justify the relatively modest annual appropriations needed to insure that those services have a reliable base income. The appropriations could be made conditional on each service's raising a matching amount, as is the case for U.S. public radio and television stations. It also would help if national, state/province and local governments[38] could provide funding to support the production of material that seeks to create bridges between ethnic minority communities and the mainstream population. Such assistance is rare, and would be a particularly appropriate expenditure of public money.

Where *private fundraising* is concerned, the ethnic services might discover that the time, money and effort they would devote to publicizing themselves and their offerings could have a beneficial effect on donor support. It is rare to find corporate or even individual donors who are willing to contribute to a venture that lacks public visibility.

Even if ethnic services generally consider themselves to be masters in the art of *economizing,* there may be ways in which changing technologies can assist in the process. Perhaps it is ironic, but as such services become better known, they may find themselves dealing with increasing numbers of requests for airtime from members of their communities, and may lack the studio space or staff assistance to honor those requests. Some of the U.K. access radio and Swedish *närradio* services have discovered that individuals and groups sometimes have their own professional recording equipment and know how to use it professionally.

Furthermore, they often would rather record in their homes or places of business, then bring the recording to the service or send it over telephone lines. The *närradio* service in Gothenberg has helped some of those users by covering the costs of upgraded phone lines, which maintains broadcast quality and is far less expensive than constructing and equipping additional studios.[39]

Networking also can be an effective way to economize, as long as it does not result in undue sacrifice of localism. We have seen a number of examples of cooperation among ethnic minority services, but one variety is a fairly recent arrival on the scene: Temporary service provided by a group of stations working together, usually with a notable event as their focal point. One example is Radio Hurakan (Hurricane), a service established for the sole purpose of covering events surrounding the meeting of the World Trade Organization (WTO) in Cancun, Mexico in September 2003. Roughly two dozen radio stations around the world, most of them with considerable ethnic minority involvement, contributed money and/or resources to support Radio Hurakan, and agreed to rebroadcast its reports as they came from the meeting and from the activities of groups protesting the WTO's policies and plans (Coyer, 2003).

The Systematic Development of Advocates

Most of the ethnic minority services I have studied feel that they have the support of the community (-ies) they serve. I already have observed that such support is vital, but in the future it is unlikely to be sufficient, especially as competition for the attention of ethnic and mainstream audiences grows. The presence of "friends in high places" can be very helpful when an ethnic service suddenly experiences a financial setback, is under threat of losing its license, or hopes to expand. Those who hold power within the community may be useful in linking the service with members of the "power elite" in the mainstream society who might support it, but the service also should develop and maintain its own list of supporters, beginning with individuals who have appeared as hosts, interviewees, discussants, and so on. They are very likely to want the service to continue, and often are willing to help it do so.

At higher levels, it may be worthwhile for the service to seek to identify the more prominent mainstream and ethnic public figures who display interest in supporting ethnic minority ventures. They may be politicians, religious or labor leaders, businesspeople, academics, government or military officials. Their statements might appear in the mainstream mass media, but some of the broader ethnic data and information services such as the U.S. Web site www.diversity.com also will publicize them. Foundations such as the Friedrich Ebert Stiftung in Germany and the Kaiser Foundation in the U.S. have long track records of supporting ethnic minority initiatives, but need to be sized up in terms of the approaches that are most likely to bring a favorable response to proposals coming from ethnic media services.

Advertising in one form or another (including program and service sponsorship) is likely to become increasingly important to ethnic minority media services, since the licenses or conditions under which most of them operate make it possible to carry advertising, even when the service is nonprofit. If ethnic services are to draw maximum benefit from this source, and at the same time avoid the pitfalls (e.g., advertiser influence over editorial policy), they will need to establish clear understandings with advertisers and sponsors regarding such things as the difference between *consultation* and *control*. (The service is open to consultation, but ultimately retains control.) I have not encountered many instances of advertisers or sponsors who have insisted upon controlling the contents of programs in which their messages appear, but I have heard ethnic service administrators express concern over their need to keep advertisers and sponsors happy, especially when there may be few of them—a common enough situation when an ethnic media service first appears. That concern seems to arise from the feeling that, if advertisers and sponsors do not get what they want, they will stop advertising and sponsoring and will influence others to do likewise. However, a service that establishes and defends its principals, although it may lose some of that support, is quite likely to attract a different category of friends in high places: Other advertisers and sponsors who applaud its willingness to take a principled stand.

The Need for Research

Most ethnic minority media services conduct very little audience research, in part because those in charge appear to regard it as too complex, too expensive, and even too intrusive. As I have indicated, it need not be any of those things, and services that have carried out such research have found it both manageable and rewarding. The ethnic media associations might consider developing guidelines for conducting research that would illustrate how to do so simply, inexpensively and sensitively,[40] and then publishing and distributing them to the services. If that could be followed up with a series of workshops on the subject, so much the better.

As I indicated more than once, there are several benefits that are associated with conducting research, and some of them have implications for the future prospects of ethnic services. Many advertisers, sponsors and foundations will expect to see something more than impressionistic evidence of the size and composition of the audience and the impact of the service's offerings on that audience. Also, the service's ability to keep its finger on the pulse of its community and its offerings in line with community needs and desires will be enhanced by knowledge gained through data that are generated by systematic research, assuming of course that the questions posed are carefully designed to elicit such information.

There is one area of inquiry where most ethnic services do little or no research at present, but where the need for it is almost certain to increase in the future: Which other ethnic media services do they compete with, and how do they fare in that competition? Ten years ago, such a question would have been largely irrelevant because there were so few situations where there were alternative choices. Now, many of the largest cities in industrialized nations have more than one electronic media service for the largest ethnic communities (South Asians in London; Hispanics in New York; Turks in Berlin, North Africans in Paris), and distribution of radio and TV stations (including ethnic stations) through the Web will increase the range of choice for ethnic minorities anywhere, as the internet becomes more widely available. That already has happened with many cable- and satellite-distributed ethnic services. Maintaining the viability of any given ethnic media service will depend more and more heavily on keeping track of the (growing) competition.

While many ethnic media services appear to be making some progress in attracting young people as participants in program-making, my general impression is that service administrators know very little about younger listeners, viewers, and internet users. Not only is this almost certain to be a growing audience; it also is the audience of the future for most ethnic services. Yet, as I indicate below, it may not be an audience with a strong interest in program material in minority languages. What it may find more attractive is material that emphasizes a "third culture" approach: Homi Bhabha's "third space" (Bhabha, 1994). That space, which is occupied by individuals who draw together elements of old and new homeland cultures as well as cultural perceptions that they themselves originate, needs to be better understood (hence the need for research) if ethnic services are serious about attracting younger audience members—and not just ethnic minority members, because the very originality of "third-space" cultural expression should make it attractive to members of the mainstream culture.[41]

Research on the role of the electronic media in promoting participation in the public sphere also is sorely lacking, and would be important to the future of ethnic media services for two reasons: First, to provide such services with concrete examples of how they might play that role if they are not already doing so, and how they might play it most effectively; and second, to provide those services with evidence that they can use to convince foundations and governments that they can be beneficial in promoting the health of civic society.

Media Proliferation and Publicity: Opportunities and Dangers

As the mediascape expands in size and complexity, there is opportunity and danger for ethnic minority media services. The *opportunity* comes in the form of greater numbers of outlets available to ethnic minority groups.[42] Granted, government regulatory agencies are not always ready to encourage ethnic services to occupy those outlets, although the friends in high places mentioned earlier in the chapter may be able to persuade agencies to insure that minority-operated services not be left out when more low-power radio or TV licenses are being issued, new networks authorized, Web sites licensed,[43] conditions set for the carriage of cable or satellite channels, and the like. To the extent that the internet remains relatively open to newcomers wishing to develop their own Web sites, regulation in the form of licensing will not be an issue, and ethnic service providers with sufficient financial resources and technical knowledge should be able to proliferate, although they will be aided in so doing if their respective community members become more numerous and avid "netizens." In short, there will be many more electronic opportunities for ethnic media services.

One of the great but little explored opportunities that well may attract ethnic minority media entrepreneurs in the future is service to the global ethnic community, or diaspora.[44] One characteristic of present-day emigration is that a number of the more prominent groups (Somalis, Vietnamese, Afghanis) have emigrated to many different parts of the industrialized world, and substantial numbers of them have taken up residence in cities such as Berlin, New York, Sydney, London, but also smaller metropolitan centers such as Minneapolis/St. Paul, Melbourne and Manchester. In some cases, they can arrange to receive feeds of their old homeland electronic media through satellites, much as Turks in Europe, South Asians in Great Britain and the United States and North Africans in Paris, have done for the past decade or longer. However, there appears to be a largely unserved market for ethnic minority services that would allow Afghani, Turkish, Vietnamese, and other émigré communities around the world to share their experiences with one another through informational and entertainment formats. Silverstone speaks of a *global commons*, served by "global media for the construction of sociality, for the creation of a minority, marginal, diasporic, presence, both locally and globally, in cultural and political space" (Silverstone, 2001: 13).

Silverstone does not provide a detailed description of what such a service might sound or look like, although he does point out that its establishment, especially as a kind of global alternative sphere, would not be easy because it would have to take into account various political and cultural conditions within ethnic communities—male dominance, generational dominance, "the politics of the inside," widely differing notions of what constitutes "home," and much else (Silverstone, 2001: 18-19). He regards the internet as particularly well-suited to this function, but sees important roles for TV, video, fax and the press. He does not deal with the always crucial issue of financial feasibility and viability, aside from mentioning the low price of operating through the internet, but he does note that a number of ethnic minority groups scattered across the globe already have begun to exchange audio- and videocassettes (many of them family-to-family, I might add) and other forms of mediated transmission, so there is at least nascent interest in the development of global services for and about minorities.

The growth of the global commons would be aided by the further development of networking services of the sort noted in Chapter 5. The Aboriginal People's Television Network referred to earlier is an example of one way to proceed, but there are others: Leasing of satellite transmission time at lower-cost off-peak periods to share radio and TV material that could be downloaded and replayed when most convenient; internet Web-streaming that could function in much the same manner. The necessary reception equipment often is not available in local ethnic minority media services currently, but costs are dropping, and those technologies are quite likely to be more accessible and affordable within the next several years. (Hopefully power supplies and telephone lines also will have become more dependable and more sophisticated in the meantime, especially in Third World nations.) It would be at least as helpful if such technologies could be used to assist ethnic service administrators in exchanging information, posing questions, and even commiserating with one another.

Opportunity does not always translate into reality, of course. The internet may be the least expensive of the electronic media, but it does take capital to develop and place a Web site, as well as to sustain it. I already have observed that the major lending institutions in industrialized nations are not fond of taking risks, especially in the present uncertain financial climate, and they tend to see ethnic media services as risky propositions. (That is one reason why I have advocated governmental start-up financing for such services, or at least for those that look to be worthy ventures but have not been able to convince the financial institutions that they are.) The scale of investment involved in establishing a global media presence for and about ethnic minorities is large enough that it would seem to require support on an international level, perhaps by a consortium of regional and international governments and quasi-governments (UN, the EU), financial institutions (the World Bank), and the more internationally minded foundations (the Friedrich Ebert Stiftung). However, small-scale starts might be made in certain instances through leasing airtime from national broadcast services that already are distributed internationally through satellite. There always is the danger of national government interference if the material exchanged among the diaspora becomes politically tendentious, but it may be worth the risk, and it would be far less expensive than establishing a full-blown service.

A global network also would be more capable of mobilizing ethnic minority opinion on such issues as outsider exploitation of local natural resources or achieving something closer to parity in international trade where minority populations are concerned. Shohat and Stam (1994) make the argument in these terms: "we would argue that it is precisely the overlapping of these circles [of minority interests] that makes possible intercommunal coalitions based on historically shaped affinities. Rather than asking who can speak, we should ask about how to speak together, and, more important, how to move the plurilog forward." They then offer the analogy of a jazz ensemble, stating that interest groups, like jazz ensembles, should strive to "foster a mutual adoption of other voices and accents" but "within intercommunal coalitions joined in shared struggles" (Shohat & Stam, 1994: 346-347).[45]

I find that *dangers* are somewhat more difficult to predict. Although financial support will remain a problem for many (most?) ethnic minority electronic media, I feel reasonably confident that the vast majority of such services will be able to stay afloat, although I suspect that there will be further consolidation in the ethnic minority commercial sector, as appears in late 2003 to be imminent for Univision and the Hispanic Broadcasting Service (radio) in the United States. Now that ethnic services have gained a foothold in most industrialized nations, it does not seem likely that their right to exist will be challenged, or at least not in any effective way. Ethnic internet services should continue to grow, even as internet connections in ethnic minority households are growing.

The opening up of media outlets has brought with it a possible danger where ethnic minority services are concerned: Governments are beginning to regard consolidation of media services with less suspicion than once was the case. The United States has seen a great deal of consolidation of electronic media ownership since passage of the Telecommunications Act of 1996, and some existing ethnic minority services such as Black Entertainment Television and Telemundo, as well as a number of ethnic minority-owned radio stations, have come under (White) corporate ownership. Whether this trend will continue is impossible to tell, and it is too early to determine whether services thus acquired become less ethnic community-minded, but this will bear watching.[46]

The advent of digital radio and television has added another candidate to the list of possible nationwide outlets for ethnic minority services—something that is bound to increase in importance as more and more ethnic minority groups spread out within their new homelands. A handful of such services already exists; two of them—the Asian Network and Radio 1Xtra—are supported by the BBC, whereas a third—African-American-owned Radio One—operates through XM Satellite Radio (U.S.). How successful any of those services will be depends largely on the adoption rate among listeners, and that rate has been quite modest thus far (less than 1% of the U.S. or U.K. populations as of late 2003). The sets themselves generally cost more than U.S. $100 (a few cost as little as $70), and would be a considerable investment for many ethnic minority households. Digital television sets are becoming much less expensive, but at the least are in the U.S.$300-400 range. What may be more daunting for ethnic minority TV operators is the high cost of equipping a digital studio.[47]

Another potential danger lies in the extent to which ethnic minority media services continue to make heavy use of "old homeland" languages. Although there is a great sense of identity in being able to use one's ethnic language, there also are indications that second- and later generation minority group members may not feel the same degree of need to hear, see and read them through the electronic media as do first-generation minorities. For example, a survey-based study (Ang et al., 2002) of five groups[48] of ethnic minority émigrés to Australia indicated that 52 per cent of first-generation émigrés listened to radio broadcasts in languages other than English, whereas only 32% of second-generation émigrés did so (Ang et al., 2002: 59). At the least, service administrators need to be aware of possible shifts in the balance of those preferring the one language or the other, especially among important target audiences.

I previously have expressed my concerns over the problems faced by recently arrived émigré groups. Those problems are serious, but not insuperable, and the solutions depend more on changes in administrative and program policy in most of the ethnic services than they do on additional financial support, welcome and appropriate though that would be. Furthermore, the present flow of émigrés, refugees, and exiles is not so huge that its accommodation by the ethnic media could not be managed with some redirection of currently available resources and some fairly modest shifts in policy. However, if world events continue in their present course, I would expect that flow to increase—not equally for all of the industrialized nations, but certainly for many of those where there already are tensions regarding immigration policy, provisions for emigre education and for health care, high unemployment (with émigrés often blamed for "taking away'" jobs, even if the mainstream populations would not touch them), and various other problems and ills that are (often mistakenly) linked with the newcomers.

If ever a situation called for the skillful use of the electronic media to educate mainstream and minority populations alike regarding each other's cultures, secular and sacred, it is this, and it is a serious issue already. If minority populations come at all close to increasing as rapidly as many have predicted in the United States and Canada and throughout western Europe as well as Australia, the need for mutual understanding will grow, even as the achievement of it becomes more complex, given the increasing number and variety of ethnic minority cultures that will be on hand. Yet the very proliferation of media outlets already noted will mean that mainstream and minority populations alike will have more media choices from which to select, and the ethnic minority media will have to work even harder to call attention to themselves.

Not surprisingly, then, I return to an old theme as I close chapter and book: The need for publicity. I have made the case for it earlier, and do not intend to repeat it here, but have only hinted at the likely magnitude of the problem as we move on through the 21st century. That makes it particularly important for the ethnic media to exert greater efforts to publicize themselves. Quite aside from the anticipated increase in the number of electronic media outlets available to the viewing, listening, and reading public (and most of those outlets will be publicizing themselves), there are the more recently arrived groups that I have just mentioned. It will be difficult enough for their members to sort through the array of available media services (it is becoming difficult enough for most of us who have grown up with that array), let alone to discover those whose services can be of direct use as well as pleasure to them. In the process, some of them hopefully will feel encouraged to participate in the public sphere. And finally, although it may be more difficult to achieve, some of the publicity may reach the eyes and ears of the mainstream public, at least some of whose members should rejoice in the discovery that there still *are* real alternatives in an increasingly corporatized and homogeneous electronic media world.

NOTES

1. PSB produced *programs* dealing with ethnic minorities are another matter. For example, French PSB mainstream television services A2 and FR3 (now France2 and France3) were quite active as producers of programs (including a number of series) about ethnic minorities during the late 1980s and early 1990s (see Frachon & Vargaftig, 1995: 144-158, for more details). Boyer and Lochard (1998) also provide helpful insights on French television's portrayal of North Africans and Blacks in suburban areas, particularly Paris. Some of the programs featured considerable ethnic minority involvement as producers, directors, writers, and actors. By the late 1990s, few such programs remained on the schedule.

2. There is a fourth category that is less common than these three, but worth noting because it helps to overcome the frequent lack of technological expertise available to those seeking to establish ethnic electronic media services. Radio and TV *technicians*, most often from the PSBs, often have volunteered their experience to help set up the ethnic services, and sometimes have been crucial in locating used equipment for them. Some have provided maintenance and repair service free of charge or at low cost. They appear to enjoy those roles because they regard the ethnic services as a social good, but many also enjoy the relative freedom to experiment with ways to get the most out of old or low-cost equipment.

3. Conversely, the absence of those characteristics can damage or even destroy the effectiveness of an ethnic minority media service. Daley and James (1992) criticize the top-down management style employed by some planners and administrators in establishing a rural television service for Alaskan natives during the 1970s, where consultation was not carefully considered and where the scheduling of steps in project development was far too rapid. Molnar (1993) details some of the administrative problems at Aboriginal Australian radio station 8KIN (Alice Springs).

4. However, changes in *execution*—the production of messages in support of goals— are to be expected, as the services assess the best ways of getting those messages across to their communities.

5. While visiting Tumeke FM in Whakatane, New Zealand in 1991, I was told by the program director that the station had revived the use of the older Maori names for the months, rather than the more recent Maori versions of the Western titles for them. However, the policy seemed to be drawing far more complaints than praise. As one young caller to the station put it, "Why don't you stop using titles that even my old granny, who speaks perfect Maori, doesn't understand?"

6. Minneapolis community radio station KMOJ-FM, operated by and largely for the Twin Cities African-American community, has had many changes in management since its debut in 1977, and a number of changes came about because the "power elite" within the community was displeased about who did and did not receive the station's attention.

7. The Moutse region is in Mpumalanga Province, east of Johannesburg. The region has nearly 50 villages and a population of about 900,000.

8. The WLBT-TV case noted in Chapter 1 gives some indication of the FCC's reluctance to remove the license of a station that clearly was not meeting the needs of a large share of its community.

9. A few earlier studies, such as Anwar (1978), do touch on some of the elements of effectiveness, such as radio listener perceptions of the quality of ethnic minority program production and the usefulness of information conveyed through specific programs. Anwar's study (of South Asia community members in Leicester, United Kingdom) features one particularly interesting and unusual dimension: The effect of audience member fluency in English ("Good," "Poor," and "None") on perceptions of programs. (Often the effects were minimal, but "Poor quality/not professional" was indicated by 13% of those with "Good" fluency and by just 1% of those with "None" [1978: 23]).

10. I find the following studies particularly insightful: Hargreaves and Mahdjoub (1997); Moragas Spa, Domingo, and Lopez (2002); Tsagarousiano (2002); Ogan (2001); Ogan and Milikowski (1998); Hargreaves (2001); Milikowski (2001); and Tsagarousiano (2001). Morley (2000) also notes several studies along those same lines.

11. The literature on participation through the media is quite rich where *development* communication is concerned. Jacobson and Servaes (1999) offer a quite comprehensive review of theories about participation. Cook and Kothari (2001) feature contributors who take a very critical approach to present practices surrounding participatory communication; many of them note the 'top-down' approaches of project directors who go through the motions of encouraging participation, but provide little meaningful opportunity for communities to become involved. (Among their justifications: "We know what's good for them," but also "The people to whom we report want certain kinds of results reported in a certain way, so we have to make sure that the project operates along those lines, whether or not the community agrees.")

12. See the Center's website (www.rds.org.gt/cmcm) as well as the Web site for the Council for Mayan Communication (www.mayacom.org). See also Gumicio-Dagron (2001).

13. See Chapter 5 for a more detailed account of this project.

14. This example was furnished by Suzanne Aubin, Dirctor, CBC Northern Service, in the course of a personal interview in Montreal, June 1994.

15. Personal viewing of video recording of *Nachbarn* at ZDF (*Nachbarn*, 1995).

16. Personal interview with Leila, Stockholm, April 2001 However, the "public sphere" in this case is limited to listeners who speak Farsi: middle-aged and older Iranians, which may exclude some of the second and third generation of those living in the Stockholm area.

17. The Kabylie are the indigenous (pre-Muslim conquest) people of North Africa, and speak Tamazight, ~~although~~ Many are bilingual in Arabic, although most of those living in France also speak French. For an interesting critical review of their experiences in receiving support from the Moroccan and Algerian governments for broadcasts in Tamazight, see Saib (2001). For a summary (also critical) of their internet activity, see Ouakrim (2001). For background on the earlier years of Kabylie broadcasting, see Ihadadden (1992).

18. A Web site linked to www.Kabyle.com—www.mondeberbere.com—also offers a number of forums. One of them, posted on June 20, 2003, dealt with the question "La langue Arabe oui, mais pourquoi?" (The Arabic language, yes, but why?). The five participants generally were somewhat to very negative about the utility of Arabic, and became quite sarcastic at times. When the convenor ("Rifino") posed

the question "For you, which discipline is best taught through Arabic?" "Lahib" responded "The Koran and the Arabic language," while "Lou" said "lying" (*mensonge*) (Translations mine). Although such a forum session might not constitute direct participation in the public sphere, it does serve to sharpen skills that will help to enable such participation.

19. An argument made by Hartley and McKee (2000: 4).

20. One particularly interesting site is the Women of Uganda Network (WOUGNET, at www.wougnet.org), which operates training programs as well as managing the site, and which has an impressive set of links.

21. See Browne (2002: 176-178); and Browne (1996: 219-221) for an indication of some of the activities and influence of ethnic minority female journalists and managers in electronic media operations.

22. Mayanis (2002) provides a good critical appraisal of the problems and prospects facing such centers. The experience of ethnic minorities and other inhabitants of the Dutch city of Moerwijk should serve as a reminder that problems with telecenters are not confined to Third World nations: The city government supported a training program for individuals, many of them ethnic minorities and the elderly, who lacked their own computers and had little or no experience with them. However, that support ended a little over a year later, and access to the computers ended as well, resulting in anger and frustration among the learners, and very likely leaving a legacy of mistrust (Hoving, 2003).

23. This is a public site, but requires a password for access to much of the tribal material, thus safeguarding tribal practices.

24. Elvin (2003: 5) states that "I took part in the recording of one of its [the BBC's online web forum, ["Question Time"] in March 2002 and was able to observe first hand [some] problems related to its editorial process and a tendency towards institutional narcissism which could undermine the very real work it has done in the field."

25. Visual images, often quite ornate, that embody certain characteristics of the sender and that the sender wishes to share with others in the group. An example would be where a female group member wishes to portray herself as a lioness, and supplies a visual image of a half-lioness-half human female.

26. Lehtonen and Heikkilä (2003) describe a project where such a "bottom-up" approach is being taken.

27. Murdock's essay is an excellent encapsulation of arguments regarding the (possible) role of the media in promoting civil society.

28. A New Zealand White broadcasting executive stated the argument in very much the same words as he gave me his views on the utility of Maori radio stations in the course of a conversation we had in Singapore in September 1991.

29. There have been instances of such broadcasts on the part of clandestine radio stations, certainly with the knowledge of their staff members and with the compliance of those governments allowing them to operate (Soley & Nichols, 1987).

30. This story was told to me by several German broadcasters, including those at Offener Kanal Berlin, Offener Kanal Hamburg, and ZDF (Second German Television) in the course of my visit to Germany in September 1995. A more complete version appears in Browne (1999b: 77-78).

31. Hans Degenhart, 5EBI's manager, told me in a March 2001 interview (Adelaide) that he instructed the broadcaster to apologize on air for her "intemperate" lan-

guage and warned her that any future incident along those lines would result in the loss of her program slot. See also Australian Broadcasting Authority (1997).

32.   One of the more unusual of these, related to me by the staff at radio station 3ZZZ, Melbourne in March 1996, involved a complaint from a Serbian group about a Croatian program that included a musical selection from the 14th century in which there was a reference to a battle between Croats and Serbs. The Serbs insisted that playing the selection was a slight on their honor, and that an apology should be issued by the Croat broadcasters. (It wasn't.)

33.   Swedish researcher Birgitta Loewander studied a number of community radio services in three Swedish cities for indications of threats or disrespectful statements directed at ethnic minority groups. She found some evidence of such statements in two of the cities (Stockholm and Malmo); a follow-up study aimed at assessing the extent of such practices revealed that they were not widespread (Loewander, 1998).

34.   Examples of such statements can be found on the Web sites of some of the European PSBs, and there is a critique of them, as well as a proposed model of how codes might be constructed, in Husband and Alam, "Codes of Practice and Media Performance" (Tuning into Diversity, 2002). Several booklets and pamphlets stress the need for "ethnic sensitivity" on the part of media professionals, journalists in particular. A few examples of the latter are Bostock (1990); King (1985); Langton (1993); and Stockwell and Scott (2000). See also Bertrand (2003).

35.   The managing director of the BBC until January 2004, Greg Dyke, made several strongly worded public pronouncements (including "I think the BBC is hideously white" in a 2001 speech) regarding the need for the Corporation to do much more to improve and expand BBC portrayals of, as well as services for, ethnic minorities. The head of the BBC's Asian Network, Vijay Sharma, noted in my April 2002 interview with her that she saw Dyke as a prime mover in the development of nationwide distribution capability for the network.

36.   Cottle (1995), in his study of BBC producers of programs about South Asians, provides a fairly pessimistic view of the ability of mainstream producers to acquire a sufficient degree of ethnic sensitivity, and of administrators' willingness to pressure them to do so. Husband and Alam (2002) point out that codes generally emphasize what *should* be done, rather than what *must* be done. Those two authors also have prepared a CD ROM containing several dozen codes and declarations of principal on ethnic minority representation. Contact The Multicultural Skyscraper (www.multicultural-skyscraper.com) for details.

37.   However, ethnic minority populations often feature lower than average internet user rates, which reduces the medium's utility where the mini-sphere and the larger public sphere are concerned.

38.   That does not rule out the possible contributions of regional and international bodies such as the EU and the United Nations. The draft Declaration prepared by the conveners of the World Summit on the Information Society contains several statements which endorse and public service broadcasting and community media (paragraphs 6b, 27a, 41f and 42f); the draft Action Plan proposes an Information and Communications Technologies for Development Fund, although details on the sources and level of financing for such a fund are not spelled out. A coalition of groups (FEMNET [Africa], AMARC, WINGS) has argued for inclusion of funding for community radio, since ICT access is likely to be slow to develop in rural areas of the developing world, whereas radio already reaches rural areas in some devel-

oping nations (Warren, 2003). The actual summit meeting (December 2003) produced many statements sympathetic to the idea of support for ICT ventures in Third World nations, but no tangible actions along those lines.

39. Personal interview, Hans Heintze, Gothenburg, May 2001. He observed that the quality of tapes varied. However, Gothenburg Närradio makes its standards clear, and rejects tapes that do not meet them, so the quality usually improves very quickly.

40. Most ethnic media research, such as there is, still is carried out by mainstream researchers or by ethnic minorities trained by such researchers, and often seems to lack the sensitivity to ways of posing questions that will (a) better ensure that ethnic minority respondents truly understand the question; and (b) feel sufficiently motivated to answer it.

41. The "Serbo-German rock band" example presented earlier illustrates one way in which third-space culture can be expressed.

42. However, there are possible roadblocks to that continued expansion. The WTO, meeting in Cancun, Mexico in September 2003, was to have discussed a revision in the General Agreement on Trade in Services (GATS) that would have the GATS include communication and audiovisual services (film, music production, the electronic media), along with media distribution services (satellite, cable, broadcast). That request had been made before, but a number of nations argued against a blanket provision and have maintained an exemption labeled the *cultural exception.* The WTO meeting broke up before a binding agreement on that provision could be adopted, but opponents of it continue to fear that, if it *were* to be adopted, it could mean that such restrictions as limits on media ownership (including foreign ownership and media cross-ownership), public service obligations, and possibly special forms of financial support for noncommercial electronic media services, could be abolished because they hinder free and open trade (Costanza-Chock, 2003).

43. In those nations that now do so or may do so in the future.

44. Scholarly treatment of the media activities of diasporic populations is available in *Hommes et Migrations* (2002) Karim (2003), Morley (2000), Naficy (1993), and Verhulst (1999). Cunningham and Sinclair (2000) cover the media activities of four diasporic communities in Australia, but say little about their development of links with their community members in other parts of the world. Dayan (1998, 1999) makes a case for careful consideration of the role of some of the "small" media (audio- and videocassettes, but also personal letters, photographs, etc.) when assessing the sorts of media that serve to link diasporic communities.

45. This passage comes from a chapter section entitled "Self-Representation and the Politics of Identity," which offers an interesting perspective on the role of media with respect to global mobilization.

46. Such concerns have been expressed in many quarters, including the American Federation of Labor (AFL) and the Congress of Industrial Organizations (CIO) in their comments to the FCC regarding cross-ownership of broadcast stations and newspapers (American Federation of Labor, 2001), and *The Black Commentator* ("Treat Corporate Media," 2003), on the need for Blacks to protest the corporatization of the media and to seek greater media access.

47. There is one possible attraction for ethnic minorities where digital TV is concerned: Some U.S. broadcasters who have digital licenses are considering the possibility of seeking the FCC's permission to subdivide the digital frequency assigned to them and create up to five separate channels of *analog* services, which would fit

within the spectrum space taken up by one digital service. If that were permitted, it could become possible for prospective ethnic minority broadcasters to lease such channels.

48.   Approximately 400 subjects each from among Filipinos, Greeks, Vietnamese, Lebanese, and Somalis; additionally, a sample of roughly 60 indigenous (Aboriginal) peoples, was surveyed, as were more than 1,400 "mainstream" Australians. The report itself provides a great deal of material about ethnic group and mainstream Australian perceptions of multiculturalism, hopes for its future, and so on. The fourth chapter, on media consumption, also indicates relatively higher use of the internet among second-generation émigrés when compared with first-generation émigrés, as one might have predicted.

Appendix:

Implications for Participation in the Public Sphere by Ethic Minorities: Some Observations on Habermas

Habermas does recognize the importance of the participation of minority groups in the public sphere, as witness the following passages from *Remarks on Discourse Ethics, Justification and Application* (translation by Ciaran Cronin):[1]

> There must be a common basis on which mutual understanding of alien cultures, belief systems, paradigms, and life forms is possible—that is, a translation *between* different evaluative languages and not merely communication among members of *the same* language group relying on reciprocal observation of alien cultures. The languages and vocabularies in which we interpret our needs and communicate our feelings must be mutually permeable. . . . (Chapter 2, p. 95, originally published as one of a set of three essays in *Erlaueterungen zur Diskursethik*, Frankfurt a/M: Suhrkamp Verlag, 1991, Ch. 6).

> the *real* citizens of contemporary liberal societies are flesh and blood individuals who have grown up in different traditions and forms of life and owe their self-understanding to competing world views. The political public sphere in which they come together to form a public body of citizens is characterized by a plurality of belief systems and interest structures and the coexistence and confrontation of life forms and individual life projects. . . . (*Remarks...*, p. 93).[2]

> [Discourse ethics] adopts the intersubjective approach of pragmatism and conceives of practical discourse as a *public* practice of *shared*, reciprocal

perspective taking: each individual finds himself compelled to adopt the perspective of everyone else in order to test whether a proposed regulation is also acceptable from the perspective of every other person's understanding of himself and the world. . . . It is only when the continued existence of this communication community, which demands of all its members an act of selfless empathy through ideal role taking, is assured that the networks of reciprocal recognition, without which the identity of each individual would necessarily disintegrate, can reproduce themselves. (*Remarks...*, Ch. 5: Morality, Society, and Ethics: An Interview with Torben Hviid Nielsen, p. 154). This is much more a discussion than it is an interview, and Nielsen begins by stating "The main topic of discussion will be your views on moral theory and ethics . . ." (p. 154).

NOTES

1. In the preface to the book, Habermas notes that "The "Remarks on Discourse Ethics" constitute the main text and derive from notes made during the years 1987 to 1990. They represent a confrontation with competing theoretical programs and are offered as a global critical evaluation of the relevant literature (p.vii).
2. Here, Habermas is summarizing and interpreting John Rawls—mostly his (unpublished ms.?) "Justice and Fairness: A Briefer Restatement," 1989.

Bibliography

Adler, Leonore & Uwe Gielen, eds. (2003). *Migration, Immigration and Emigration in International Perspective.* Westport, CT: Praeger.

Aksoy, Asu & Kevin Robins (2003). "Banal transnationalism: The difference that television makes." In Karim Karim, ed., *The Media of Diaspora: Mapping the Globe,* 89-104. London: Routledge.

Albert-Honore, Sharon (1996). "Empowering Voices: KUCB and Black Liberation Radio." In V. T. Berry & C. L. Manning-Miller, eds., *Mediated Messages and African-American Culture,* 201-217. Thousand Oaks, CA: Sage.

Ali, Shujat (2001). Group Managing Director of Asian Sound Radio, Manchester. Letter to Tessa Jowell, Secretary of State for Culture, Media and Sport, 20 August.

Alia, Valerie (1999). *Un/Covering the North: News, Media and Aboriginal People.* Vancouver, BC: University of British Columbia Press.

American Federation of Labor & Congress of Industrial Organizations (2001). "Comments Before the Federal Communications Commission in the Matter of Cross-Ownership of Broadcast Stations and Newspapers, December 4, 2001." Retrieved from jyudken@aflcio.org, October 11, 2003.

Ananthakrishnan, S.I. (1994). "The development of local radio and ethnic minority initiatives in Norway." In Charles Husband, ed., *A Richer Vision,* 106-126. Paris: UNESCO.

Anderson, Benedict (1991). *Imagined Communities: Reflections on the Origins and Spread of Nationalism.* London: Verso.

Andrews, Bart & Arghus Juilliard (1986). *Holy Mackeral! The Amos n' Andy Story.* New York: E.P. Dutton.

Ang, Ien, Jeffrey Brand, Greg Noble & Derek Wilding (2002). "Living Diversity: Australia's Multicultural Future." Report to the Special Broadcasting Service, Sydney: SBS.

Anwar, Muhammad (1978). *Who Tunes In To What? A Report on Ethnic Minority Broadcasting.* London: Commission for Racial Equality.

Anwar, Muhammad & Anthony Shang (1982). *Television in a Multi-Racial Society.* London: CRE (Commission on Racial Equality).

Appadurai, Arjun (1996). *Modernity at Large: Cultural Dimensions of Globalisation.* Minneapolis: University of Minnesota Press.

Aster, Howard & Elzbieta Olechowska, eds. (1998). *Challenges for International Broadcasting: The Audience First?* Oakville ON: Mosaic Press.

Australian Broadcasting Authority (1997). "Report of Investigation, Greek Community Program, Community Radio Service 5EBI Adelaide" (File No. 97/0612, Complaint No. 9903).

Barber, John & Alice Tait, eds. (2001). *The Information Society and the Black Community.* Westport, CT: Praeger.

Barlow, William (1999). *Voice Over: The Making of Black Radio.* Philadelphia, PA: Temple University Press.

Barnsley, Paul (1997). "Aboriginal radio proposal loses out." *Native American Press/Ojibwa News,* December 5: 5.

Baughman, James (1985). *Television's Guardians: The FCC and the Politics of Programming, 1958-1967.* Knoxville: University of Tennessee Press.

Beaud, Paul (1980). *Community Media?* Strasbourg: Council of Europe.

Benmayor, Rina & Andor Skotnes, eds. (1994). *Migration and Identity* (International Yearbook of Oral History and Life Stories, Vol. 3). Oxford: Oxford University Press, 1994.

Berrigan, Francis (1977). *Access: Some Western Models of Community Media.* Paris: UNESCO.

Berry, Venise T. & Carmen L. Manning-Miller, eds. (1996). *Mediated Messages and African-American Culture.* Thousand Oaks, CA: Sage.

Bertrand, Claude-Jean (2003). *An Arsenal for Democracy: Media Accountability Systems.* Cresskill, NJ: Hampton Press.

Bhabha, Homi (1994). *The Location of Culture.* London: Routledge.

Black Rose (pseudonym) (n.d.). "Zoomin'—Zoom Black Magic Radio—The Story of Zoom." Retrieved from www.theroc.org/roc-mag/textarch/roc-16/roc16-06, October 20, 2003.

Bogle, Donald (2001). *Prime Time Blues: African Americans on Network Television.* New York: Farrar, Straus & Giroux.

Bosch, Tanja (2003). "Radio, Community and Identity in South Africa: A Rhizomatic Study of Bush Radio in Cape Town." Unpublished PhD dissertation, Ohio University, Athens.

Bostock, Lester (1990). "The Greater Perspective." Sydney, Australia: Special Broadcasting Service.

Bostock, Lester (1993). "From the Dark Side: Survey of the Portrayal of Aborigines and Torres Strait Islanders on commercial television." Sydney, Broadcasting Service.

Boyer, Henri & Guy Lochard (1998). *Scenes de television en banlieues, 1950-1994.* Paris: Editions Harmattan.

Braun, Rainer (1994). "MultiKulti—Integration und Information." *MAZ,* September 17.

Brook, James (2000). "Old Traditions on New Network: Igloos and Seals." *The New York Times,* February 11: A4.

Browne, Donald (1963). "Radio Guinea—A Voice of Independent Africa." *Journal of Broadcasting* 7(2): 113-122.

Browne, Donald (1982). *International Radio Broadcasting: The Limits of the Limitless Medium.* New York: Praeger.

Browne, Donald R. (1984). "Alternatives for Local and Regional Radio: Three Nordic Solutions." *Journal of Communication* 34(2): 36-55.

Browne, Donald (1988). *What's Local About Local Radio?* London: International Institute of Communications (Communications Monograph No. 1).

Browne, Donald (1991). "Local Radio in Switzerland: The Limits of Localism." *Journal of Broadcasting and Electronic Media* 35(4): 449-464.

Browne, Donald (1996). *Electronic Media and Indigenous Peoples: A Voice of Our Own?* ✓ Ames: Iowa State University Press.

Browne, Donald (1998). "Tower of Babel or Multicultural Tapestry? Ethnic Minorities and International Broadcasting." In Howard Aster and Elzbieta Olechowska, eds., *Challenges for International Broadcasting: The Audience First?,* 171-179. Oakville, ON: Mosaic Press.

Browne, Donald (1999a). *Electronic Media and Industrialized Nations: A Comparative Study.* Ames: Iowa State University Press.

Browne, Donald (1999b). "The Snail's Shell: Electronic Media and Emigrant Communities." *Communications* 24(1): 61-84.

Browne, Donald (2002). "Minority Electronic Media Services and Minority Manners of Presentation." In Nicholas W. Jankowski, ed., *Community Media in the Information Age,* 165-185. Cresskill, NJ: Hampton Press.

Buenger, Reinhard (1995). "Offen füer Neues." *agenda* (magazine of the Grimme Institute), 18: 46.

Buettner, Christian & Berthold Meyer, eds. (2001). *Integration durch Partizipation: "Ausländische Mitbuerger" in demokratischen Gesellschaften* (Integration Through Participation: "Foreign Co-Citizens" in Democratic Societies). Frankfurt: Campus Verlag.

Calhoun, Craig, ed. (1992). *Habermas and the Public Sphere.* Cambridge, MA: MIT Press.

Cantor, Louis (1992). *Wheelin' on Beale.* New York: Pharos Books.

Carmen Marquez, Lucia del (1993). "The Uses of Radio by Ethnic Minorities in Mexico: A Study of a Participatory Project." Unpublished PhD Dissertation, University of Texas at Austin.

Castells, Manuel (2001). *The Internet Galaxy: Reflections on the Internet, Business and Society.* Oxford UK: Oxford University Press.

Cisler, Steve, ed. (1998). "The Internet and Indigenous Groups." Special issue of *Cultural Survival Quarterly 21*(4).

Clarity, James (1994). "Gaelic Now Trips Off Ireland's Silver Tongues." *The New York Times*, September 16, p. A4.

Classen, Steven (1996). "Broadcast Law and Segregation: A Social History of the WLBT-TV Case." Unpublished PhD dissertation, University of Wisconsin, Madison.

CLOT-TV (2002). "Associo d'Amics de la Radio y la TV de CLOT." Descriptive statement prepared by CLOT-TV for distribution at annual meeting of OURMedia, Barcelona, July.

Coleman, Stephen (2002). "BBC Radio Ulster's Talkback Phone-in: Public Feedback in a Divided Public Space." In Nicholas W. Jankowski, ed., *Community Media in the Information Age*, 107-122. Cresskill, NJ: Hampton Press.

Community Radio Manual (1999). Newlands, South Africa: Open Society Foundation, December.

Cook, Bill & Uma Kothari, eds. (2001). *Participation: The New Tyranny?* London & New York: Zed Books.

Contreras Baspinero, Alex (2003). "Venezuela's Catia TV Illegally Raided and Shut Down," *Narco News Bulletin*, July 14, transmitted to OURMedia member list by clemencia@OU.EDU.

Cormack, Mike (1995). "Broadcasting and the Politics of Cultural Diversity: The Gaelic Television Debate in Scotland." *European Journal of Cultural Policy 2*(1): 43-54.

Cormack, Mike (1998). "Minority Language Media in Western Europe: Preliminary Considerations." *European Journal of Communication 13*, 1: 33-52.

Costanza-Chock, Sasha (2003). "Cancun Forum on Communication Rights vs. 'Free Trade.'" Press release, retrieved from OURMEDIA-L@LISTS.OU.EDU, September 8.

Cottle, Simon (1995). *Television and Ethnic Minorities: Producer's Perspectives*. Aldershot, UK: Avebury.

Cottle, Simon, ed. (2000). *Ethnic Minorities and the Media: Changing Cultural Boundaries*. London: Open University Press.

Couldry, Nick & James Curran, eds. (2003). *Contesting Media Power: Alternative Media in a Networked World*. London: Rowman and Littlefield.

Coupe, Bronwyn & Andrew Jakubowicz (1993). "Nextdoor Neighbors: A Report for the Office of Multicultural Affairs on Ethnic Group Discussions of the Australian Media." Canberra: Office of Multicultural Affairs, Department of the Prime Minister and Cabinet, Commonwealth of Australia.

Coyer, Kate (2003). "Report on Radio Hurakan." Retrieved from OURMEDIA-L@LISTS.OU.EDU, September 11.

Craft, Stephanie (2000). "The Impact of Diverse Broadcast Station Ownership on Programming." Unpublished PhD dissertation, Stanford University, Stanford, CA.

Crang, Mike, Phil Crang & Jon May (1999). *Virtual Geographies: Bodies, Space and Relations.* London: Routledge.

Cruise O'Brien, Rita (1976). "Professionalism in Broadcasting: Issues of International Dependence" and "Professionalism in Broadcasting: Case Studies of Algeria and Senegal." Brighton, UK: Institute of Development Studies, University of Sussex, Discussion Papers DF 100 and DF 101, December.

Cumberbatch, Guy & Samantha Woods (1994). *Ethnic Minorities on Television.* London: Independent Television Commission.

Cunningham, Stuart & John Sinclair, eds. (2000). *Floating Lives: The Media and Asian Diasporas.* Brisbane: University of Queensland Press.

Curran, James (1991). "Rethinking the Media as a Public Sphere." In Peter Dahlgren & Colin Sparks, eds., *Communication and Citizenship*, 27-57. London: Routledge.

Curran, James & Michael Gurevitch, eds. (1991). *Mass Media and Society.* London: Edward Arnold.

Currie, Willie & Michael Markovitz (1993). "The People Shall Broadcast: The Struggle for a Post-apartheid National Television Culture." In Tony Dowmunt, ed. *Channels of Resistance*, 90-105. London: BFI.

Dahlgren, Peter (1991). "Introduction." In Peter Dahlgren & Colin Sparks, eds., *Communication and Citizenship*, 1-24. London: Routledge.

Dahlgren, Peter (1995). *Television and the Public Sphere.* London and New York: Routledge.

Dahlgren, Peter & Colin Sparks, eds., (1991). *Communication and Citizenship: Journalism and the Public Sphere in the New Media Age.* London: Routledge.

Daley, Patrick & Beverly James (1992). "Ethnic Broadcasting in Alaska: The Failure of a Participatory Model." In S. Riggins, ed., *Ethnic Minority Media*, 23-43. Newbury Park, CA: Sage.

Daniels, Therese & Jane Gerson, eds. (1989). *The Colour Black.* London: British Film Institute.

Dates, Janette & William Barlow, eds. (1990). *Split Image: African Americans in the Mass Media.* Washington DC: Howard University Press.

Davies, Chris Lawe (1998). "Multicultural Broadcasting in Australia: Policies, Institutions and Programming, 1975-1995." Unpublished PhD dissertation, University of Queensland, Australia.

Davies, John (1994). *Broadcasting and the BBC in Wales.* Cardiff, Wales: University of Wales Press.

Davila, Arlene (2001). *Latino, Inc.: The Marketing and Making of a People.* Berkeley: University of California Press.

Day, Julia (2002a). "BBC pours [one million pounds] into 'Asian Archers.'" *The Guardian*, October 28. Retrieved from http://guardian.co.uk, September 28, 2003.

Day, Julia (2002b). "Theatre boss handed 'Asian Archers.'" *The Guardian*, November 5. Retrieved from http://guardian.co.uk, September 28, 2003.

Dayan, Daniel (1998). "Particularistic Media and Diasporic Communications." In Tamar Liebes & James Curran, eds., *Media, Ritual and Identity*, 103-113. London: Routledge.

Dayan, Daniel (1999). "Media and Diasporas." In Jostein Gripsrud, ed., *Television and Common Knowledge*, 18-33. London: Routledge.

DeChicchis, Joseph (1992). "Current State of the Ainu Language." *Journal of Multilingual and Multicultural Development 16*, 1 and 2.

DeMay, Joel (1991). "Culture and Media Use in Saskatchewan Indian Country." *Canadian Journal of Communication 16*: 417-430.

DeSipio, Louis (2003). "Latino Viewing Choices: Bilingual Television Viewers and the Language Choices They Make." Report to the Tomas Rivera Policy Institute (Los Angeles, CA), May 2003.

Dines, Gail & Jean Humez, eds. (1995). *Gender, Race and Class in Media: A Text-Reader*. Thousand Oaks, CA: Sage.

Dowmunt, Tony (1993). *Channels of Resistance: Global Television and Local Empowerment*. London: British Film Institute.

Downing, John (2001). *Radical Media: Rebellious Communication and Social Movements*. Thousand Oaks, CA: Sage.

Downing, John (2002). "The Independent Media Center Movement and the Anarchist Socialist Tradition." In Marc Raboy, ed., *Global Media Policy in the New Millennium*, 215-232. Luton, UK: University of Luton Press.

Downing, John (2003). "Independent Media Centers: A Multi-Local, Multi-Media Challenge to Global Neo-Liberalism." In Nick Couldry & James Curran, eds., *Contesting Media Power*, 243-257. London: Rowman and Littlefield.

Downing, John & Charles Husband (2002). "Intercultural Communication, Multiculturalism and Social Inequality." Paper presented at the Annual Conference of the International Association for Mass Communication Research, Barcelona, Spain.

Dugdale, Joan (1979). *Radio Power: A History of 3ZZ*. Melbourne: Hyland House.

Eggerking, Kitty & Diana Plater, eds. (1992). "Signposts." Sydney: Australian Centre for Independent Journalists.

Elizade, Ricardo Omar (1996). "Pirate Radio: Voices of Discontent." *Frontera*, 4. Retrieved from www.infoshop.org/texts/seizing/radio_latino under the title "Radio Latino," January 7, 2004.

Eltis, David, ed. (2002). *Coerced and Free Migration: Global Perspectives*. Stanford, CA: Stanford University Press.

Elvin, Pascoe (2003). "Question Time: TV Debate Goes Online." Paper presented at EMTEL Conference on New Media and Everyday Life in Europe, London, April.

Ely, Melvin (1991). *The Adventures of Amos n' Andy: A Social History of an American Phenomenon*. New York: Free Press.

Entman, Robert & Andrew Rojecki (2000). *The Black Image in the White Mind: Media and Race in America*. Chicago, IL: University of Chicago Press.

Everitt, Anthony (2002). "Access Radio: An Interim Evaluation of 15 Access Projects." London: Radio Authority.

Everitt, Anthony (2003). *New Voices: An Evaluation of 15 Access Radio Projects.* London: Radio Authority.

"Eyes on Henry Hampton" (1995). *The New Yorker,* January 23.

Fairchild, Charles (2001). *Community Radio and Public Culture: Being an Examination of Media Access and Equity in the Nations of North America.* Cresskill, NJ: Hampton. Press.

Fallow, Mike (1993). "No, Not That Tiwai." *Southland Times* (Invercargill, New Zealand), November 1: 2.

Federal Communications Commission (1978). *Public Notice.* 1 F.C.C. 2d 393, 394.

Federal Communications Commission (1983). "In the Matter of Amendment of the Commission's Rules to Allow the Selection From Among Certain Competing Applications Using Random Selection or Lotteries Instead of Comparative Hearings." Washington, DC: Federal Communications Commission.

Fero, K. (1990). *Agence IM'media: A report on immigrants and media in France.* London: Migrant Media Collective/Greater London Arts.

Frachon, Claire & Marion Vargaftig, eds. (1995). *European Television: Immigrants and Ethnic Minorities.* London: John Libbey.

Fraser, Nancy (1992). "Rethinking the Public Sphere: A Contribution to the Critique of Actually Existing Democracy." In Craig Calhoun, ed., *Habermas and the Public Sphere,* 111-133. Cambridge, MA: MIT Press.

Froehling, Oliver (1999). "Internauts and Guerilleros: The Zapatista Rebellion in Chiapas, Mexico and its Extension into Cyberspace." In Mike Crang et al., eds., *Virtual Geographies,* 164-177. London: Routledge.

Gabin, Capuchin (2001). "La culture berbere sur la toile." *Afrik.com,* June 25. Retrieved from www.Afrik.com/journal/dossier/?dossier-9013-7, November 14, 2003. Translation mine.

Gallagher, Margaret & Lilia Quindoza-Santiago, eds. (1994). *Women Empowering Communication.* New York: International Women's Tribunal Center.

Georgiu, Myria (2002). "Les diasporas en ligne." In *Hommes et Migrations,* No. 1240, 10-18.

Gibson, Owen (2002). "A Truly World Wide Web?" *The Guardian,* May 20.

Giddens, Anthony (1984). *The Constitution of Society: Outline of a Theory of Structuration.* Cambridge, UK: Polity Press.

Gillespie, Marie (1995). *Television, Ethnicity, and Cultural Change.* London and New York: Routledge.

Girard, Bruce, ed. (1992). *A Passion for Radio: Radio Waves and Community.* Montreal: Black Rose Books.

Girard, Bruce, ed. (2003). *The One To Watch.* Rome: Food and Agriculture Organization (FAO). Available at: rural-radio@fao.org.

Givanni, June, ed. (1995). *Remote Control.* London: British Film Institute.

Glaisne, Risteard o (1982). *Raidio na Gaeltachta.* Indreadbhan, Galway, Ireland: Clo Chois Fharraige.

Gohring, Nancy (2003). "On the Reservation, the Web Plays Dream Maker." *The New York Times,* June 5: E5.

Golding, Peter (1974). "Media Role in National Development." *Journal of Communication 24* (3): 39-51.

Golding, Peter (1991). "Media Professionalism in the Third World: The Transfer of an Ideology." In James Curran and Michael Gurevitch, eds., *Mass Media and Society,* 291-308. London: Edward Arnold.

Gomez, Gustavo (2003). "Catia TV estara nuevamente al aire." Retrieved November 14, 2003 from www.comunica.org/pipermail/crisal_comunica.org /2003-July

Gonzalez, Alberto & Gloria Flores (2003). "Tejana Music and Cultural Identification." In Alberto Gonzalez, Marsha Houston & Victoria Chen, eds., *Our Voices,* 4th ed., 37-42. Los Angeles: Roxbury.

Gonzalez, Alberto, Marsha Houston & Victoria Chen, eds. (2003). *Our Voices: Essays in Culture, Ethnicity and Communication,* 4th ed. Los Angeles, CA: Roxbury.

Gooskens, Ineke (1992). "Experimenting with Minority Television in Amsterdam." In Nicholas W. Jankowski et al., eds., *The People's Voice,* 225-234. London: John Libbey.

Gordon, Janey (2000). *The RSL: Ultra-Local Radio.* Luton, UK: University of Luton Press.

Gorfinkel, Edric (1992). "Making Waves with CASET." In Bruce Girard, ed., *A Passion for Radio,* 201-212. Montreal: Black Rose.

Gorter, Dirk, ed. (1989). *Fourth International Conference on Minority Languages, Vol. 1: General Papers.* Clevedon, UK: Multilingual Matters.

Government of Australia, Committee of Review of the Special Broadcasting Services (1985). "Serving Multicultural Australia: The Role of Broadcasting— Appendices." Canberra: Australian Government Publishing Services.

Government of Australia (1974). "Independent Inquiry Into Frequency Modulation Broadcasting." Canberra: Australian Government Publishing Service, March.

Government of New Zealand, Ministry of Broadcasting (1989). "Directive to the Broadcasting Commission," June 1. Wellington: New Zealand Government Publishing Services.

Government of South Africa (2000). "The Media Development Diversity Agency: Promoting media development and diversity, and access to information in South Africa—A Draft Position Paper." Pretoria, South Africa: Government Printing Service.

Grame, Theodore (1980). *Ethnic Broadcasting in the United States.* Washington, DC: American Folklife Center, Library of Congress, Publication No. 4.

Gray, Herman (1995). *Watching Race: Television and the Struggle for "Blackness."* Minneapolis: University of Minnesota Press.

Griffiths, David (1976). "Autocracy in the Airwaves." Centre for the Study of Educational Communication and Media, *Media Centre Papers*, 4. Bundoora, Victoria, Australia: LaTrobe University.

Grin, François (1989). "The Economic Approach to Minority Languages." In Dirk Gorter, ed., *Fourth International Conference on Minority Languages*, 153-174. Clevedon, UK: Multilingual Matters.

Grin, François (1997). "Market Forces, Language Spread and Linguistic Diversity." In Miklos Kontra, Robert Phillipson & Tove Skutnabb-Kangas, eds., *Language: A Right and a Resource*, 169-186. Budapest, Hungary: Central European University Press.

Grin, François & Francois Vaillancourt (1999). *The Cost-Effectiveness Evaluation of Minority Language Policies: Case Studies on Wales, Ireland and the Basque Country.* Flensburg, Germany: European Centre for Minority Issues (ECMI) Monograph # 2, November.

Gripsrud, Jostein, ed. (1999). *Television and Common Knowledge.* London: Routledge.

Guimary, Donald (1975). *Citizen's Groups and Broadcasting.* New York: Praeger.

Gumicio-Dagron, Alfonso (2001). *Making Waves. Stories of Participatory Communication for Social Change.* New York: The Rockefeller Foundation.

Guyot, Jacques (2001). "Une Chaine Breton Privee." *Mercator MediaForum* 5: 8-21.

Habermas, Jürgen (1989/orig. 1962). *The Structural Transformation of the Public Sphere.* Cambridge, MA: MIT Press.

Habermas, Jürgen (1995). Remarks made in a seminar held at Stanford University and recorded in *Stanford Law Review* 47: 849-853.

Ha-il, Kim (1992). "Minority Media Access: Examination of Policies, Technologies and Multi-ethnic Television and a Proposal for an Alternative Approach." Unpublished PhD dissertation, University of California, Los Angeles, CA.

Hall, Edward (1959). *The Silent Language.* New York: Doubleday.

Hall, Stuart (1997). *Representation: Cultural Representations and Signifying Practices.* Thousand Oaks, CA: Sage.

Hall, Stuart & Paul du Gay, eds. (1996). *Questions of Cultural Identity.* Thousand Oaks, CA: Sage.

HAM (Hamburgischen Anstalt füer neue Medien), eds. (2001). *Medien—Migration—Integration.* Berlin: VISTAS Verlag.

Hamamoto, Darrell (1994). *Monitored Peril: Asian Americans and the Politics of TV Representation.* Minneapolis: University of Minnesota Press.

Harding, Richard (1979). *Outside Interference: The Politics of Australian Broadcasting.* Melbourne: Sun Books.

Hargreaves, Alec (2001). "Diasporic Audiences and Satellite Television: Case Studies in France and Germany." In Karen Ross, ed., *Black Marks*, 139-156. Aldershot, UK: Ashgate.

Hargreaves, Alec (n.d. but likely 2001). "Racism, Cultural Diversity and the Media in France." Retrieved from ahargrea@mailer.fsu.edu, November 29, 2003.

Hargreaves, Alec & Dalila Mahjoub (1997). "Satellite Television Viewing Among Ethnic Minorities in France." *European Journal of Communication 12,* 4.

Harris, Leslie & Associates (2002). "Bringing a Nation Online: The Importance of Federal Leadership." Washington, DC: The Leadership Conference on Civil Rights Education Fund and the Benton Fund, July.

Hartley, John & Alan McKee (2000). *The Indigenous Public Sphere: The Reporting and Reception of Aboriginal Issues in the Australian Media.* Oxford, UK: Oxford University Press.

Hassanpour, Amir (2003). "Diaspora, Homeland, and Communication Technologies." In Karim Karim, ed., *The Media of Diaspora,* 76-88. London: Routledge.

Heatta, Odd Mathis (1984). "NRK's Samisk Sendinger, 1946-1984." Unpublished MA thesis, University of Tromso, Tromso, Norway.

Heatta, Nils Johan (2003). Director, NRK Sami Radio and TV, Karasjok, Norway. E-mail to author, January 8.

Hein, Kurt (1988). *Radio Baha'i Ecuador: A Baha'i Development Project.* Oxford, UK: G. Ronald.

Herkstroeter, Dirk (1995). "Die Entwicklung der Landesmediengezetze." *Rundfunk und Fernsehen 42,* 1:60-81.

Hind, John & Stephen Moss (1985). *Rebel Radio: The Full Story of British Pirate Radio.* London: Pluto Press.

Hirsch, Paul (1977). "Occupational, Organizational and Institutional Models in Mass Media Research: Toward an Integrated Framework." In Paul Hirsch, Peter Miller & F. Gerald Kline, eds., *Strategies for Communication Research,* 6, 13-42. Beverly Hills, CA: Sage.

Hirsch, Paul, Peter Miller & F. Gerald Kline, eds. (1977). *Strategies for Communication Research,* 6, Beverly Hills, CA: Sage.

Hoege, Helmut (1994). "Weltradio reicht nur bis Mitte." *TAZ,* December 20.

Hoffman-Riem, Wolfgang (1996). *Regulating Media: Licensing and Supervision of Broadcasting in Six Countries.* New York: Guilford.

Hommes et Migrations (Nov.-Dec. 2002). Issue No. 1240 (a special issue on internet activities of émigré populations).

Horn, Frank, ed. (1999). *Sami and Greenlandic Media (Juridica Lapponica 22).* Rovaniemi, Finland: The Northern Institute for Environmental and Minority Law, University of Lapland.

Hornik, Robert (1988). *Development Communication: Information, Agriculture and Nutrition in the Third World.* New York: Longman.

Horten, Gerd (2002). *Radio Goes to War.* Berkeley: University of California Press.

House of Representatives, U.S. Congress (1995). Statement of William E. Kennard, General Counsel, FCC to the Subcommittee on Oversight of the House Committee on Ways and Means, 103rd Congress, 1st Session. Washington, DC: U.S. Government Printing Office.

Hoving, Desiree (2003). "Enhancing the quality of life in a living lab: Moerwijk (the Hague)." Paper presented at EMTEL Conference on New Media and Everyday Life in Europe, London, April.

Howkins, John (1983). "Basques Use Radio to Speak Their Own Language." *InterMedia 11*(3): 49-50.

Hughes, Stella (2003). "Community Multimedia Centers: Creating Digital Opportunities For All." In B. Girard, ed., *The One to Watch*, 76-89. Rome: FAO.

"Human Rights Radio Back on Air in Springfield" (n.d., but likely 2001). Retreived from website of Champaign Independent Media Center, www.ucimc.org/newswire/display_any/334, November 10, 2003.

Husband, Charles, ed. (1994). *A Richer Vision: The Development of Ethnic Minority Media in Western Democracies.* London: John Libbey.

Husband, Charles (2000). "Media and the Public Sphere in Multi-Ethnic Societies." In Simon Cottle, ed., *Ethnic Minorities and the Media*, 199-214. London: Open University Press.

Husband, Charles and Yunis Alam (2002). "Codes of Practice and Media Performance: A Systems Approach." In *Tuning Into Diversity*, 250-285.

Ihaddaden, Zahir (1992). "The Postcolonial Policy of Algerian Broadcasting in Kabyle." In Steven Riggins, ed., *Ethnic Minority Media*, 243-255. Newbury Park, CA: Sage.

Independent Broadcasting Authority (n.d., but likely 1995). "Independent Broadcasting Authority Report on the Production and Viability of Public Broadcasting Services." Pretoria, South Africa: Independent Broadcast Authority.

Independent Communications Authority of South Africa (2003). "Discussion Paper on Low Power Sound Broadcasting." Sandton, South Africa: ICASA, February 28.

Inglis, Kenneth (1983). *This Is the ABC.* Melbourne: Melbourne University Press.

Ismond, Patrick (1994). "Ethnic Minority Media Production in Relation to British Media Policies." Unpublished PhD dissertation, University of Bradford, Bradford, UK.

Ismond, Patrick (1995). "From AsiaVision to AsiaNet" and "Identity TV." In Simon Cottle, ed., *Television and Ethnic Minorities*, 197-193 and 194-208. Aldershot, UK: Avebury.

Jacobs, Ronald (2000). *Race, Media and the Crisis of Society: From Watts to Rodney King.* Cambridge, UK and New York: Cambridge University Press.

Jacobson, Thomas & Jan Servaes, eds. (1999). *Theoretical Approaches to Participatory Communication.* Cresskill, NJ: Hampton Press.

Jakubowicz, Andrew, ed. (1994). *Racism, Ethnicity and the Media.* Sydney: Allen & Unwin.

Jakubowicz, Andrew and Kerie Newell (1995). "Which World? Whose/Who's Home?: Special Broadcasting in the Australian Communication Alphabet." In Jennifer Craik, Julie James Bailey and Albert Moran, eds., *Public Voices, Private Interests: Australia's Media Policy*, 130-146. St. Leonard's, AU: Allan & Unwin.

Jankowski, Nicholas, ed., with Ole Prehn (2002). *Community Media in the Information Age: Perspectives and Prospects.* Cresskill, NJ: Hampton Press.

Jankowski, Nicholas, Ole Prehn & James Stappers, eds. (1992). *The People's Voice: Local Radio and Television in Europe.* London: John Libbey.

Jhally, Sut [producer] (1996). *Race: The Floating Signifier.* Northampton, MA: Media Education Foundation. (60 minute video)

Jhally, Sut & Justin Lewis (1992). *Enlightened Racism: The Cosby Show, Audiences, and the Myth of the American Dream.* Boulder, CO: Westview Press.

Kamalipour, Yahya & Theresa Carilli, eds. (1998). *Cultural Diversity and the U.S. Media.* Albany: State University of New York Press.

Karam, Robert & Arlene Zuckernick (1992). "A Study of Audiences for Aboriginal Community Radio: A Profile of Four Northern Ontario Communities." Ottawa: Ministry of Culture and Communications, April.

Karim, Karim H., ed. (2003). *The Media of Diaspora: Mapping the Globe.* London: Routledge.

Keane, John (1996). *Reflections on Violence.* London: Verso.

Keith, Michael (1995). *Signals in the Air: Native Broadcasting in America.* Westport, CT: Praeger.

Keller, David (1993). "Community Radio—The USA." *pbx* (Journal of the Public Broadcasting Association of Australia), February:12.

Kepplinger, Hans & Thomas Hartmann (1989). *Stachel oder Feigenblatt.* Frankfurt: IMK, 1989.

King, Michael (1985). "Kawe Korero: A Guide to Reporting Maori Activities." Pukekohe, New Zealand: New Zealand Journalists' Training Board.

King, Russell and Nancy Wood, eds. (2001). *Media and Migration: Constructions of Mobility and Difference.* London and New York: Routledge.

Kleinstüeber, Hans (2001). "Habermas and the Public Sphere: From a German to a European Perspective." In *The Emergence of the European Public Sphere* (2001). Special issue of *JAVNOST: The Public 8* (1).

Knutson, J.W. (1998). "Rebellion in Chiapas: Insurrection by Internet and Public Relations." *Media, Culture and Society 20*(3): 507-518.

Kolar-Panov, Dona (1997). *War and the Diasporic Imagination.* New York: Routledge.

Kontra, Miklos, Robert Phillipson & Tove Skutnabb-Kangas, eds. (1999). *Language, A Right and a Resource: Approaching Linguistic Human Rights.* Budapest, Hungary: Central European University Press.

Krasnow, Erwin (1997). "A Case for Minority Tax Certificates." *Broadcasting & Cable*, December 15: 80.

Krasnow, Erwin, Lawrence Longley & Herbert Terry (1982). *The Politics of Broadcast Regulation*, 3rd ed. New York: St. Martin's Press.

Kristof, Nicholas (1996). "Japan's Forgotten People Are Trying to be Heard." *The New York Times*, October 5: A6.

Land, Jeff (1999). *Active Radio: Pacifica's Brash Experiment.* Minneapolis: University of Minnesota Press.

Langton, Marcia (1993). "Well, I Heard It on the Radio and Saw It on the Television." North Sydney: Australian Film Commission.

Lasar, Matthew (1999). *Pacifica Radio: The Rise of an Alternative Network.* Philadelphia, PA: Temple University Press.

Lee, Rachel & Sau-ling Cynthia Wong, eds. (2003). *Asian America.Net: Ethnicity, Nationalism and Cyberculture.* New York: Routledge.

Lehtonen, Pauliina & Heikki Heikkilä (2003). "Citizens Consulting the Infocracy: The Appropriation of ICT and Participatory Ideas in Finland.." Paper presented at EMTEL Conference on New Media and Everyday Life in Europe, London, April.

Lemke, Claudia (1995). "Maori Involvement in Sound Radio Broadcasting, 1915 to 1958." Unpublished MA thesis, University of Auckland, Auckland, New Zealand.

Lewis, Peter (1977). *'Different Keepers': Models of Structure and Finance in Community Radio.* London: International Institute of Communications.

Lewis, Peter, ed. (1993). *Alternative Media: Linking Global and Local.* Paris: UNESCO, Reports and Papers on Mass Communication No. 107.

Lewis, Peter & Jerry Booth (1989). *The Invisible Medium: Public, Commercial and Community Radio.* London: Macmillan Education Ltd.

Liebes, Tamar & James Curran (1998). *Media, Ritual and Identity.* London: Routledge.

Lilienthal, Volker (1995). "Die Gremienplage." *Kirche und Rundfunk,* 61 and 64.

Lind, Rebecca (2003). *Race/Gender/Media: Considering Diversity Across Audience, Content and Producers.* Boston, MA: Pearson, Allyn and Bacon.

Linder, Laura (1999). *Public Access Television: America's Electronic Soapbox.* Westport, CT: Praeger.

Loewander, Birgitta (1998). "Racism in the community radio?" Stockholm, Sweden, Granskningsnaemnden foer radio och TV (supervisory body for *närradio* services). Retrieved from www.gnr.se, September 16, 2003.

Lopez, Bernat (2002). "Expectations of the Net: Vilaweb as a Successful Case Study of an On-Line Medium in a Lesser-Used Language." *Mercator Media Forum* 6: 37-61.

Mabuza, Ernst (2003). "Icasa Seeks Input On Low-Power Radio." *Business Day* (Johannesburg, South Africa), March 3.

MacDonald, J. Fred (1979). *Don't Touch That Dial: Radio Programming in American Life.* Chicago, IL: Nelson-Hall.

Madden, Kate (1989). "'To be nobody else...' An analysis of Inuit broadcasting attempts to produce culturally sensitive video programming to help preserve Inuit culture, 1983-85." Unpublished PhD dissertation, Pennsylvania State University, University Park, PA.

Madden, Kate (1992). "Video and Cultural Identity: The Inuit Broadcasting Corporation Experience." In Felipe Korzenny, Stella Ting-Toomey & Elizabeth Schiff, eds., *International and Intercultural Communication Annual, 16: Mass Media Effects Across Cultures,* 165-184. London: Sage.

Makinwa, Bunmi (2003). Report. *The Drum Beat* (publication of The Communication Initiative), June 9, retrieved from www.comminit.com, September 16, 2003.

Malik, Sarita, ed. (2001). *Representing Black Britain: Black and Asian Images on Television.* Thousand Oaks, CA: Sage.

Mason, Laurie, Christine Bachen & Stephanie Craft (2001). "Support for FCC Minority Ownership Policy: How Broadcast Station Owner Race or Ethnicity Affects News and Public Affairs Programming Diversity." *Communication Law and Policy 6*, 1: 37-73.

Mayanis, Meddie (2002). "The African Community Telecenters: In Search of Sustainability." Retrieved from www.developmentgateway.org, December 4, 2003.

Maybury-Lewis, David, ed. (1998). "Aboriginal Media, Aboriginal Control." Special issue of *Cultural Survival Quarterly, 22/2*.

"Mbanna Kantako: Human Rights Radio Network" (2002). International Movement Against All Forms of Discrimination and Racism, Home Page Interview, Springfield, IL, February. Retrieved from www.imadr.org/interview/mbanna.1, November 6, 2003.

Mayugo, Carme (2002). "Local TV stations, work in progress." Paper delivered at OURMedia Conference, Barcelona, Spain, July.

McBride, Sean (1980). *Many Voices, One World: Communication and Society Today and Tomorrow.* Paris: UNESCO.

McChesney, Robert (1993). *Telecommunications, Mass Media and Democracy.* New York: Oxford University Press.

McDowell, William (1992). *The History of BBC Broadcasting in Scotland, 1923-1983.* Edinburgh: Edinburgh University Press.

McKinley, Michelle & Lene Jensen (2003). "In Our Own Voices: Reproductive Health Care Programming in the Peruvian Amazon." *Critical Studies in Media Communication 20*, 2: 180-203.

McKinney, Eleanor (1966). *The Exacting Ear: The Story of Listener-Sponsored Radio.* New York: Pantheon Books.

McPhail, Thomas (1987). *Electronic Colonialism: The Future of International Broadcasting and Communication.* Newbury Park, CA: Sage.

McPhail, Thomas (2001). *Global Communication: Theories, Stakeholders and Trends.* Boston, MA: Pearson, Allyn and Bacon.

Meadows, Michael (1992). *A Watering Can in the Desert: Issues in Indigenous Broadcasting Policy in Australia.* Sydney: Hodder and Stoughton.

Means Coleman, Robin (1998). *African-American Viewers and the Black Situation Comedy.* New York: Garland.

"(The) Media and the Roma in Contemporary Europe: Facts and Fictions" (1996). Report on a Project on Ethnic Relations-sponsored conference, Prague, September 19-22, 1996. Available at www.per-usa.org/rommedia.

"Media Pack: Black Britain" (2002). www.adrevenue.co.uk, November 14.

Meyer, Vicki (2001). "From Segmented to Fragmented: Latino Media in San Antonio, Texas." *Journalism and Mass Communication Quarterly,* 78, 2: 291-306.

Michaels, Eric (1986). *The Aboriginal Invention of Television in Central Australia, 1982-1986.* Canberra, ACT: Australian Institute of Aboriginal Studies.

Mickiewicz, Ellen (1988). *Split Signals.* New York: Oxford University Press.

Milam, Lorenzo (1974). *Sex and Broadcasting: A Handbook on Starting a Radio Station for the Community,* 3rd ed. San Diego, CA: Dildo Press.

Milikowski, Marisca (2001)). "Learning about Turkishness by Satellite: Private Satisfactions and Public Benefits." In Karen Ross, ed., *Black Marks,* 125-137. Aldershot, UK: Ashgate.

Mohacsi, Viktoria (1999). "Inside the box." *Roma Rights* 4: 5. Available at: www.errc.org/rr_nr4_1999.

Mohammadi, Annabelle Sreberny and Ali Mohammadi (1994). *Small Media, Big Revolution: Communication, Culture and the Iranian Revolution.* Minneapolis: University of Minnesota Press.

Molnar, Helen (1993). "The Democratization of Communications Technology in Australia and the South Pacific: Media Participation by Indigenous Peoples." Unpublished PhD dissertation, Monash University, Victoria, Australia.

Molnar, Helen & Michael Meadows (2001). *Songlines to Satellites: Indigenous Communication in Australia, the South Pacific and Canada.* Annandale, NSW (Australia): Pluto Press.

Montgomery, Kathryn (1989). *Target: Prime Time. Advocacy Groups and the Struggle Over Entertainment Television.* New York: Oxford University Press.

Moragas Spa, Miquel de & Maria Corominas (1992). "Spain, Catalonia: Media and Democratic Participation in Local Communication." In Nicholas W. Jankowski et al., eds., *The People's Voice,* 186-197. London: John Libbey.

Moragas Spa, Miquel de & Carmelo Garitaonandia, eds. (1995), *Decentralization in the Global Era: Television in the Regions, Nationalities and Small Countries of the European Union.* London: John Libbey.

Moragas Spa, Miquel de, Carmelo Garitaonandia & Bernat Lopez, eds. (1999). *Television on Your Doorstep: Decentralization Experiences in the European Union.* Luton, UK: University of Luton Press.

Morley, David (2000). *Home Territories: Media, Mobility and Identity.* London: Routledge.

Moseley, Christopher, Nicholas Ostler & Hassan Ouzzate, eds. (2001). *Endangered Languages and the Media.* Bath, UK: Foundation for Endangered Languages.

Mowlana, Hamid & Margaret Frondorf, eds. (1992). *The Media as a Forum for Community Building.* Washington, DC: Paul H. Nitze School of Advanced International Studies, Program on Social Change and Development.

Mullan, Bob (1996). *Not a Pretty Picture: Ethnic Minority Views of Television.* Aldershot, UK: Avebury.

Murdock, Graham (1999). "Rights and Representations: Public Discourse and Cultural Citizenship." In Jostein Gripsrud, ed., *Television and Common Knowledge,* 7-17. London, UK: Routledge.

Murphy, Brian (1983). *The World Wired Up.* London, UK: Comedia.

Naficy, Hamid (1993). *The Making of Exile Cultures: Iranian Television in Los Angeles.* Minneapolis: University of Minnesota Press.

Navarrete, Lisa & Charles Kamasaki (1994). *Out of the Picture: Hispanics in the Media.* Washington, DC: National Council of La Raza.

Navarro, Mireya (2003). "Latino TV Embraces Reality Shows." *The New York Times,* September 8: B1.

Nihoniho, Anthony & Neville Young (1993). "Survey for Te Reo Iriraki ki Otautahi 90.5 FM." Christchurch, New Zealand: Te Reo Iriraki ki Otautahi, March.

Nordenstreng, Kaarle & Herbert Schiller (1993). *Beyond National Sovereignty: International Communication in the 1990s.* Norwood, NJ: Ablex.

Noriega, Chon (2000). *Shot in America: Television, the State and the Rise of Chicano Cinema.* Minneapolis: University of Minnesota Press.

"Nunavut Our Land" (2003). News release. *Isuma News,* May 30. Retrieved from http://isuma.ca/news/053003, October 15, 2003.

Ofori, Kofi (1999). "When Being Number 1 Is Not Enough: The Impact of Advertising Practices on Minority-Owned and Minority-Formatted Broadcast Stations" (report to the Office of Communications Business Opportunities, Federal Communications Commission (USA), March 2, 1999. Document obtained from www.civil-rightsforum.org/fccadvertising).

Ogan, Christine (1993). "Listserver Communication During the Gulf War." *Journal of Broadcasting and Electronic Media 37,* 2.

Ogan, Christine (2001). *Communication and Identity in the Diaspora: Turkish Migrants in Amsterdam and Their Use of Media.* Lanham, MD: Lexington Books.

Ogan, Christine & Marisca Milikowski (1998). "Television Helps to Define 'Home' for the Women of Amsterdam." *Media Development 45*(3): 13-21.

Olson, Scott (1984). "Devolution and Indigenous Mass Media: The Role of Media in Inupiat and Sami Nation-Building." Unpublished PhD dissertation, Northwestern University, Evanston, IL.

O Siochru, Sean & Bruce Girard, with Amy Mahan (2002). *Global Media Governance: A Beginner's Guide.* Lanham, MD: Rowman & Littlefield.

Ouakrim, Mohamed (2001). "Promoting the Maintenance of Endangered Languages through the Internet: The Case of Tamazight." In Christopher Moseley et al., eds., *Endangered Languages and the Media,* 61-67. Bath, UK: Foundation for Endangered Languages.

Panos West Africa (2002). "The Oral Testimony Radio Project of Panos, West Africa." Press release from Panos West Africa. Retrieved from www.comminit.com/st2003/sld-8419, December 4, 2003.

Parker, Lonnae O'Neal (2003). "Hon, Guess Who's Coming to Dinner?" *Washington Post,* May 28: C1.

Persaud, Babita (2002). "Sabado Gigante stars to hit Ybor." *St. Petersburg Times,* December 1: 1.

Peters, John D. (1993). "Distrust of Representation: Habermas on the Public Sphere." *Media, Culture and Society 15*(4): 541-571.

Phelan, John (1987). *Apartheid Media: Disinformation and Dissent in South Africa.* Westport, CT: Lawrence Hill.

Portney, Kent (1986). *Approaching Public Policy Analysis.* Englewood Cliffs, NJ: Prentice-Hall.

Price, Vincent & Joseph Cappella (2003). "Conversations at Random: New Possibilities for Studying Public Opinion Online." Paper presented at Conference on New Research for New Media, sponsored by University of Minnesota School of Journalism and Mass Communication, Institute for New Media Studies, Minneapolis, MN, September 4-6.

Raboy, Marc, ed. (2002). *Global Media Policy in the New Millennium.* Luton, UK: University of Luton Press.

Raidio Telefis Eirann (RTE) (2001). "One World Radio," pamphlet. Dublin: RTE.

Ray, William (1990). *FCC: The Ups and Downs of Radio-TV Regulation.* Ames: Iowa State University Press.

"Resolution" (2001). www.lulac.org/Issues/Resolve/2001/NBC.

Riano, Pilar, ed. (1994). *Women in Grassroots Communication: Furthering Social Change.* Thousand Oaks, CA: Sage.

Riggins, Steven, ed. (1992). *Ethnic Minority Media: An International Perspective.* Newbury Park, CA: Sage.

Rios, Diana & Ali Mohamed, eds. (2003). *Brown and Black Communication: Latino and African-American Conflict and Convergence in Mass Media.* Westport, CT: Praeger.

"Rising Voices: Minorities and the Future of Soviet and American Television" (1991). *Media Studies Journal 5*, 4, 203-215.

Rivas-Rodriguez, Maggie (2003). *Brown Eyes on the Web.* New York: Routledge.

Rock on Olympia [author pseudonym] (2002). Posted on www.morelater.com/kaos/forum/messages/204. Retrieved November 22, 2003.

Rodriguez, America (1999). *Making Latino News: Race, Language, Class.* Thousand Oaks, CA: Sage.

Rodriguez, America (1996). "Objectivity and Ethnicity in the Presentation of the Noticiero Univision." *Critical Studies in Mass Communication,* March: 59-81.

Rodriguez, Clara, ed. (1998). *Latin Looks: Images of Latinos and Latinas in the U.S. Media.* Boulder, CO: Westview Press.

Rodriguez, Clemencia (2001). *Fissures in the Mediascape: An International Study of Citizen's Media.* Cresskill, NJ: Hampton Press.

Ross, Karen (1996). *Black and White Media.* Cambridge, MA: Polity Press.

Ross, Karen, ed. (2001). *Black Marks: Minority Ethnic Audiences and Media.* Aldershot, U.K.: Ashgate.

Ruohuoma, Erja (1995). "Sami Radio Programming and Audiences in Finland, Sweden and Norway." Helsinki, Finland: YLE.

Russell, Adrienne (2001). "Chiapas and the New News: Internet and Newspaper Coverage of a Broken Cease-Fire." *Journalism: Theory, Practice and Criticism 2*, 2.

Russinov, Rumyan (1999). "Campaigning for Romani Media in Bulgaria." *Roma Rights 4*: 5, www.errc.org/rr_nr4_1999.

Sagot, Rene (2002). "Kabyles sûr le Net." In *Hommes et Migrations*, No. 1240, 29-34.

Saib, Jilali (2001). "Maintenance & Promotion of Berber: The Role of the Electronic Media." In Christopher Moseley et al., eds., *Endangered Languages and the Media*, 40-46. Bath, UK: Foundation for Endangered Languages.

Sakolsky, Ron (1992). "Zoom Black Magic Liberation Radio." In Bruce Girard, ed., *A Passion for Radio*, 106-113. Montreal: Black Rose.

Savage, Barbara (1999). *Broadcasting Freedom: Radio, War and the Politics of Race.* Chapel Hill: University of North Carolina Press.

Schiller, Herbert (1969). *Mass Media and American Empire.* New York: A.M. Kelley.

Schlesinger, Philip (1991). *Media, State and Nation.* Newbury Park, CA: Sage.

Schneckener, Ulrich (1994). "Radioprogramm in babylonischer Sprachenvielfalt." *Frankfuerter Rundschau*, September 14.

Seefeld, Kathi (1994). "Radio Multikulti geht am Montag auf Sendung." *Neues Deutschland* (Berlin), September 17: 18.

Sharipkov, Oleg (2002-03). "IT News in Russia: Penza Association of Refugees and Forced Migrants." *Communication Technology Review*, Winter. Retrieved from www.comtechreview.org/fw2002, December 28, 2003.

Shohat, Ella & Robert Stam (1994). *Unthinking Eurocentrism: Multiculturalism and the Media.* London and New York: Routledge.

Silverstone, Roger (2001). "Finding a Voice: Minorities, Media and the Global Commons." *Emergences 11*(1):

Singhal, Arvind & Everett Rogers (2003). *Combatting AIDS: Communication Strategies in Action.* Thousand Oaks, CA: Sage.

Singhal, Arvind & Everett Rogers (2004). *Entertainment-Education and Social Change.* Mahwah, NJ: Erlbaum.

Soley, Lawrence (1999). *Free Radio: Electronic Civil Disobedience.* Boulder, CO: Westview Press.

Soley, Lawrence & John Nichols (1987). *Clandestine Radio Broadcasting.* New York: Praeger.

Solovyova, Julia (n.d. but likely 1999). "Russia: Multiethnic Radio." *Transitions.* Retrieved from Transitions website www.ijt.cz, January 15, 2000.

Soruco, Gonzalo (1996). *Cubans and the Mass Media in South Florida.* Gainesville, FL: University Press of Florida.

Sonnenberg, Urte (1994). "'Mini-FM,' Community Radio and Local Television Stations." Paper presented at the Annual Convention of the International Association for Mass Communication Research, Seoul, South Korea.

Special Broadcasting Service (1984). "Submission to Committee of Review, April 1984." Sydney: Special Broadcasting Service.

Spoonley, Paul & Walter Hirsh (1990). *Between the Lines: Racism and New Zealand Media.* Auckland, NZ: Heinemann Reed.

Sreberny, Annabelle (1999). *Include Us In.* Leicester, UK: Centre for Mass Communications Research. Available through the website of the Broadcasting Standards Commission (www.bsc.co.uk).

Sreberny, Annabelle & Karen Ross (1995). *Black Minority Viewers and Television.* Leicester, UK: Centre for Mass Communications Research.

Sterngold, James (1992). "This Man Has Dream [sic.]: It's Downright Un-Japanese." *New York Times,* August 19: A4.

Stevens, Geoffrey (n.d.). "Unbundling the Word 'Community'." Course materials for Fourth Year Theory Work, Rhodes University, South Africa. Retrieved from http://journ.ru.ac.za/radio/theory4.htm, October 10, 2003.

Stevenson, Nick (2002). *Understanding Media Cultures,* 2nd ed. London, UK and Thousand Oaks, CA: Sage.

Stiles, Mark & Associates (1985). "Broadcasting and Canada's Aboriginal Peoples." Report to the Task Force on Broadcast Policy. Ottawa: Canadian Radio-Television and Telecommunications Commission.

STOA (2002). "The Netherlands and Media Policy." In *Tuning Into Diversity,* 387-428. Available on www.multicultural.net/index.asp.

Stocker, Edward (1984). "A History of Multilingual Broadcasting in Sydney and Melbourne, Australia, 1975-1980." MA thesis, San Francisco State University, San Francisco, CA.

Stockwell, Steven & Philip Scott (2000). "All-Media Guide to Fair and Cross-Cultural Reporting." Brisbane: Australian Key Centre for Cultural and Media Policy, Griffith University.

Süeddeutscher Rundfunk (1993). "SDR Ausländerbefragung 1993—Erste Ergebnisse." Stuttgart, Germany: Sueddeutscher Rundfunk.

"Telemundo purchase OK'd" (2002). (Miami) Herald.com, April 11, www.miami.com/mld/miamiherald.

Ter Wal, Jessika, ed. (2002). *Racism and Cultural Diversity and in the Mass Media: An Overview of Research and Examples of Good Practice in the EU Member States, 1995-2000.* Vienna: European Research Centre on Racism and Xenophobia.

Thede, Nancy & Alain Ambrosi, eds. (1991). *Video the Changing World.* Montreal: Black Rose Books.

Thomas, Eric (1992). "Canadian Broadcasting and Multiculturalism: Attempts to Accommodate Ethnic Minorities." *Canadian Journal of Communication 17:* 281-300.

Thomas, Ned (2001). "Two Breton Voices on Radio." *Mercator Media Forum 5:* 107-114.

Thornley, Phoebe (2002). "The Early Days of Community Radio: Elites, Ordinary People and 'Community of Interest.'" Paper presented at annual conference of the Community Broadcasting Association of Australia, November.

"3ZZZ Youth Program" (1998). *NEMBC Newsletter* (National Ethnic and Multicultural Broadcasters Council), Spring.

Tillotson, Kristen (2004). "Ethnic TV." *Minneapolis Star Tribune,* January 8: E3.

Tomaselli, Ruth, Keyan Tomaselli & Johan Muller (1985). *Broadcasting in South Africa.* New York: St. Martin's Press.

Tomlinson, Timothy (1994). "The Development of Local and Religious Radio in Norway and Sweden." Unpublished PhD dissertation, University of Minnesota, Minneapolis, MN.

Torres, Sasha, ed. (1998). *Living Color: Race and Television in the United States.* Durham, NC: Duke University Press.

Torres, Sasha (2003). *Black, White and in Color: Television and Black Civil Rights.* Princeton, NJ: Princeton University Press.

Townsend, Mike (1996). Human Rights (Radio). *Washington Post,* March 15, Retrieved from www.liberationradio.net/articles/history/human, March 17, 2003.

Townsend, Mike (1999). "Kantako's Human Rights Radio Continues to Defy Thought Police." Retrieved from A-Infos (anarchist news service), www.ain-fos.ca/99/nov/ainfos00303, November 10, 2003.

Townsend, Mike (2000). "BAD NEWS." Retreived from mediageek website www.mediageek.org/archives/000526 (posted by Paul, December 3, 2000), November 10, 2003.

"Treat Corporate Media Like the Enemy & No Free Pass for Black Radio" (2003). *The Black Commentator 40* (May 1). Retrieved from ERAM@MAEL-STROM.STJOHNS.EDU, May 23, 2003.

Tsagarousianou, Roza (2001). "A Space Where One Feels at Home." In Russell King and Nancy Wood, eds., *Media and Migration,* 152-172. London, UK: Routledge.

Tsagarousiano, Roza (2002). "Ethnic Community Media, Community Identity and Citizenship in Contemporary Britain." In Nick Jankowski, ed., *Community Media in the Information Age,* 209-230. Cresskill, NJ: Hampton Press.

Tuning into Diversity—Immigrants and Ethnic Minorities and Mass Media: Representation and Policies (2002). Retrieved from www.multicultural.net, November 15, 2003

"Turkey Allows Broadcasting of Kurdish-Language Shows (2002)." *New York Times,* November 21, A5.

Turner, Terence (1991). "Visual Media, Cultural Politics and Anthropological Practice." *Independent 14:* 1.

UNESCO (1986). *Mass Media and the Minorities.* Paris: UNESCO.

U.S. Commission on Civil Rights (1977 and 1979). *Window Dressing on the Set and Window Dressing on the Set: An Update.* Washington, DC: U.S. Commission on Civil Rights.

U.S. Court of Appeals (1966). Office of Communication of the United Church of Christ vs. FCC. 359 F.2d 994 (D.C. Cir. 1966).

U.S. Court of Appeals (1969). Office of Communication of the United Church of Christ vs. FCC. 425 F.2d 543 (D.C. Cir. 1969).

U.S. Department of Commerce (2002). "A Nation Online: How Americans Are Expanding Their Use of the Internet." Washington, DC: Department of Commerce.

Vallverdu, Francese (1995). "The Catalan Used on Television." *Mercator Media Forum 1*: 65-76.

Vargas, Lucila (1995). *Social Uses and Radio Practices*. Boulder, CO: Westview Press.

Veldkamp Markonderzoek (1995). "Media-onderzoek etnische groepen 1995." Amsterdam: Markonderzoek.

Verhulst, Stefaan, ed. (1999). "Symposium: Globalisation and Diasporic Communication," special issue of *JAVNOST: The Public* 6(1).

Vertovec, Steven (1996). "Berlin Multikulti: Germany, 'Foreigners' and 'World Openness.'" *New Community* 22(3): 381-399.

Voss, Friedrich (2001). "Radio Multikuturell: Beitraege des Hoerfunks zur Foerderung multikultureller Vielfalt." *ARD Jahrbuch* (Yearbook of the Association of German Public Broadcasters).

Wajid, Sara (2000). "Article 13 of the Amsterdam Treaty and the Media." International Federation of Journalists website www.ifj.org/working/issues/racism/res under "Research 2000."

Walker, Jesse (2001). *Rebels on the Air: An Alternative History of Radio in America.* New York: New York University Press.

Wambui, Mercy (2003). Brief report on Development Through Radio Project, Sierra Leone. *Pula: A Newsletter on Women and ICT's in Africa,* 2 (August), retrieved from www.apcafricawomen.org/pula2, December 4, 2003.

Warren, Frieda (2003). "World Summit on the Information Society." Retrieved from OURMEDIA@LISTS.OU.EDU, September 12, 2003.

Weissman, Steven (1981). "The FCC and Minorities: An Evaluation of FCC Policies Designed to Encourage Programming Responsive to Minority Needs." *Columbia Journal of Law and Social Policies* 16(4): 561-589.

White, Shirley, ed. (2003). *Participatory Video: Images That Transform and Empower.* Thousand Oaks, CA: Sage.

Whiteduck Resources Inc. & Consilium (2003). "Northern Native Broadcast Access Program (NNBAP) & Northern Distribution Program (NDP) Evaluation." Ottawa: Department of Canadian Heritage.

Wilkins, Ivor & Hans Strydom (1979). *The Broederbond.* New York: Paddington Press.

Wilson, Clint, Felix Gutierrez & Lena Chao (2003). *Racism, Sexism and the Media,* 3rd ed. Thousand Oaks, CA: Sage.

Wilson, G. Thomas II (2001). "The New Model of Black Media Entrepreneurship: BET Holdings, Inc." In John Barber & Alice Tait, eds., *The Information Society and the Black Community,* 95-110. Westport, CT: Praeger.

Wilson, Lisa (1988). "Minority and Gender Enhancements: A Necessary and Valid Means to Achieve Diversity in the Broadcast Workplace." *Federal Communications Law Journal 40*, 1.

Withers, Charles (1984). *Gaelic in Scotland, 1698-1981*. Edinburgh: John Donald.

Witherspoon, John & Roselle Kovitz (2000). *A History of Public Broadcasting.* Washington, DC: Current (The Public Telecommunications Newspaper).

Wober, J. Mallory & Said Fazel (1984). "Citizens of Ethnic Minorities, Their Prominence in Real Life and on Television." London: Independent Broadcasting Authority.

Author Index

Subject Index*

A

Access radio, 40, 205
  in Norway, 40
  in Sweden, 40
  in United Kingdom, 40-41
Access television (*see also* Offener
  Kanale), 28, 42, 59
Advertisements, 147-148, 207
African National Congress (South
  Africa), 87
Ainu (Japan), 36-37(n49)
AIROS (American Indian Radio on
  Satellite), 29, 168
Alaska, 213(n3)
"Alba" (Inuit), 164
AMARC (Association Mondiale,
  Canada), 72, 216(n38)
"American Family" (US), 99
"Amos n' Andy" (US), 19
Anderson, Benedict, 11
APTN (Aboriginal Peoples Television
  Network-Canada), 29, 43, 53, 118,
  209-210

Arabic (*see also* Middle East
  Broadcasting Centre), 58
ARD (Association of German Public
  Broadcasters) ethnic minority programs, 10, 90-91
Article 91, 72, 74
AsiaVision (UK), 139(n15)
Audience composition, 167, 171-172
  mainstream audiences, 116-117
Audience research
  centers, 171
  sensitivity, 140(n24), 217(n40)
  specific studies, 107(n12), 171-172,
  186, 211, 214(n9)
Audiocassettes
  in Iranian Revolution, 43
  in South Africa, 43-44
AwazFM (South Asian, Scotland), 40,
  135

B

Barcelona Televisio, 61
BBC (British Broadcasting Corporation)

---

*With few exceptions, this index does not include the specific topic areas featured in the main chapter subtitles. Neither does it contain entries for the phrase *public sphere*, which appears in a very large number of pages throughout the text. Program titles are indicated with quotation marks.

Printed in the United States
28943LVS00003B/160-177

9 781572 736054